King Alf

MW01007874

King Alfred's Book of Laws

A Study of the Domboc *and Its Influence on English Identity, with a Complete Translation*

Todd Preston

McFarland & Company, Inc., Publishers

Jefferson, North Carolina, and London

LIBRARY OF CONGRESS CATALOGUING-IN-PUBLICATION DATA

Preston, Todd.
    King Alfred's book of laws : a study of the Domboc and its
influence on English identity, with a complete translation /
Todd Preston.
       p.   cm.
    Includes bibliographical references and index.

    ISBN 978-0-7864-6588-0
    softcover : acid free paper ∞

    1. Law, Anglo-Saxon.   2. Alfred, King of England, 849–899.
    3. Great Britain — Politics and government — 449–1066.
    4. Law — England — History — To 1500.   I. Title.
    KD543.P74 2012
    340.5'50942 — dc23   2012007134

BRITISH LIBRARY CATALOGUING DATA ARE AVAILABLE

On the cover: King Alfred the Great statue in Wantage, England
(Photograph by Philip Jelley)
Front cover design by David Landis (Shake It Loose Graphics)

Manufactured in the United States of America

McFarland & Company, Inc., Publishers
  Box 611, Jefferson, North Carolina 28640
  www.mcfarlandpub.com

Table of Contents

Preface

For students of the early Middle Ages, King Alfred is a figure who looms large at the intersection of literature and history. Most famously, Alfred is the ruler who brought learning back to England at the end of the ninth century after the depredations of decades of Viking invasion. As a result, analysis of Alfred's canon has focused heavily on his religious and philosophical texts, with his law code, or *Domboc*, receiving relatively scant notice until fairly recently. However, the *Domboc* is a fascinating text in itself, which can tell us a great deal about how Alfred ruled his people, and how he was perceived in subsequent centuries.

This book analyzes King Alfred's *Domboc* (literally "judgment-book") as an important foundation narrative for both the Anglo-Saxons and, later, the English. Alfred's text serves as a key illustration of the interconnected processes of forging royal, cultural, and national identities through legislation. Its goal is to delineate an Alfredian theory of law in the context of contemporary kingship literature. This will be accomplished by arguing that both the act and content of legislation are essential elements of kingship, instrumental in forging royal and national identities through political and ideological self-fashioning. In its analysis of the original incarnation of Alfred's *Domboc*, the study focuses on the prevalence and dominance of *bot* (compensatory feud) language throughout the text. In contrast to Alfred's received reputation as a thoroughly Christian king, the monarch's specific language choices in legislation forward royal and national images primarily identified by secular cultural forces.

This text also examines the influence of Alfred's law code following his death at the beginning of the tenth century. An investigation of the texts and contexts of the reappearance of Alfred's *Domboc* in the late eleventh and early twelfth centuries illuminates the role the *Domboc* plays in the formation and strategic invocations of national identity in the wake of conquest. Law collections *I-II Cnut* (following the Danish conquest), and the *Instituta Cnuti* and the *Quadripartitus* (following the Norman conquest), use the *Domboc* to facilitate the transition to post-conquest rule and legitimize their dominion over the Anglo-Saxons. Conversely, the compilers of the twelfth-century *Textus Roffensis* employ the *Domboc*'s connection to an Anglo-Saxon past in an effort to confirm their pre-conquest claims to rights and holdings. In the sixteenth century, Protestant reformers use the *Domboc* to tie the English Church and English common law to an authorizing native past. Archbishop Matthew Parker's Protestant reform tract *A Testimonie of Antiquitie*, and William Lambarde's collection of English law, the *Archaionomia*, both employ the *Domboc* to link their religious and legal campaigns to validating Anglo-Saxon precedent.

In examining the texts and contexts surrounding the appearances of King Alfred's *Domboc* from its inception to its eventual publication in print, I have attempted to bring together the major voices in the fields of early English law and literature. However, one stumbling block I came across early in my studies was a lack of a complete English translation of the *Domboc* in a single source, which would include Alfred's entire prologue as well as the complete codes of Alfred and the appended law code of his royal forbear, King Ine. To help remedy that difficulty, the above analysis is followed by an unannotated diplomatic edition and translation of the text of the *Domboc* from Cambridge, Corpus Christi College 173, the earliest and one of the most complete manuscripts of the law-book. Not intended as a scholarly edition of the *Domboc*, this translation is meant only to serve as an initial ready reference to the contents of the law code.

As in any endeavor of this nature, both thanks and apologies are in order. As for thanks, many belong to my colleagues at the Pennsylvania State University and Lycoming College for their support in my writing of the manuscript, but the most belong to the unstinting encouragement of my wife and boys: Susan, Michael, and Jack. As for apologies, they are from me for any lapses in translation or interpretation in the following text, which are surely all my own.

Introduction

Perhaps the most intimate picture we have of King Alfred's (871–899) practice of law comes from the Fonthill Letter.[1] In the letter, the writer depicts Alfred hearing a legal case as "cing stod, ðwoh his honda, æt Weardoran innan ðon bur" ([the] king stood, [and] washed his hands, within the chamber at Wardour).[2] This rather informal portrait of the king, hands dripping into a washbasin as he hears the particulars of the case, is key to understanding the way in which law functioned for Alfred, his people, and those who would claim Alfred's legal legacy in the future. Alfred's law, although part of an abstract continuum of legislation from a real or imagined past through the present and into the future, was also a living text, operating at the intersection of the regal and the commonplace. The Anglo-Saxons were a people of law, and that legislation had a direct connection to their lives. Moreover, Alfred not only refashioned this law in response to the distinct needs of his kingship and his people in his *Domboc*, or lawbook, but his legislation was also recontextualized and redeployed by those who came after the Anglo-Saxons for their own particular purposes. As David Pratt notes of the king, "every age has reinterpreted his ninth-century memory" (*Political Thought* 1) to suit their own purposes or needs. Alfred's stature as a ruler and as a symbol of Anglo-Saxon ideals and culture therefore makes him and his *Domboc* a productive locus for an inquiry into the function of Anglo-Saxon lawmaking for both the Anglo-Saxons themselves as well as their cultural and political heirs.

Whereas previous studies of the literary canon of Alfred, King of Wessex have focused on his translations of, and prefaces to, such texts as Pope Gregory's *Regula pastoralis* and Boethius' *Consolation of Philosophy*, an investigation of Alfred's *Domboc* shows the important role the text plays in defining both king and kingdom.[3] Historically, scholars have generally undervalued the *Domboc* as a crucial element of the king's canon.[4] How-

3

ever, an analysis of the contents and uses of King Alfred's law-book will demonstrate that the *Domboc* was an important source of cultural identity for the Anglo-Saxons and, eventually, the English as a nation. To this end, the *Domboc* will be examined as a literary text in a series of significant historical contexts: the late ninth century, the twelfth century, and the late sixteenth century.

The late ninth century was the period of Alfred's reign and the initial inscription of the *Domboc*, which most likely dates to within three or four years on either side of the year 890.[5] The text consists of a historical preface, Alfred's complete law code, and the appended law code of Ine (688–726). In this original incarnation of the text, the *Domboc* operates as a foundation narrative for the Anglo-Saxons as both a legislative product of Alfred's kingship and an expression of Anglo-Saxon culture. Positioning the king as the ultimate arbiter of Anglo-Saxon legislation, the text presents legislation as a means to recount the religious and political origins of the Anglo-Saxon people while providing a set of laws representative of their culture's core values. A close reading of the *Domboc* reveals the concept of financial compensation, represented through the Anglo-Saxon term *bot*, to be an important marker of Anglo-Saxon cultural identity. Investigating the role of *bot* in the laws is central to an understanding of the text's function as a cultural and political statement of national identity.

The link between the law-book and national identity forms the basis for the *Domboc*'s reappearance in the late eleventh and early twelfth centuries. The importance of this period to the present study hinges upon *Domboc*'s utility in the wake of conquest. Both the Danish conquerors of the eleventh century and the Norman conquerors of the twelfth century seized upon the *Domboc* as a text linking legislation to an authorizing past. They used the law-book to legitimize their respective claims to rule. Cnut (1016–1035), for example, initiates his reign over the Anglo-Saxons by issuing a law code (*I-II Cnut*) containing excerpts of Alfred's *Domboc*. This legislative correlation of Cnut's rule with that of the earlier Anglo-Saxons ameliorated the shock of conquest and legitimized the new king's rule through association with the Anglo-Saxon royal line.

Anglo-Normans of the twelfth century followed the Danish example of post-conquest legislation by issuing the *Instituta Cnuti* (c. 1080), which collected and expanded upon *I-II Cnut*, including yet more excerpts from the *Domboc* to again tie the current administration to an Anglo-Saxon precedent. The entire text of the *Domboc* also surfaced in Norman legal encyclopedias of the time, such as the *Quadripartitus* (c. 1100), in an effort to establish the continuity of rule from Anglo-Saxon to Norman administrations. Yet the conquered native Old English speaking scribes of the twelfth century also reproduced Alfred's law-book in combination with other legal and historical texts in an effort to legitimize both real and spurious pre-conquest claims to rights and holdings. Such was the case of Rochester Priory's *Textus Roffensis* (c. 1123), a manuscript combining a legal encyclopedia, royal genealogy, and cartulary with the aim of bolstering the priory's claims to pre-conquest entitlements.

However, foreign conquest has not been the only impetus to reproduce the *Domboc*. The late sixteenth century marks the first time Old English texts, and Alfred's law in particular, came into print (as opposed to earlier manuscript transmissions). The impetus for printing Alfred's laws was the transfer of English royal power from the Catholic Mary I (1553–1558) to the Protestant Elizabeth I (1558–1603). At this time the *Domboc* appeared in both a religious tract, Archbishop Parker's *A Testimonie of Antiquitie* (1566), and also a legal encyclopedia, William Lambarde's *Archaionomia* (1568). This re-emergence of the *Domboc* signals the significant role Alfred's text played in invoking a connection to Anglo-Saxon roots in the negotiation of English national identity during the Reformation.

At each of these points on the timeline, Alfred's *Domboc* served particular literary, cultural, political, and religious ends. Each new audience and regime used the *Domboc* to its own best advantage. As such, the text provides a window on the way law functions in the creation and maintenance of governmental administrations. Further, Alfred's *Domboc* can serve as a point of entry into the relationship between legal texts and authority, as the law code significantly participates in the establishment of royal and ecclesiastical legitimization. An investigation of the law code offers insight into a kind of secular, royal authority that is not entirely negotiated through Carolingian models of kingship, nor completely mediated by Christianity.[6] Rather, the significant redeployments of the laws help to define an important aspect of English rule: the making and perpetuation of a perceived native/indigenous Germanic approach to Anglo-Saxon royal authority.[7]

The *Domboc*, therefore, functions as a foundation narrative through the interconnected processes of forging both royal and national identities. As such, legislation is a means by which a king can forward an image of himself and his realm, establishing both the social order as well as an identity for himself and his subjects. As Pratt helpfully summarizes, "Law as written text gave force to shared identity, in multiple accounts of ethnic or corporate unity" (*Political Thought* 215). This process of self-identification depends upon both the larger action of enacting legislation and the particulars of that legislation's content. Subsequently, an examination of the significant occasions of the *Domboc*'s textual history (its earliest manuscript context, its redeployment following the Danish and Norman conquests, and its first appearance in print in the sixteenth century), demonstrates how people reproduced the *Domboc* to serve particular social, political, and institutional ends contingent upon that identifiably Anglo-Saxon national identity. In essence, the *Domboc* emerges as a document that is continually used as part of a project to reconfigure an English/Anglo-Saxon national identity that is both drawn from the past even as it is shaped by contemporary circumstances.

To best understand the *Domboc*'s functions over the years, it is necessary to consider a number of fundamental problems in the study of Anglo-Saxon laws. First, legal historians usually agree that laws were recorded as part of a dispute or issue that demanded the restatement of an existing verbal statute, or as a summation of unwritten conventions.[8] Therefore, the extant laws do not represent a complete code, but only a record of those laws demanding special attention. However, this model of legislation is only partial. It does not obviate the political function of the issuing of a law code. Disseminating his law code was a significant political act that helped to secure Alfred's place among great English kings.[9] Even when a law code was inscribed as an adjunct to unwritten norms, its very inscription served as a powerful political statement.

Further, of those laws that were put into writing, the codes either do not necessarily agree with one another or are now represented only by fragments.[10] In some cases, complete codes are lost from the existing manuscript record, even though their prior existence is recognized in surviving documents. Additionally, these remaining codes and fragments are not necessarily the initial, legal recordings of the laws directly from a ruler or legislative body. Rather, both time and place separated these laws from their probable royal or legislative inception. Moreover, the extant laws are copies that were generally produced and stored at religious houses, not legislative institutions. They were also usually copied a good deal later than the enactment or inscription of their exemplars.[11] Anything said about Anglo-Saxon law codes must be tentative in light of these difficulties.[12]

All of the above caveats certainly apply to the study of Alfred's law code. However, these difficulties do not necessarily preclude an interpretation of the significance of the *Domboc*'s production and reproductions. The fact that its extant laws may not reflect the complete written and oral record of the laws of Alfred's reign, in fact, may provide important clues as to what kinds of law carried enough import to be committed to the relatively costly vehicle of manuscript inscription. In the same vein, the preservation of entire or partial codes over time can serve as testimony not only to the serendipity of manuscript survival, but also to the significance of some of their contents or overarching ideology.

Alfred's *Domboc*, for example, survived the centuries at least partly due to multiple copying (nineteen extant manuscripts). These manuscript copies of the *Domboc* appear, however, specifically in centuries marked by conquest or substantial internal changes that threaten cultural cohesiveness. When the culture is challenged, from within or without, the law-book, as a cultural icon, serves as a link to a common ancestry that provides continuity for the conquered and stability for the secular and clerical leaders wielding the text. Finally, the preservation of the surviving manuscripts in ecclesiastical settings highlights the importance of the content of the text even while it clarifies the relationships between sacred and secular authorities, emphasizing the co-dependence of one upon the other.

The *Domboc* contains laws of both clerical and secular concern. The text begins with an Old English translation of large sections from the Decalogue (Exodus 20:1–17, 23). Sections of the Book of the Covenant (Exodus 21:2–16, 18–22:11, 16–29, 31–23:9) follow, expanding on material in the Decalogue. These sections are followed by Alfred's history of the law of God as it passed from Moses to Christ, from Christ to the apostles, and finally from the apostles to holy bishops and wise men. Alfred then tells how secular rulers adapted these laws and how he "togædere gegaderode" (gathered together) (*Af El.* 49.9) the laws of which he and his councillors approved.

The laws gathered in the *Domboc* are primarily concerned with managing disruptions of the social order through conditional restitution. Most establish the payment for compensation in an if-then formula. For example: "Gif hwa ymb cyninges feorh sierwe [...] sie he his feores scyldig 7 ealles þæs ðe he age" (If anyone plots against the king's life [...] let him be liable of his life and all that he owns) (*Af.* 4). Fully half of the laws pertain to specific bodily injuries: "Gif him mon aslea oþer eare of, geselle

XXX scill. to bote" (If a man strikes off another man's ear, give 30 shillings to compensate) (*Af.* 46). Alfred follows his laws with the laws of another West Saxon king, Ine. Alfred likely includes Ine's laws in the *Domboc* because of the source and content of the older law code. As opposed to earlier extant Kentish laws like those of Æthelberht (reigned 560–616) or Wihtræd (reigned 691–725), Ine's code is a West Saxon law code, just like Alfred's. As such, its inclusion is in keeping with Alfred's interest in authorizing origins. Moreover, the content of Ine's code complements Alfred's laws.

Most of Ine's code has the same conditional if-then structure as Alfred's laws, with perhaps more of an emphasis in content on theft and managing slaves. For example: "Gif hwa stalie, swa his wif nyte 7 his bearn, geselle LX scill. to wite. Gif he ðonne stalie on gewitnesse ealles his hierdes, gongen hie ealle on ðeowot" (If anyone steals without his wife and children knowing, he pays 60 shillings to the king. If he then steals with his whole household knowing, they all go into slavery) (*Ine* 7–7.1). Ine's laws, then, serve as an appropriate complement to Alfred's law code in both form and content.

In addition to its content, the *Domboc*'s manuscript history also helps to illustrate the function of Alfred's law-book over time. Of Alfred's laws in Old English, six extant manuscripts survive:

- Cambridge, Corpus Christi College 173 (the "Parker Chronicle")
- Cambridge, Corpus Christi College 383
- London, British Library Cotton Nero A. i
- London, British Library Cotton Otho B. xi
- London, British Library Burney 277
- Rochester Cathedral Library A. 3. 5 (the *Textus Roffensis*)[13]

Additionally, Alfred's law code was twice translated into Latin:

- *Instituta Cnuti* III[14]
  - Rochester Cathedral Library A. 3. 5
  - London, British Library Cotton Titus A. 27
  - Paris, Bibliothèque Nationale, Colbert 3,860
  - Oxford, Bodleian, Rawlinson C. 641
- *Quadripartitus*[15]
  - London, British Library Cotton Domitian viii
  - London, British Library Royal 11.B.ii

- London, British Library Additional 49366
- London, British Library Cotton Titus A.xxvii
- Manchester, John Rylands Library, Lat 420
- London Collection[16]
  - ★ London, British Library Cotton Claudius D.ii
  - ★ Manchester, John Rylands Library, Lat 155
  - ★ Cambridge, Corpus Christi College MSS 70+258
  - ★ Oxford, Oriel College, 46

The extant manuscripts of the Old English text give testament to the varied survivals of the law code. Cambridge, Corpus Christi College (CCCC) 173, the *Parker Chronicle*, contains the earliest copy of the law code (c. 890–1000), and is one of the two complete manuscript versions, including all 120 sections, as numbered in the manuscripts.[17] The only other manuscript to contain a complete copy is Rochester A.3.5, the *Textus Roffensis*, the latest copy of the laws (c. 1122).[18] Aside from these two complete texts, the *Domboc*'s textual life was more troubled.

British Library (BL) Cotton Otho B. xi, for example, was severely damaged in the Cotton Library fire of 1731. Luckily, its readings were salvaged thanks to a mid-sixteenth-century transcription by Laurence Nowell.[19] BL Cotton Nero A. i. contains only the capitula to the laws.[20] CCCC 383 contains, as numbered in the manuscripts, Alfred's law sections 4 (partial) through 37 (partial) and sections 39 (partial) through the end of Alfred's code (section 43). This manuscript also preserves Ine's code in its entirety.[21] Finally, BL Burney 277 contains the very end of Ine's prologue (section 44) through Ine's law section 47 (partial).[22] BL Burney 277 should be considered a manuscript of Alfred's laws, even though it contains only a segment of Ine's code, as Ine's code is known elsewhere only through its transmission with Alfred's law code. These fragmentary survivals of Alfred's law-book in Old English show the susceptibility of early texts to the ravages of time.

Yet Alfred's *Domboc* had an added bulwark against the vagaries of manuscript survival: its reproduction in Latin legal compilations. Just as Alfred chose "þa ðe me ryhtoste ðuhton, ic þa heron gegaderode" (those [laws] that seemed to me the rightest, [and] I gathered together those [laws] herein) (49.9), so the compilers of the Latin *Quadripartitus* and the *Instituta Cnuti* gathered Alfred's law code into their own.[23] Of course, the interpretation of a compilation can be problematic. Just as there is a question as to what role Alfred himself played in the actual writing of the texts attributed to him, so there needs to be caution in assuming that the various compilations of his law code reflect a single, identifiable intelligence.[24] The governing methodologies behind the compilation of a given manuscript can range from "grab bags, with texts [...] collected and copied into a manuscript for no discernable reason" to texts where "there clearly is an organizational principle behind the arrangement of texts in an Old English codex" (F. C. Robinson 23–24).

To interpret every collocation of texts as necessarily meaningful is as dubious as ignoring the possibilities of codicological commentary. Especially in its Latin incarnations, Alfred's code coexists with other legal codes in a way that begs comparison with them. His *Domboc* is presented in its entirety in all the *Quadripartitus* manuscripts, with the exceptions of John Rylands Library, MS Lat 420, and Cotton Domitian viii. The latter manuscript is incomplete, ending after only one quire in the midst of Alfred's code. The former lacks its initial two quires, picking up the text with Ine's code as appended to Alfred's.[25] In both cases, it may be safe to assume the remainder of Alfred's code would be found in the missing quires. Alternately, Alfred's laws are more selectively incorporated into the *Instituta Cnuti*, suggesting the compiler's focus on particular laws over wholesale reproduction of the text.

The specific content of the laws plays an important function in defining Alfred's role as king and the identity of his realm. Therefore, an examination of the laws both as a cohesive whole and as individual statutes will demonstrate their significance in the fashioning of Alfred's kingship. Further, such an investigation of this legislation's manuscript contexts and initial print incarnations will show their link to contemporary and subsequent ideas of West Saxon and English national identities.

A close examination of the manuscripts of the codes and their subsequent redeployments can help to reveal the implied associations between legal material and clerical, genealogical, and historical narratives. Thus, the law code can be seen to be working both within and against traditional conceptions of genre, revealing the possible forms and functions of early medieval prose more fully. More specifically, such an investigation can trace the function of legislation through its hybrid literary and official employments of the vernacular. The law code, in this fashion, serves as a nexus of language and ideology. This intersection accounts for Alfred's continued portrayal as a kind of Anglo-Saxon Renaissance man, as anachronistic a label as it may be, while simultaneously demanding a closer appraisal of the historical moment in which this work was compiled. In turn, a closer appraisal must also be made of the continuing invocations of that historical moment over the centuries. Finally, an inquiry into the presentation of the laws of King Alfred can explain how their several representations figure in the continuing negotiations of an English national, cultural, and literary identity.

Accordingly, the first chapter provides contexts for the subsequent reading of the *Domboc* by examining the intersections of kingship, law, and national identity in ninth-century Wessex, the time of its creation and original inscription. For Alfred, lawmaking is more than the mere codification of legal statutes. Both the act *and* the content of legislation are essential functions of kingship, instrumental in forging royal and national identities. Alfred's debt to both native and continental models of kingship emphasizes the codification of law as an essential function of kingship. Comparisons of Alfred's *Domboc* to Bede's *Historia ecclesiastica*, Asser's *Vita Alfredi*, Einhard's *Vita Karoli*, the Old English *Exodus*, and earlier Anglo-Saxon legislation illuminate the model of royal legislation Alfred tries to forward in his text. The codification of law in the *Domboc* emerges as having both specific political and ideological functions. Politically, the *Domboc* establishes the king's administrative station and governmental function. Ideologically, the *Domboc* forwards a West-Saxon national identity dependent upon a Mosaic model of covenant.

The next chapter shows that Alfred's *Domboc* is primarily indebted to the secular cultural practice of adjudication dependent upon the *bot* system. This is a system of compensation based on remuneration for social transgressions. The *Domboc* builds a cumulative case for the importance of Anglo-Saxon cultural practice to Alfred's kingship and kingdom, as evidenced by the pervasive use of the language of *bot*. Alfred translates portions of the Old and New Testaments in terms of the *bot* system. He also reconciles the cultural roles of lord and king through the mechanics of the *bot* system. His dependence upon the *bot* system in legislation also mediates his relationship to prior rulers as legislators. This reliance upon a culturally identifiable Anglo-Saxon form of jurisprudence lays the foundation for future incarnations of the text.

The third chapter investigates the reappearance of Alfred's *Domboc* in the late eleventh and early twelfth centuries, illuminating the role the *Domboc* plays in the formation and strategic invocations of national identity. Alfred's promotes a West-Saxon national identity through his use of kingship and kinship terminology in the text's historical preface. This may explain why the *Domboc*, in whole or in part, appears in the laws of Cnut (*I-II Cnut*), William the Conqueror (reigned 1066–87) (*Instituta Cnuti*), and Henry I (reigned 1100–35) (*Quadripartitus*) following the Danish and Norman conquests of the Anglo-Saxons. The representation of the king and his realm through their specific connection to an Anglo-Saxon national identity is in turn employed by these later rulers as a legitimizing link to a native royal authority. Finally, the case of Rochester Cathedral's *Textus Roffensis* serves as an example of the reproduction of Alfred's *Domboc* for specific institutional ends that are contingent upon the text's expression of a legitimizing national identity.

The final chapter provides an analysis of the circumstances surrounding the *Domboc's* first appearances in print, excerpted in Matthew Parker's 1566 *A Testimonie of Antiquitie* and printed fully in William Lambarde's 1568 *Archaionomia*. Parker's and Lambarde's texts are two of a number of reproductions of Anglo-Saxon texts executed by the archbishop's circle in the mid-1560s that directly participate in the formation of a Protestant English national identity. Through the transcriptions and editions of the archbishop and his circle, these men invoke Alfred's law code in the interests of redefining the English nation by recalling the king's connection to a native legitimizing authority.

Parker's main project in the *Testimonie* is to foster the study of early English history and language in an effort to reinforce the foundations of the recently established Church of England. Thus, his collection includes texts that serve as both religious inspiration and nationalistic propaganda. The *Domboc* extract is instrumental in this effort and should be read in this context as a conduit through which a particularly Anglo-Saxon royal authority is called upon at a critical juncture of the redefinition of English national identity. Both Lambarde and Parker reproduce the text to supply their countrymen with a link to an authorizing native past. For Parker, that link is to the practices of the early English Church that coincide with Protestant doctrine. For Lambarde, the *Domboc* supplies a connection to early English law, emphasizing the native legislation over a Roman model. Both translator-editors manipulate the text in the service of promoting a specific Anglo-Saxon cultural heritage for the religion and law of Elizabethan England.

Alfred's *Domboc*, then, emerges as a critical element of the king's canon in the formation of both royal and national identities. In particular, it is the *Domboc*'s presentation of a validating native authority that accounts for its repeated reinscription and eventual publication at times of national and cultural crisis. Large cultural changes due to political and religious upheavals call for national unification to provide a sense of safety and social cohesion in uncertain times. A shared past is one route to a sense of unity, and that is what the *Domboc* provides. In the face of foreign invasion, foreign conquest, and religious reformation, Alfred's law book serves as a conduit to an affirming shared past.

CHAPTER 1

Kingship, Law, and National Identity in Ninth-Century Wessex

Understanding the function of King Alfred's *Domboc* at the time of its inscription necessitates a theory of law that examines the intersections of kingship, law, and national identity in ninth-century Wessex. The ideals and practices of Alfred's kingship determine the ideological and political functions of his version of Anglo-Saxon law. In turn, the principles and performance of his kingship and his use of law together fundamentally shape the burgeoning sense of a West-Saxon national identity during Alfred's reign. The connections between the practice of Anglo-Saxon kingship, the function of Anglo-Saxon law, and the growing conception of a West-Saxon national identity in ninth-century Wessex lay the conceptual foundation for a discussion of the importance of the *Domboc*'s role as both an important product and source of culture.

I argue for an Alfredian theory of law in which both the act and content of legislation are essential elements of kingship and are instrumental in forging royal and national identities. A consideration of the *Domboc*'s role in representing these elements of law shows that the king's law-book is instrumental in the contemporary fashioning of Alfred's royal identity, as well as the identity of his West-Saxon kingdom. The codification of law in the *Domboc* establishes royal and national identities through ideological and political functions. Ideologically, the *Domboc* forwards a model of kingship authorized by Christian ideals, but actualized through Anglo-Saxon juridical cultural practice.[1] Since Alfred begins his text with Moses, the Old English *Exodus* serves as an instructive analog to Alfred's own negotiation of biblical ideals and Anglo-Saxon cultural norms in rulership.[2]

Alfred's use of an apostolic letter, Acts of the Apostles, 15:23–29, provides further context for this negotiation and directly speaks to the role of the written text in governance. Politically, the *Domboc* establishes the king's station and governmental function and forwards a West-Saxon national identity through describing the scope of his realm. Thus, the *Domboc* emerges as a crucial text to the understanding of Alfred's conception and execution of kingship.

The Current Scholarly Model

The perception of Alfred's creation of the *Domboc* has been problematized by the king's association with Carolingian kingship.[3] However, the Carolingian model of royal legislation is not the sole template at work in Alfred's context, as the example of Charlemagne illustrates. In his *Vita Karoli*, Einhard lists the many accomplishments of the Carolingian Charlemagne, including the emperor's attention to the law of his people: "cogitavit quae deerant addere et discrepantia unire, prava quoque ac perperam prolata corrigere" (he [Charlemagne] intended to add what they lost and to reconcile discrepancies, and also to correct the improperly and incorrectly cited).[4] However, the task proved too unruly for the emperor, who resigned himself to getting the law available to him into writing: "Ominum tamen nationum, quae sub eius dominatu erant, iura quae scripta non erant describere ac litteris mandari fecit" (Yet of all of the nations that were under his rule, he made it to be commanded that the laws which were not written were to be written out and [collected in] books).[5] Einhard's description of Charlemagne's codification of law emphasizes the act of inscription over the mastery of content. Even though Charlemagne could not effect the inclusions and corrections he initially wanted, the emperor nonetheless commands an imperfect inscription for the sake of totality.

One can mistakenly assume that Alfred follows Charlemagne's example, insofar as Alfred's stated aim is to also assemble a relatively comprehensive body of legislation: "Ic þa Ælfred cyning þas togædere gegaderode 7 awritan het, monege þara þe ure foregengan heoldon, ða ðe me licodon; 7 manege þara þe me ne licodon ic awearp mid minra witena geðeahte" (I, Alfred king, then gathered these [laws] together and commanded [my witan] to write down many of those [laws] that our predecessors held,

16

which to me seemed good; and many that did not seem good to me I set aside with my wise men's counsel) (*Af El.* 49.9).[6] Like Einhard's Charlemagne, the primary legislative goal in Alfred's case could wrongly be seen as prioritizing inscription over the manipulation of content. Indeed, the preface to his law code emphasizes that Alfred merely "gegaderode" (gathered together) laws as the king. Any inference of authorial interference by the king is explicitly downplayed: "ic ne dorste geðristlæcan þara minra awhut fela on gewrit settan" (I did not dare to presume to set much of my own [laws] at all in writing).[7] Such statements could be erroneously construed as to remove Alfred's person from his legislative work, limiting the connection between the contents of his *Domboc* and his practice of kingship. In this inappropriate application of the Carolingian model to Alfredian practice, the personalizing royal authority becomes muted in reference to the contents of legislation. Through the forced mapping of Carolingian practice onto Alfred's *Domboc*, legislation comes to be seen as large, monolithic set pieces whose contents are of less particular interest than the deployments of the laws as sealed comprehensive units.

Patrick Wormald articulates this symbolic function of legal inscription as he argues that the act of early western European lawmaking, as noted above, is more important than the content or organization of the laws themselves.[8] In this view, a law code's content and organization is secondary to the political significance of a ruler's effort to get a law code in his name on the books as a symbol of legitimate regality.[9] Following J. M. Wallace-Hadrill, Wormald argues, "Germanic kings made laws, first and foremost, partly in order to emulate the literary legal culture of the Roman and Judaeo-Christian civilization to which they were heirs, and partly in order to reinforce the links that bound a king or dynasty to their people." (Wormald, "*Lex*" 136).[10] This point of view argues that the primary function of issuing laws in the ninth century was not to legislate, but to assert the legitimacy of the lawmaker's royal standing.[11] In doing so, law links the lawgiver to a self-identified cultural heritage, establishing an ideological setting to which the lawgiver hopes to conform. Simultaneously, law identifies and reaffirms the lawgiver's political station and relationship to his subjects as he defines them. However, the undervaluing of the importance of the content of Alfred's law code does not take into account its significant role in shaping both Alfred's royal image and the emerging sense of national identity among the West Saxons.[12] While Wormald devotes his argument primarily to the level of the *act* of lawgiving, an examination of the content and contexts of the *Domboc* shows that political and ideological functions of the law are written into both the preface to the text and the individual laws as well. Specifically, the contents of these elements of the text show King Alfred to be using detail to establish both royal and national identities.

Law and Ideology: The Mosaic Model

Ninth-century Anglo-Saxon law is ideological in its shaping of royal and national identity through appeals to a self-chosen cultural inheritance. The power of this ideological appeal cannot be underestimated. As Pierre Bourdieu argues, "one of the major powers of the state is to produce and impose [...] categories of thought that we spontaneously apply to all things of the social world — including the state itself" (35). The state is therefore able to wield an active role in its own categorization through legislation: "the site par excellence of the concentration and exercise of symbolic power" (Bourdieu 47). In the case of Alfred's Wessex, the concentration of symbolic power is evident in the preface to his law code. In order to create an authorizing identity for himself and his kingdom, Alfred presents a cultural heritage that traces a direct line from Moses, through Christ and his apostles, and ultimately to the West Saxons and his own person. In the act of directly connecting his legislation to a Judeo-Christian tradition of sanctified legislation, Alfred is a legislative innovator. Alfred is the first Anglo-Saxon king on record to use his legislation to articulate a specific Anglo-Saxon identity constructed through a narrative of kingdom formation.

Earlier Kentish and West Saxon laws, of which Alfred was aware, show the beginnings of using legislation to inscribe culture and most likely informed his own approach to legislation.[13] The Kentish Wihtræd (691–725) and the West Saxon Ine (688–726) both offer brief discursions on the nature of lawmaking and its connection to culture.[14] In both Wihtræd's and Ine's brief prefaces to their respective codes, the kings acknowledge the communal nature of legislating. For Wihtræd, lawmaking includes input from an "eadriga geheahtendlic ymcyme" (a deliberative assembly of the prosperous) (*Wi Prolog*). For Ine, a similar group of legislative helpers is defined as "eallum minum ealdormannum 7 þæm ieldstan witum minre þeode 7 eac micelre gesomnunge Godes þeowa" (all my ealdormen and the chief councillors of my people and also a great collection of God's servants) (*Ine Prol.*). Through their law codes, these early kings delineate the communal mechanics of lawmaking and their political station in reference to it. Including the procedure of lawmaking within the law code itself signals the importance of legitimizing law based on its adherence to accepted cultural practice. As John G. H. Hudson notes, Anglo-Saxon laws are not only "signs of royal intention or aspiration, but of social practice" (35). Kings do not legislate from above their culture, but from within it.

However, Alfred goes further. Like Ine and Wihtræd, he uses his *Domboc* to preserve current cultural practice, showing that he is aware of his position within the culture and able to manipulate his role for his own ideological ends. He identifies himself both generally as "cyning" (king) (*Af. El.* 49.9) and specifically as "Westseaxna cyning" (king of the West Saxons) (*Af. El.* 49.10), and works cooperatively with "eallum minum witum" (all of my councillors) (*Af. El.* 49.10). Yet Alfred does not stop with simply inscribing culture, but uses his legislation to shape his culture by translating selections of the Old and New Testaments, tracing the history of the Church coming to England, and describing his own method of gathering laws to encode.

Alfred contextualizes his legislation in terms of the dissemination of holy law throughout the *Domboc*'s historical preface. The *Domboc* begins with Moses: "Dryhten wæs sprecende ðas word to Moyse 7 þus cwæð: Ic eom dryhten ðin god" (God was speaking these words to Moses and thus said: I am the Lord your god) (*Af. El. Pro.*). After the presentation of the Old Testament laws, Alfred reminds us that "Þis sindan ða domas þe se ælmihtega God self sprecende wæs to Moyse" (These are the laws which almighty God himself was speaking to Moses) (*Af. El.* 49). He then reminds the reader that Christ came not "ðas bebodu to brecanne ne to forbeodanne, ac mid eallum godum to eacanne" (to break or forbid these laws, but with all good to reinforce them) (*Af. El.* 49). Christ's recasting of Old Testament laws in light of the New Dispensation was then taken by the apostles "geond ealle eorðan to læranne" (through all the earth to teach [them]) (*Af. El.* 49.1). In turn, "þa wurdon monega seonoðas geond ealne middangeard gegaderode, 7 swa geond Angelcyn" (then were many synods gathered throughout all of middle-earth, and also throughout the English race) (*Af. El.* 49.7) Alfred went to these laws and "þas togædere gegaderode" (gathered these together) (*Af. El.* 49.9) as the basis of his own laws.

The cumulative effect of this preface is the forging of an ideological project that places Alfred's West Saxons as explicit heirs to a Judeo-Christian kingdom of both man and God. In the *Domboc*'s preface, "the account of devine law is largely replicated, but within the framework of English lawgiving" (Pratt, *Political Thought* 227). Through this preface, Alfred and his subjects are metonymically assigned the honored place of the Old Testament Israelites: God's chosen people.[15] Further, Alfred, as king, figures as an Anglo-Saxon apostle, bringing holy law to his people. By placing these Old and New Testament examples of lawgiving as preface to his own law code, Alfred engages an ideological agenda to proclaim his kingdom as God's kingdom.

This agenda is evident in Alfred's choice of Old Testament material for his preface. Alfred begins the *Domboc* by translating a large part of the book of Exodus, chapters 20 through 23:19. These chapters follow the disclosure on Mount Sinai of God's law to Moses, including the Decalogue (the Ten Commandments) and the Book of the Covenant (specific stipulations surrounding the Commandments). The book of Exodus is a powerfully meaningful text for the Anglo-Saxons. As Malcolm Godden argues, "For the Anglo-Saxons the Old Testament was a veiled way of talking about their own situation. [...It] offered them a means of articulating the ways in which kingship, politics, and warfare relate to the rule of God" ("Biblical" 225).[16] Alfred exemplifies this approach to Old Testament literature by invoking Mosaic law, and the figure of Moses, to establish his ideological project of forwarding his rule as that over God's chosen people.

Alfred's commencing of his *Domboc* with this structure invites the comparison between his earthly rule and the heavenly rule of God. The Decalogue and the Book of the Covenant are in the form of a lord-man pledge. In the Exodus, the Covenant is "a conditional divine pledge to be Israel's God (as her Protector and Guarantor of her blessed destiny); the condition: Israel's total consecration to the Lord as his people (his kingdom) who live by his rule and serve his purposes in history" (Barker and Burdick 19).[17] More generally, such biblical pledges manage the relationship between lord and subject. The lord claims absolute sovereignty and requires service and loyalty from his subject. In return the subject receives protection and succor, but such treatment is conditional upon the subject's fidelity.[18] In initiating his *Domboc* with a recounting of the covenant between the Old Testament God and the Israelites, Alfred establishes a template for his own earthly rule. God proclaims that he shall be "faciens misericordiam in milia his qui diligunt me et custodiunt preacepta mea" (granting mercy to thousands, to those who love me and keep my commandments) (Exodus 20:6).

Alfred similarly establishes sovereignty over those who swear allegiance to him. Indeed, the very first of Alfred's laws regards the keeping of one's "að and wedd" (oath and pledge) (*Af.* 1), presumably including the principal oath of loyalty to one's king.[19] The parallel dictates of allegiance called for by God and by an earthly king provide a consonant template for a basic element of kingship, the lord-man pledge.

The comparison between earthly and divine covenants is more than merely symbolic. Wormald seems to underestimate Alfred in arguing for a predominantly symbolic relationship between these covenants. He contends that the *Domboc* "proclaimed the destiny of a kingdom that had survived God-given punishment, and might now enter its inheritance. If this was Alfred's point, it may have mattered less that his laws, seen as *laws*, were miscellaneous in content and erratic in arrangement. The objective would have been to get *any* West Saxon law into writing" (Wormald, *Making* 427). Certainly, there is a symbolic relationship between the Israelites of the book of Exodus and the Anglo-Saxons. Nicholas Howe's treatment of the Old English (OE) *Exodus* as evidence of the aligning of Anglo-Saxon and Israelite histories along the theme of migration myth provides ample evidence of the symbolic power of the book of Exodus story for the Anglo-Saxons.[20] However, Alfred did more than unreflectively place a section of the book of Exodus at the start of his text for symbolic effect. He manages the text in such a way as to make its particular contents more consonant with the values of his audience. The inclusion of Mosaic law is of symbolic importance, but the king's treatment of it tailors it further for his specific ideological purposes to promulgate a royal and national image.[21]

Moreover, the very calling up of Moses' character has specific ideological implications for Alfred's text. By first turning to Moses, the primary authoritative Judaic lawgiver, Alfred invokes a key figure of the intersection of earthly and heavenly rule. Beginning the *Domboc* with God's words to Moses stresses the relationship between divine progenitor and human authority.[22] Moses, as opposed to Christ, is a son of man. He is God's representative on earth, but is, himself, completely human. An earthly king could not hope to completely emulate Christ, an incarnation of God on earth. However, he could hope to aspire to Moses' station: that of human being authorized to act as intermediary between God and the people he leads. While scholars have widely commented upon the influence of Mosaic law upon Alfred's law code, the significance of Moses' symbolic role merits further investigation.[23]

The OE *Exodus* can provide a helpful insight into the Anglo-Saxon perception of Moses' role as a human intermediary for God and, by extension, into how Alfred may have been employing this pivotal figure as both a sacred and secular model of leadership. Alfred appears to have been aware of the typological portrayal of Moses in which the OE *Exodus* participates, as the patriarch's character in the Old English poem is strikingly close to the image Alfred forwards of himself in the *Domboc*.[24] Yet it is impossible to directly place the OE *Exodus* text in Alfred's hands. However, it is not improbable to conjecture that the depiction of Moses portrayed in the OE *Exodus* may well have been available to him, through either the Mosaic typological tradition or the poem itself.

In addition to the symbol Moses provides Alfred, the king translates Mosaic law in a rhetorical move that relates the law-giving power of a spiritual leader (Moses) to that of a secular leader (Alfred). This may be especially relevant to Moses' portrayal in the *Exodus*, if, in fact, his "importance is not personal but political–as leader of the people or mediator between the people and God–for this is a *political* history" (Walzer 12). Alfred's evoking of the Moses of the Old English poem versus that of the biblical book of Exodus is significant in the resulting scope of the king's identification with the patriarch. The action of the poem focuses primarily on the Israelites' flight across the bed of the Red Sea (Exodus 13:20–14.11), ending with the distribution of treasure on the far shore. In the OE *Exodus*, the patriarch's failure to reach the Promised Land is not addressed. Rather, the role of Moses as an effective spiritual and military leader of a united people is the focus of the poem as it "celebrates the collective group bound together by a common religion and plight" (Howe, *Migration* 76). Such a vision of Moses would be particularly relevant to Alfred, besieged as he was by pagan invaders. Moses' role as leader of a beleaguered people looking for succor parallels Alfred's portrayal of his own kingdom in another Alfredian text.

The king offers a model of his kingdom strikingly similar to the situation of the Israelites of the OE *Exodus* in his preface to the *Regula pastoralis*. He re-imagines the more perfect times of his forebears: "hu ða kyningas ðe ðone onwald hæfdon ðæs folces [on ðam dægum] Gode & his ærendwrecum hersumedon; & hie ægðer ge hiora sibbe ge hiora siodo ge hiora onweald innanbordes gehioldon, & eac ut hiora eðel gerymdon; & hu him ða speow ægðer ge mid wige ge mid wisdome" (how the kings who had authority over this people [in those days] obeyed God and his representatives; and they both kept their peace, and their morality, and their authority at home and also extended their country; and how they succeeded both in war and in wisdom).[25] Moses, as God's "mouthpiece" in the OE *Exodus*, is analogous to God's "representatives" for the Anglo-Saxons in Alfred's preface in the *Regula pastoralis*. Both serve the function of bearing God's law to humanity.

The roughly analogous positions of Alfred and Moses as lawgivers and as representatives of authority are evident in the way in which "the king was seriously considering the law of Exodus in relation to the conditions of his own time" (Whitelock, *English Historical Documents* 362–63). This is especially appropriate given the typological use of Moses in the *Exodus*. By referring to Moses as "manna mildost" (*Exodus* 550), Charles Wright argues that "the *Exodus*-poet thus took advantage of a coincidence of biblical authority and poetic tradition: an alliterative phrase which would have implied an ideology of kingship at once Germanic and Christian" (443). If such a depiction of the patriarch in the OE *Exodus* is any gauge of the ninth-century West Saxon conception of Moses, Alfred's use of Mosaic law at the outset of his *Domboc* further cements the symbolic relationship between the Israelites of the book of Exodus and the Anglo-Saxons.

Alfred's use of Moses here hinges upon the patriarch's ethos as a divinely ordained *martial* leader, a point too often glossed over. For example, Sarah Foot argues that Alfred's use of Moses is merely "legislating here overtly in the tradition of a Christian king, against an historical background of Old Testament lawgiving" (32). However, Alfred is actually using Moses as a figure imbued with the values and characteristics of a good Anglo-Saxon secular leader. Forged by Judeo-Christian culture, the Moses of the OE *Exodus* has to act in accordance with Anglo-Saxon cultural practice. In presenting Moses as the progenitor of law in accordance with God's dictates, Alfred is also trading upon the Anglo-Saxon portrayal of Judeo-Christian figures in terms of the Germanic heroic idiom.

Moses, in the OE *Exodus*, is described in terms familiar to Germanic heroic poetry.[26] Much as the "Dream of the Rood" presents a stunning example of Christ as warrior, in which he is described as *ellen* (brave) (34), *strang and stiðmod* (strong and resolute) (40), and *modig* (bold) (41), the OE *Exodus* gives us a Moses with qualities both Biblical and Germanic.[27] Moses, in the *Exodus*, "wæs leof Gode, leoda aldor, / horsc ond hreðergleaw, herges wisa, / freom folctoga" (was loved by God, a leader of the people,

/ wise and prudent, the leader of the army, / a bold commander) (12–14a). By God, Moses "gesealde wæpna geweald wið wraðra gryre; / ofercom mid þy campe cneomaga fela, / feonda folcriht" (was given command of weapons against the fierceness of the hostile ones; / overcame many nations (tribes) by means of that struggle, / the common law of enemies) (20–22a). The emphasis on personality traits valued in Anglo-Saxon leaders accommodates scriptural characters to Alfred's own milieu. Through scripture and secular poetry, Moses is associated with both spiritual and earthly leadership.

The rhetorical position afforded by such a dual sacred and secular leadership is in keeping with Alfred's treatment of proper leadership in his translation of Gregory's *Regula pastoralis*, where Alfred merges the roles of secular ruler and sacred teacher.[28] Indeed, for Alfred a key aspect of a ruler is to be a godly man who leads by the example of righteous living. Through incorporating the figure of Moses into his *Domboc*, Alfred fulfills the ideological function of law to firmly attach his rule to that of a self-selected cultural forebear.

Law and Ideology: The Apostolic Model

Christ receives rather less attention than Moses does in Alfred's preface, as the king appears more comfortable focusing on the earthly conduits of God's authority. Alfred glosses over Christ's life relatively quickly to focus on the savior's message and its dissemination through the proselytizing of the apostles. Alfred briefly considers Christ in paragraphs *Af El.* 49 through *Af El.* 49.1 of the preface to his law code to mark a transition from a focus on the Old Testament to the New. As Moses was the human conduit for the Ten Commandments, so Christ emerges as the (at least partly) human medium for bringing God's law to humanity in the New Testament (*Af El.* 49). However, Alfred moves quickly past Christ's physical lifetime. While Moses' personal role in lawgiving spans sections *Af El.* 1– 49, Christ's life from when he "on middangeard cwom"(came to middle-earth) (*Af El.* 49) to the time of "his þrowunge" (his suffering [on the cross]) (*Af El.* 49.1) takes only six lines in the manuscript (CCCC 173).[29] Rapidly passing over Christ's physical travails allows Alfred to more effectively address his main conceptual point, Christ as teacher.

In the text, the language of rulership is the language of instruction. Although small, the brief section of the preface relating Christ's life contains a key change in Alfred's language and model of legislation. The commanding "bebead" (to command) of Mosaic law (*Af El.* 49) becomes the instructional "læranne" (to teach) of Christian law (*Af El.* 49.1). Such a change in rhetoric follows Alfred's view of rulership as expressed in his translation of the *Regula pastoralis*. As his translation states: "se cræft þæs lareowdomes bið cræft ealra cræfta" (the craft of teaching is the craft of all crafts).[30] Above all, effective leaders are effective *lareowas* (teachers).

The use of Matthew 15:17 at this juncture underscores Alfred's own conception of the function of his law code and the image of himself he transmits through it.[31] Alfred translates Matthew 15:17 thus: "he cwæð, þæt he ne come no þas bebodu to brecanne ne to forbeodanne, ac mid eallum godum to eacnne" (he [Christ] said, that he did not come to break nor to annul these laws, but with all goodness to bring [them] forth) (*Af El.* 49). To this translation Alfred adds, "7 mildheortnesse 7 eaðmodnesse he lærde" (and he taught mercy and kindness) (*Af El.* 49). Alfred, like Christ, portrays himself as a conduit for a higher authority: "Ic þa Ælfred cyning þas togædere gegaderode 7 awritan het, monege þara þe ure foregengan heoldon" (I, Alfred king, then gathered these [laws] together and commanded to write down many of those [laws] that our predecessors held) (*Af El.* 49.9). Alfred also portrays himself as one who has not come to rewrite the wisdom of the ages, as "ic ne dorste geðristlæcan þara minra awuht fela on gewrit settan, forðam me wæs uncuð, hwæt þæs þam lician wolde þe æfter us wæren" (I did not dare to presume to set much of my own [laws] at all in writing, because it was unknown to me what of this would be pleasing to those who were [to come] after us) (*Af El.* 49.9). The humility, genuine or not, that Alfred displays in his portrayal of his own role in lawmaking is consonant with that of Christ's role in recasting the Mosaic law of the book of Exodus 5:1–48 in Matthew 5:17–48.[32]

In this way, Alfred, like Christ, presents himself as a leader only insofar as he might make the old law meaningfully comprehensible to a new, later audience. Alfred mirrors Christ's approach to law, making plain the tie between the two lawgivers and furthering his ideological agenda to cast his own rule as that over God's chosen people: just as Christ adapts Mosaic law for the Christians, so Alfred adapts Mosaic law for the Anglo-Saxons.

Specifically, Alfred's translation of Matthew 5:17 mirrors the king's role as an adapter of texts "þa þe niedbeðearfosta sien eallum monnum to wiotonne" (which are most necessary for all men to know).[33] Again like Christ, Alfred has not come to overthrow the Old Law, but to meaningfully reconcile it to his present need for the creation of a kingdom and a collective identity for his people. Likewise, Alfred is not replacing the image of Moses as warrior-ruler, but leavening it with a ruler's need to also be compassionate and instructive. His aim, like Christ's, is to approach rulership in the manner of teacher, just as Christ refigures, but does not reject, Mosaic law in the Sermon on the Mount (Matthew 5:17–48). As the dates for the drafting of the *Domboc* and Alfred's translation of the *Regula pastoralis* are roughly contemporaneous, it is no surprise that the drive to educate his subjects should be found in both texts.[34]

Indeed, the language of teaching permeates this transition section of the preface, and teaching is fundamentally linked to Alfred's conception of kingship. It then comes as no surprise that Alfred describes Christ's in terms of how "he lærde" (he taught) (*Af El.* 49) upon his arrival on earth. Following his death on the cross, the apostles also display their leadership in terms of teaching. They "tofarene wæron geond eallum eorðan to læranne" (were dispersed throughout all of the earth to teach) (*Af El.* 49.1). When they rejoined one another, they sent an apostolic letter to Syria and Cilicia "Cristes æ to læranne" (to teach Christ's law). Alfred's kingship is marked by a similar drive. The king's educational program is evidence of the instructional nature of royal authority. Alfred's letter prefacing his translation of the *Regula pastoralis* states "þæt we eac sumæ bec, þa þe niedbeðearfosta sien eallum monnum to witonne, þæt we þa on þæt geðiode wenden þe we ealle gecnawan mægen" (that we also translate some books, which are most necessary for all men to know, into that language we all are able understand).[35] Alfred's law code is evidently closely related to, if not part of, this educational program. The model text he offers in his preface to the *Regula pastoralis* for a work worthy of translating is the "æ" (law) that was "ærest on Ebreisc geðiode funden" (first found translated into Hebrew).[36]

Through this comment, Alfred specifically ties translation of the biblical law to a nationalistic project. Translation is more than lexical and linguistic: it is political. As Alfred relates, "Ond eac ealla oðræ Cristnæ ðioda sumne dæl hiora on hiora agen geðiode wendon" (And also all other Christian nations translated some part of them [the Judeo-Christian laws] into their own language).[37] Alfred here identifies a parity between national identity, linguistic identity, and political stability. The slippage between the two identities occurs in Alfred's description of prior translations. His use of "Ebreisc" (Hebrew) refers specifically to the language, but he identifies the "Creacas" (Greeks) by nationality, while his identification of the Romans, "Lædenware" necessitates the use of a word for a national identity that includes an identification of language as a component part. The linguistic and textual form of law becomes an integral part of Alfred's shaping of a connected national identity and royal image through legislation.

In the move from a verbal legislation to its textual transmission, Alfred is presenting himself not only as a leader, like Christ or Moses, whose authority is legitimized through the source of his law, but also as a ruler whose authority, like that of the apostles, is being significantly cast in a corrective and authoritative textual form. Alfred does this through the presentation of the apostolic letter found in the Acts of the Apostles, 15:23–29. This section of Alfred's preface overtly seems to be occupied with the mechanics of the acceptance of God's law and the spreading of it by His earthly agents. First, through Christ, and then through the apostles and clergy, Alfred is tracing the dissemination of God's law from its most holy incarnation, the actual word of God, to the work of what were considered historical figures, the apostles. The mission of spreading God's word and law, Alfred realizes from Matthew 10:6 and 28:19, is tied to recognizing nationhood.[38] Alfred realizes this as the content of the letter he chooses speaks to the function of his own law code in terms of his role as leader of a unified group. As Judith Butler argues, a "speaker renews and reinvigorates the linguistic tokens of a community" through speech (39). Alfred's textual authority does not come from creating an entirely new text, but rather in re-inscribing an accepted cultural authority.

In the apostolic letter, the apostles assert the authority of the text when they first note a problem that has arisen from the verbal dissemination of God's law to Syria and Cilicia: "we geascodon, þæt ure geferan sum mid urum wordum to eow comen 7 eow hefigran [wisan budon] to healdanne þonne we him budon, 7 eow to swiðe gedwealdon mid ðam mannigfealdum beodum, 7 eowra sawla ma forhwerfdon þonne hie geryhton" (we have learned that some of our fellow disciples have come to you with our words, and commanded you to keep more oppressive customs than we commanded them, and too exceedingly have led you astray with these manifold commands, and have more perverted your souls than they have set them right) (*AfEl.* 49.3). The apostles' solution to the problem was that "sendon hie ærendgewrit to him" (they [the apostles] sent a written message to them [the Syrians and Cilicians] (*AfEl.* 49.2), to authorize the true carriers of the law, Paul and Barnabus, together with Judas and Silas (*AfEl.* 49.3–

4; Acts 15:25–27). The authority of the text empowers Paul, Barnabus, Judas, and Silas as legitimate representatives of God's law.

Alfred's choice of inserting Acts 15:23–29 at this point in his preface provides a model of authority based on textuality that he hopes to employ in his own laws. Alfred's translation of the authorizing apostolic letter more clearly defines the cultural norms of its recipients in terms of Judeo-Christian law. For Alfred's written law code, the text implies a continuum of legitimizing authority. This power originates with Moses' governing of the Israelites and is re-actualized by Alfred's own West-Saxon reign that is authorized, at least in part, by its very textuality.

Alfred's move from verbal dictate to textual authorization in written law appears in the sequence of the texts he translates. The law of God given to Moses in the section of Exodus that is translated by Alfred (20:1–23:13) was originally an oral one. It is not until Exodus 24:3 that Moses finally inscribes God's laws for the Israelites.[39] Similarly, when Alfred refers to Christ's Sermon on the Mount (Matthew 5:17), he is recalling an oral confirmation of the old law. In this text, Christ prefaces each section of his recounting of Mosaic law with the phrase "audistis quia dictum est" (you have heard that it has been said).[40] The apostles are Alfred's first example of a textually transmitted law, and the crucial link in Alfred's chain of authority. Through strategically invoking written influence via the insertion of Acts 15:23–29, Alfred presents an image of himself as spanning the hazily defined border between the written and unwritten sources of power. In doing so, he negotiates the space between Christian and Germanic legal traditions through the mixed medium at the foundation of his *Domboc*. He takes advantage of the authorial power of verbal law even as he legitimizes the textual vehicle for his own law because it facilitates operating the legislative machinery of his reign.[41] As ruler over a putatively Christian people who live in a world of Germanic cultural practices, Alfred prefaces his law in such a way as to fortify his legitimacy on both fronts.

The text of the apostolic letter itself is testament to Alfred's attempt to authorize his enlisting of a Christian heritage for his own ideological ends. In his translation of Acts 15:28 the apostles assert that "Þæm halgan Gaste wæs geðuht 7 us þæt we nane byrðenne on eow settan noldon ofer þæt ðe eow nedþearf was to healdanne" (It seemed good to the Holy Spirit and to us that we should not set any burden on you beyond that which was a necessary thing for you to hold) (*Af El.* 49.5). In presenting this text at the outset of his law code, Alfred shows that thoughtful leaders realize the disjuncture between the ideals of heavenly law and the reality of human fallibility.[42]

Although Alfred emphasizes the importance of teaching, education is effective only insofar as the audience can assimilate it. A key to effective leadership, in this model, is to steer a middle course and provide one's followers the kind and amount of law that is both in keeping with God's dictates and attainable by earthly subjects. "Whether recited or read, by king, bishop or newly literate ealdorman," Wormald argues, "the law-book aimed for an overall impact on the collective unconscious by juxtaposing familiar customs, judgments and decrees with perceptibly similar laws of God" (*Making* 427). In appealing to both Germanic customary laws and Christian strictures, Alfred makes an ideological link between the two cultures.

By invoking Mosaic law, apostolic lawgiving, and synodic history, Alfred clearly establishes an ideological agenda that casts his lawgiving as continuing Judeo-Christian tradition. In the Old Testament, law passes from God to Moses, and from him to the Israelites. In the New Testament, Mosaic law is refigured through the New Dispensation and passes from Christ to his apostles, and then from the apostles to the people. Eventually, holy law reaches the people Alfred identifies as the *Angelcynn* via the synods of "middle-earth," drawing a close correlation between the political and religious uses of the term *Angelcynn*.

First, *Angelcynn* appears in the *Domboc* to identify a people who "Cristes geleafan onfengon" (took Christ's faith) (*AfEl.* 49.7), capping the king's ideological project to cast his realm as that of the chosen people. The word *onfon* (to take) that Alfred uses here intensifies the connection between religious and political unity. This word is regularly used in connection with baptism, establishing a religious connotation for the term. Additionally, one of *onfon's* constituent elements, the word *fon* (to take), regularly appears as political a term in the *Anglo-Saxon Chronicle*,[43] usually in the construction "feng to rice" (succeeded [took] to the throne [kingdom]).[44] In becoming the *Angelcynn*, Alfred's people are succeeding to a kingdom much as adherents to Christianity are assured a place in the "regnum caelorum" (kingdom of heaven) (Matthew 5:19).

However, Alfred also seizes upon the political connotation of the word. In the *Domboc*, the politically constructed *Angelcynn* are specifically connected to the rules of Ine, Offa, and Æthelberht. Alfred cites the sources of his laws as coming from "oððe on Ines dæge, mines mæge, oððe on Offan Mercna cyninges oððe on Æðelbryhtes, the ærest fulluhte onfeng on Angelcynne" (either in Ine's day, kinsman of mine, or in Offa's [time], king of Mercia, or in Æthelberht's [time], who first accepted baptism among the Angelcynn) (*Af. El.* 49.9). The *Angelcynn* represent a people ideologically united in faith and culture, and politically constituted of the respective peoples of Wessex, Mercia (exclusive of those within the Danelaw), and Kent who come to live under Alfred's rule. Alfred acknowledges the delicate political position of including conquered peoples under the umbrella of his expanding rule. This rapid change of context and connotation of the term *Angelcynn* signals a shift in Alfred's presentation of his *Domboc* from the ideological project of the preface to a political one.

Law and Politics

As *cyning* (*Af El.* 49.9, 10), Alfred provides a picture of the politics of his administration through the lens of lawmaking. Making clear the machinery of jurisprudence of his realm serves to foster a sense of community and unity. He specifically delineates his administrative role as ruler and identifies the ethnic and faith-defined scope of his rule. He does this through emphasizing the role of accepted Anglo-Saxon cultural practices in his lawmaking.

Alfred is careful to point out that lawmaking is directed by the king, but dependent upon the approbation of his *witan*. The king highlights the importance of the *witan*'s role as a signal of his adherence to Anglo-Saxon cultural norms. Alfred is the one who "þas togædere gegaderode 7 awritan het" (gathered together these [laws] and commanded [them] to be written down) (*Af El.* 49.9), but his selection is influenced by "minra witena geðeahte" (the advice of my councillors) (*Af El.* 49.9), and his ultimate case for the rightness of his laws is that he "eallum minum witum þas geeowde, 7 hie ða cwædon, þæt him þæt licode eallum to healdanne" (showed these [laws] to all my councillors, and they then said that it pleased them all to observe [the laws]) (*Af El.* 49.10). After providing Old and New Testament examples of lawgiving, as well as explaining the role of ecclesiastical dissemination of law, the final voice of the preface to his law code is that of the *witan*, authorizing the law code by ratifying it in a specifically Anglo-Saxon milieu.

The law code also provides evidence of Alfred's political agenda in defining his realm. In the same section of the preface in which Alfred first identifies his title as king and the role of his councillors in lawmaking, he also initiates a political delineation of his kingdom: pairing his self-definition as king with the definition of his realm.[45] The *Angelcynn* who accepted Christianity and incorporated laws into their *sinoðbocas* (synod-books) are recontextualized in terms of political affiliations as Alfred chooses laws that come from "oððe on Ines dæge, mines mæge, oððe on Offan Mercna cyninges oððe on Æðelbryhtes, ðe ærest fulluhte onfeng on Angelcynne" (either in Ine's day, kinsman of mine, or in Offa's [time], king of Mercia, or in Æthelberht's [time], who first accepted baptism among the English race) (*Af. El.* 49.9). Here, Alfred is careful to emphasize the kin-based authorization of his relationship to Ine (688–726) as "mines mæges" (kinsman of mine) (*Af. El.* 49.9). As the *Anglo-Saxon Chronicle* relates, "Ða feng Ine to Seaxna rice, þes cyn geð to Ceardice" (Then Ine succeeded to the kingdom of the [West] Saxons, whose ancestry goes back to Cerdic).[46]

Alfred's kin-relationship to Ine, and thereby ultimately to Cerdic, the founder of the West Saxon royal house, underwrites his legitimate claim to the ancestral lands of Wessex.[47] However, since he also rules over people who could identify themselves as Mercian or Kentish, he reinforces his right to govern them as well by establishing the connection between his law and the laws of these other regions. For example, Alfred credits Offa (758–96), "Mercna cyninges" (king of Mercia), as a source for his law code. He also makes reference to Æthelberht, a Kentish king (560–616), as the first of the *Angelcynn* (English race) to accept baptism, neatly tying together the threads of legislation, national identity, and religious approbation all in one reference.

Politically, Alfred's attaching the genesis of his law code to the legal traditions of Wessex, Mercia, and Kent figures the king as a legitimate authority over the peoples of these regions.[48] In reality, Alfred's debt to Offa is difficult to ascertain, as no law code of Offa is extant.[49] Æthelberht's contribution is easier to find. His earlier Kentish code provides Alfred with his injury tariff (*Af* 44–77).[50] By the time of the writing of his law code, addressing Mercia and Kent as independent regions was anachronistic, for the *Domboc* was written between the late 880s and the early 890s, when Alfred has been king of Wessex for over a decade.[51] English Mercia submitted to Alfred's sovereignty by 883, and Kent submitted to his grandfather Ecgbert in 823.[52] However, the submissions of Mercia and Kent did not culturally homogenize these domains into Wessex; they operated to different degrees as subordinate, but roughly parallel, sub-kingdoms. Alfred's control over Mercia was a gradual process, contingent upon both his military might and his cultural accommodations.[53] Similarly, his brothers recognized the separation between Kent and Wessex even as they sought the consolidation of sub-kingdoms that Alfred eventually accomplished.[54] Both Æthelberht (860–65) and Æthelred (865–71) issue charters under the title of "king of Wessex and Kent."[55] While Mercia and Kent are nominally and administratively subject to Alfred, these sub-kingdoms still have enough separate identity to merit Alfred's assertion of creating a law code indebted to their legal traditions. He affirms his own ancestral kingship as "Westseaxna cyning" (king of the West Saxons) (*Af El.* 49.10), but also styles himself simply as a *cyning* (king) with authority to employ the previous legislation of his subject sub-kingdoms, Mercia and Kent.[56]

In his preface, Alfred thus emphasizes the scope of his rule: references to the *Angelcynn* reinforce his dominion over Anglian Mercia, the title *Westseaxna cyning* does the same for Wessex and Kent, while the simple term *cyning* allows for a consolidation of rule over all these regions and their peoples. Through presenting these various titles in reference to his realm, Alfred asserts authority through a measured accommodation of those subject to him.

Alfred's choice to mention Æthelberht as the first of the *Angelcynn* to receive baptism draws a significant link between the political and ideological functions of his law code. Æthelberht is an *Angelcynn* insofar as his rule extends from the Kentish homeland north to the Humber, encompassing Anglian territory.[57] His rule over a kingdom of disparate cultural sub-groups makes him a politically significant role model for Alfred to invoke, but why stress Æthelberht as the first to be baptized of the *Angelcynn*? The answer lies in Bede's *Historia ecclesiastica*, which Alfred most probably knew well.[58] Contrary to Alfred's assertion, Bede does not state that Æthelberht was the first to be baptized, only that he was one "inter alios" (among others).[59] It is Alfred who promotes Æthelberht to the "ærest fulluhte onfeng on Angelcynne" (first [who] accepted baptism among the English race) (*Af El.* 49.9). The reason is linked to another salient fact about Æthelberht that Bede notes in the *Historia*. Æthelberht "drecreta illi iudicorum [...], cum consilio sapientum constituit; quae conscripta Anglorum sermone hactenus habentur" (decreed judgments [to his people] [...], established with the consultation of wise men; which, having been written in the language of the English, are kept to this day).[60] Æthelberht, like Alfred, authored a law code in English with the aid and approval of his *witan*. Calling upon Æthelberht as lawmaker underscores the political function of the law code and its link to Anglo-Saxon legislative protocol. Law defines the administrative role of the king in adjudication. Recasting Æthelberht as the *ærest* (first) among the *Angelcynn* to receive baptism does the ideological work of placing the Kentish king as a shaper of King Alfred's national culture. In Æthelberht, Alfred invokes a model of expansive kingship over a populace of varied cultural backgrounds united through the king's leadership in governance and culture. In his preface, Alfred transforms Æthelberht into a shaper of cultural identity.

Sarah Foot persuasively argues that Alfred's law is "an amalgam of the collected laws of the previous kings of Kent, Mercia and Wessex [...used in...] his attempt to make his West-Saxon and Mercian people into one *gens*" (32–33); in this case, an *Angelcynn*. Her argument holds as law, in this instance, roughly functions as one of the "large cultural systems" Benedict Anderson argues as a source of national identity (12). It comes from a large stock of unwritten mores and customs that shapes both the content of the laws and the administrative system that codifies them. Alfred, in recapitulating earlier laws such as Æthelberht's, only "makes explicit the practice [of recapitulation] already visible in the laws of earlier kings" (Richards, "Anglo-Saxonism" 48). Alfred's *Domboc* operates in the crystallizing moment when the fluid field of cultural identities meets the shaping power of political authority.

CHAPTER 2

Reading the Laws: The *Domboc* in Its Earliest Context

In the late ninth century, the *Domboc* does much more than simply codify legislation for Alfred and his subjects. Rather, its content acts as a foundation narrative for the West Saxons as a people and defines the unique character of Alfred's kingship over them. The *Domboc* forges an identity for the West Saxons, beholden to a Christian heritage and its ideals, but put into action by means of Anglo-Saxon jurisprudence. A close reading of the *Domboc* shows Alfred's kingship and kingdom to be more than a pale reflection of his Carolingian neighbors, but a distinctive amalgamation of native Christian and secular cultures.[1] Alfred carefully uses legislation to define his role as king, the limits of his kingdom, and the cultural norms of his people. Ultimately, the particular representation of king, kingdom, and people in the *Domboc* establishes a markedly Anglo-Saxon society to which future English monarchs will turn in times of national crisis.

The impact of the *Domboc*'s function on Alfred's role as king is governed by the link between legislation and royal image. As Louis Marin argues, "the king is only truly king, that is, monarch, in images. They are his *real* presence. A belief in the effectiveness and operativeness of *his* iconic signs is obligatory" (8). For Marin, the language or visual image representing the king serves as the locus of royal power because it signifies the potential for force, the wherewithal to impose power on another.[2] The importance of the *Domboc* as legislation lies in its linguistic representation of the king (signifying the potential for force behind its text), and the cultural effect of legitimizing the king's regality through representing this power. The most prevalent instrument of royal power in the *Domboc* is the *bot* system. Therefore, a close study of Alfred's *Domboc* and his use of the *bot* system can establish the importance of the text in forming Alfred's contemporary royal image and the concomitant shaping of the West Saxons as a cohesive people under his rule.

Understanding the mechanics and cultural connotations of the *bot* system is fundamental to accurately assessing the impact the *Domboc* has in shaping Alfred's kingship, kingdom, and culture. In a legal context, the Old English word *bot* means "compensation (made for infraction of the law or received injury)" (Healey, Venezky and Cameron).[3] For the Anglo-Saxons, the *bot* system is a compensatory system of conflict resolution.[4] It is a set of socially sanctioned cultural practices related to and perhaps derived from the Scandinavian system of dispute settlement that allows for retribution, vengeance, and financial compensation for injury against persons or property.[5] This practice may well belong to what Pratt identifies as "[n]inth-century Anglo-Saxon legal expertise derived fundamentally from customary experience [...]. Some of its character may be preserved in the notion of *folcriht* ["common law"], apparently referring to commonly accepted practices of justice" (*Political Thought*, 217). Alfred's repeated invocation of the *bot* system in the *Domboc* has a direct impact on the characterization of king and kingdom. First, the prevalence of *bot* language forwards an image of the king whose functional role is not primarily that of a Christian ruler, as in a Carolingian model, but as an arbiter of Anglo-Saxon justice. Second, such a secular depiction of the king has significant repercussions for the shaping of a West Saxon national identity, since it illuminates the intimate connection between royal, national, and cultural identities. Alfred's use of the language of feud and compensation in the laws establishes a royal image for himself and a national identity for the West Saxon people that is indebted to the ideals of secular Anglo-Saxon society.[6]

Alfred's use of the language of the *bot* system illustrates the relationship between language and the image of authority. In the *Domboc*, the sentence structure of legislation is largely that of force held in abeyance. Throughout the text, the judgments of the *Domboc* are expressed in a conditional "if-then" fashion: "Gif hwa ymb cyninges feorh sierwe [...] sie he his feores scyldig 7 ealles þæs ðe he age" (If anyone plots against the king's life [...] let him be liable of his life and all that he owns) (*Af.* 4). Twenty-one of the forty-eight Mosaic injunctions, seventy-five of the seventy-seven of Alfred's laws, and fifty-six of the seventy-six of Ine's laws contain such a grammatical structure.[7] Fully eighty-nine percent of the statues in the *Domboc* have a conditional format. The prevalence of this rhetorical maneuver underscores the authority of the legislator based on the threat of violence behind the law. This pervasive conditional language of the *Domboc* is one of force held in check contingent upon submission to authority. Alfred, as king, personally wields both the administrative power his subjects must obey and the punitive violence they fear.

As Michel Foucault argues, "crime attacks the sovereign: it attacks him personally, since the law represents the will of the sovereign; it attacks him physically, since the force of the law is the force of the prince" (47).[8] The sovereign's use of force in response to such an attack "requires redress for the injury that was done to his kingdom [...], but it also requires that the king take revenge for an affront to his very person" (Foucault 48). The potential for force is directly linked to both the person and function of the king. The relationship between the person of the king and the law is evident in Alfred's use of *wite* in the laws. *Wite* is a component of the *bot* system in which a fine is paid directly to the king for the breaking of his law. For example: "Gif mon twyhyndne mon unsynninge mid hloðe ofslea, gielde se ðæs sleges andetta sie wer 7 wite" (If a man with a band of robbers slays a two-hynd man, let he that confesses of the slaying pay the monetary compensation for the man's life [to his kin] and the fine to the king) (*Af.* 29).[9] Such a pairing of royal and communal claims on the offender underscores the personal connection between the ruler and his law.

Attaching royal power in legislation to the person of the king, by means of the language of the *bot* system, has implications for the ideological and political functions of the text. As Patrick Wormald argues, in trying to interpret the mixture of old and new legal material in the written law codes of early western European peoples, the very act of legislation is ideological.[10] Although Wormald's approach can undervalue the specific content of legal texts, it does provide an instructive template for a larger function of early legislation. In his model, early legal texts operated on a symbolic level to specific ideological ends. For Alfred, Wormald argues that the primary function of the king's *Domboc* is not to legislate. That is, it is not meant to serve as a written guide to the actual practice of adjudication.

Rather, in Wormald's view, the chief purpose of the *Domboc* is to serve as a powerful symbol of Alfred's kingship during a period in which the king was threatened from without and trying to forge a cohesive realm among his culturally heterogeneous subjects within.[11] For Wormald, the *Domboc* functions as "the aggressive weapon of a new state" in the political and ideological connotations of inscribing law, more than in the text of the law itself (*Making* 429).[12] It was more politically significant for Alfred to get a law code in his name as a symbol of legitimacy, according to Wormald, than it was for the king to worry overmuch about that code's actual content.[13]

An important effect of creating such a symbolic image of the king is the extension of that symbolism to the nation as a whole. Alfred's *Domboc* represents the personal power of the sovereign, yet is also among those laws which "have been thought to express a very narrow self-consciousness linked to nationality" (McKitterick 15).[14] Evidence of this self-conscious national identity lies in Alfred's identification of his realm and people. Alfred titles himself "Westseaxna cyning" (king of the West Saxons) (*Af El.* 49.10), circumscribing his scope of influence to that of a specific socio-political identification.[15] Moreover, Alfred's use of the term *Angelcynn*, the English race, speaks to a self-conscious sense of cultural identity.[16] As Sarah Foot argues, "through his promotion of the term *Angelcynn* to reflect the common identity of his people in a variety of texts dating from the latter part of his reign, and his efforts in cultivating the shared memory of his West Mercian and West Saxon subjects, King Alfred might be credited with the invention of the English as a political community" (25). The king is an instrumental figure in forming national identity.[17] However, there is more to the process of forming a national identity than overt prop-agandizing. The prevalence of *bot* language throughout the *Domboc* also forges a national identity on a sub-textual level.

Benedict Anderson argues, "nationalism has to be understood by aligning it, not with self-consciously held political ideologies, but with the large cultural systems that precede it" (12).[18] However, as evidenced by the *Domboc*, self-conscious ideologies and large societal systems are not mutually exclusive. Alfred does include self-conscious nationalistic language through the terms *Angelcynn* and *Westseaxna cyning*, but he simultaneously provides evidence of a "large cultural system" at work: that of a feud-based culture, what Hyams characterizes as "a culture permeated by a resistant notion of direct personal action against perceived wrong" (*Rancor*, 109). Anderson defines such "cultural systems" as "taken-for-granted frames of reference" for a given community (12). The *bot* system of compensation is an aspect of Anglo-Saxon feud-based culture that easily fits Anderson's definition. References to the payment of *wergild* in compensation for a man's life occurs in every extant Anglo-Saxon law code up to and including Alfred.[19] By Alfred's day, the *bot* system of compensation for injury was such a commonplace that the king ascribes its provenance to the early synods of Christian bishops and wise men.[20] In Benedict's terms, the *bot* system of remuneration for death or injury qualifies as a large cultural system operant in shaping the developing national identity of Alfred's Wessex.

Alfred is both in control of and subject to the narrative he authorizes in the *Domboc*. The coexistence of explicit and implicit forces fashioning national identity through the language of the *Domboc* marks a narrative circularity of reference in which, as Homi Bhabha argues, "the position of narrative control is neither monocular or monologic" (301).[21] As Alfred forges and forwards his own image through the *Domboc*, so does he craft an image of the nation he rules. The terms *Westseaxna cyning* and *Angelcynn* attest, respectively, to both operations. Concurrently, the text of the *Domboc* is shaped by the larger cultural system of *bot*. The image of the king becomes the touchstone for the identity of the nation, even as the cultural systems of the nation define the means of propagating the royal image. The result is a loop of reference in which the potential exists for the king's image to symbolically embody the nation.[22]

However, given this role of the *Domboc* in creating both the image of the king and the identity of the nation as a whole, Wormald perhaps too broadly states the function of the text. As he argues, "[w]hether recited or read, by king, bishop or newly literate ealdorman, the law-book [of King Alfred] aimed for an overall impact on the collective consciousness by juxtaposing familiar customs, judgements and decrees with perceptibly similar laws of God" (Wormald, *Making* 427). Yet the *Domboc* reveals more than juxtaposition of secular and sacred law to effect an "overall impact." As Paul Hyams finds, Alfred's reign may be an early source of a kind of kingship manifesting "a high degree of royal authority and control in the maintenance of law and order by the king qua king" (*Rancor*, 100). This model of royal control illuminates Alfred's careful and intensive recasting of his sacred sources as creating a specific royal image, and developing an emerging sense of West Saxon national identity. Alfred's apparent care in translation points to the *Domboc* as a document providing meaning for both king and kingdom, not only as a single monolithic symbol.

Specifically, Alfred's handling and creating of individual laws shows an assimilation of Judeo-Christian traditions and beliefs into secular Anglo-Saxon cultural practice through the prominent use of the language of the *bot* system, ultimately privileging the secular over the sacred. The language of the *bot* system permeates the *Domboc* as a shaping source of West Saxon national identity within the text. Alfred rewrites Mosaic law in accordance with his ninth-century Anglo-Saxon milieu, re-imagines the New Dispensation to validate the Anglo-Saxon *bot* system, and enlists the punitive sanctions of the Christian Church in the service of secular law.[23] Accordingly, the *Domboc* is a text which creates and promulgates an image of Alfred that is primarily contingent upon his role as a secular Anglo-Saxon king through his intensive use of the language of the *bot* system.

Mercy in Alfred's Canon

In light of the king's translations of religious and philosophical works, the function of law as force held in abeyance can readily be misconstrued as Christian mercy. That the *Domboc* speaks to the dispensation of worldly justice risks just such a perfunctory mapping of the sacred missions of the biblical translations in the text onto the Anglo-Saxon laws in Alfred's *Domboc*. Such a process privileges a sacred reading over a secular one, skewing the image of the king and his kingdom. Superficially, it would seem that invoking Christian mercy in the translations would mitigate or even obviate the need for coercive and corrective force in judgment. Forgiveness and clemency, rather than execution or retribution by remuneration, would become the operative force in legislation. Accordingly, Alfred's claim that lawmaking should operate in harmony with "ðære mildheortnesse þe Crist lærde" (that mercy which Christ taught) (*Af El.* 49.7) could be taken at face value. However, in his translations of Augustine's *Soliloquies*, Boethius' *Consolation of Philosophy*, and Gregory's *Regula pastoralis*, Alfred distinguishes three different kinds of mercy, or *mildheortnesse*: that which God shows humanity, that which lay people show one another, and that which earthly leaders show their charges.[24] God's mercy and the mercy of lay humanity are abstract in their concern with forgiveness and redemption. The mercy of earthly rulers, however, is explicitly tied to the concrete demands of administration, reflecting Alfred's treatment of mercy in the *Domboc*.

Alfred equates mercy with an effective administrative policy of compliance and loyalty through accommodation. God's mercy towards humanity is a feature of all three translations, in each case governing the abstraction of salvation. In the *Consolation*, "God nylle for his mildheort-nesse nan unaberendlice broc him an settan" (God, through his mercy, does not wish to set on them [evil-doers] any unbearable affliction), so as not to chase them from the path of righteousness.[25] In this case, God's "mildheortnesse" is a translation of the original's "sapiens dispensatio" (wise administration).[26] In order to compel obedience effectively, a wise ruler does not challenge the norms of his subjects' culture so much as to dissuade their obedience.

However, if such accommodation is not enough to ensure compliance, and transgressions occur, mercy is again employed to retain his followers. In Chapters 52 and 53 of the *Regula pastoralis*, God extends His mercy towards those who "mildheortlice bioð gehealdne æfter hiora ðurhtogenum synnum" (are mercifully kept after carrying through their sins).[27] If mercy can not keep people from straying, it can ensure their continued place in God's community despite their sins. Mercy is the final engine of expiation. In the *Soliloquies*, mercy appears as God's instrument of redemption in the narrator's prayer of honor and supplication: "þæt ðu me for ðinre mild-heortnesse alyse and gefreolsige" (that you, through your mercy, redeem and deliver me).[28] The goal of God's mercy is the abstract forgiveness of sins, by its very nature intangible. This mercy is characterized by encour-agement to serve God through accommodation and forgiveness.

However, humanity's use of mercy is more concrete in application than God's example shows. In the *Soliloquies*, mercy is one of the "creftas" (crafts) by which a man can "gefastna þa eagan þines modes on gode" (fas-ten the eye of your mind on God) so to better govern his reason.[29] It is an abstract means by which people can come to know God better. Neverthe-less, mercy also has a practical application for humanity; it helps to govern human relationships. According to the *Consolation*, for humanity "þæt wære ryht þæt hiora ælc gulde oþrum edlean ælces weorces æfter his gewyrhtum, þæt is þæt mon lufode þone godan, swa swa riht is þæt mon do, 7 mildsige þam yfelum" (that would be right that all of them requite to others recompense of every deed according to his merits; that is that one should love the good, just as it is right that one should do, and show mercy to the evil).[30] Alfred renders this passage from the more compact Latin: "dilige iure bonos et miseresce malis" (rightfully love good men and feel pity for evil men).[31]

The king activates the passive sense of the Latin *miserescere* (to feel pity for), which implies an internal state. By translating it into the more active Old English *miltsian* (to show mercy), he makes the action external: an interaction between the good and the wicked, exactly the purview of an earthly monarch. As opposed to simply feeling pity for evil men, Alfred's translation calls for showing mercy to them. His translations of the *Soliloquies* and the *Consolation* portray mercy among mortals as a tool of social and spiritual maintenance.

For earthly rulers, mercy is exclusively a practical tool of worldly governance. In Alfred's preface to the *Soliloquies*, he invokes mercy in the relationship between lord and subject, in which a man may "bocland and æce yrfe þurh his hlafordes miltse geearnige" (earn bookland and eternal heritage through his lord's mercy).[32] The placement and content of this mention of mercy is significant. As a part of Alfred's putatively original preface to the translation of the *Soliloquies*, the appearance of mercy in this context is less likely to have been part of a corrupted exemplar.[33] Alfred's use of the term *milts* places mercy in a specific secular and royal context. Mercy is the vehicle by which a lord grants bookland: "grants of considerable portions of land made by kings to bishops and religious houses, or to lay nobles. [...] conferr[ing] a larger dominion than was known to customary law" (Pollock and Maitland 60). Despite the abstract and philosophical nature of the text he is about to translate, Alfred attaches mercy to earthly rulership in terms of a concrete function of royal administration: the transfer of property and the rights attached to such transactions.

Another administrative implementation of mercy is in the managing of the good and the wicked. Alfred illustrates this function of mercy in his translation of chapters 16 and 17 of the *Regula pastoralis*.[34] Gregory presents Paul as an example to show that "he geleornode hu he scolde oðrum monnum miltsian ðe he geðoht hu he wolde ðæt mon him miltsode gif he suelc wære" (he learned how he should show mercy to other men when he thought how he wished that one would show mercy to him if he was such a one).[35] As in his translation of the *Consolation*, Alfred uses the Old English *miltsian* (to show mercy) to translate the Latin *miserere* (to pity, feel sorry for), only now the executor of this mercy is an earthly ruler.[36] The more active Old English verb suits the action of the passage. As an earthly leader, Paul must be demonstrably humane and merciful towards his charges, just as he would have others be merciful to him: he must lead by example. Alfred imports this concept of mercy as an object example of equitable judgment in the preface to his *Domboc*: "he nanum men ne deme þæt he nolde ðæt he him demde" (he should not judge to any man that [which] he would not [have] judged to him[self]) (*Af El.* 49.6). To lead effectively on earth, both Paul and the king must rule by example.

However, this example must not be beyond the reach of a leader's charges. Accommodating his followers' limitations is another tool of worldly governance Alfred incorporates into his administrative style. In the king's translation of the *Regula pastoralis*, Paul recognizes that an example is more easily followed if it is familiar. He considers this in his effort to convert the Jews: "Ðone ic wæs mid Iudeum ic wæs suelc hie" (When I was with the Jews, I was like them).[37] Paul wants the Jews to follow his example in coming to Christ, so he adopts some of their customs to give him more leverage as a member of the Jewish community.

Indeed, Alfred employs this same rhetorical device when he translates an apostolic letter to Antioch in his preface to the *Domboc*, which states: "þæt we nane byrðenne on eow settan noldon ofer þæt ðe eow neððearf wæs to haldanne" (that we [the apostles] should not set any burden on you [the citizens of Antioch] beyond that which was a necessity for you to keep) (*Af El.* 49.5). The apostles recognize that to demand too much of the citizens of Antioch could chase them from the Church. Rather, the apostles seek to win the citizens' submission to Christ by ruling lightly.

By including this letter in his preface, Alfred preserves Gregory's portrayal of a merciful leader. Such a ruler can put himself in the position of his subjects in judgment. He also recognizes to what extent his subjects are willing to bend to his dictates, and to what extent a ruler's dictates need to bend to the norms of his subjects in order to ensure compliance. Alfred's translation of the *Consolation* attests to God accommodating His subjects to ensure their fidelity, and thereby their salvation. Given Alfred's familiarity with Boethius' text, it is little wonder that Alfred would recognize the possibility that the concrete expression of mercy in governance can yield the abstract end of salvation.

Alfred presents the apostolic letter to endorse accommodation of the societal norms of his subjects. For earthly leaders, effective rule exists "ðone sio ryhtwisnes & sio mildheortnes hi gegadrige on ðæm anwalde ðæs recceres" (when righteousness and mercy are gathered together in the authority of the ruler).[38] For Alfred, mercy must become part of authority, although it is subject to the personal power of the ruler based upon the possibility of force.

Mercy and Bot *in the Mosaic Preface*

While the Judeo-Christian focus of Alfred's preface to the *Domboc* may lead one to think that Christian mercy is the guiding force of the king's law code, in actuality mercy becomes sublimated to force as the language of the *bot* system dominates the mechanics of juridical practice.[39] Although Alfred did have a very real intellectual and philosophical debt to his continental Carolingian neighbors, ultimately, his *Domboc* is ultimately more directly governed by the influence of local cultural practices.[40] The successive archbishops of Rheims, Hincmar (845–882) and Fulk (882–900), may have had some effect on Alfred's thinking and subsequent text, but as Nelson suggests for a variety of supposed Carolingian influences, these influences may "be explained quite well wholly or largely in terms of indigenous ideas or traditions" ("A King Across the Sea" 50).[41] The "indigenous […] tradition" of *bot* best explains Alfred's modifications to his source text, without need of a Carolingian source. Reassessing the relative roles of mercy and *bot* in the *Domboc* is a necessary and instructive first step in understanding how the text shapes the representation of Alfred's kingship and kingdom.

In each section of Alfred's translation of the Mosaic laws, the king maps his native cultural milieu onto his scriptural exemplar. He uses legislation as a means to shape the character of his kingship and his kingdom in accordance with Anglo-Saxon cultural practice. When the text of Alfred's biblical source agrees with the Germanic cultural practices of the ninth-century Anglo-Saxons, the text remains substantively unchanged. Correspondingly, when the text is in contrast or is not readily adaptable to Germanic Anglo-Saxon cultural customs or ideals, it is excised or revised to bring it more clearly into line with those practices or values. If, as Malcolm Godden argues, "for the Anglo-Saxons the Old Testament was a veiled way of talking about their own situation […that…] offered them a means of considering and articulating the ways in which kingship, politics and warfare related to the rule of God" ("Biblical" 225), then Alfred is translating the Mosaic laws to conform to contemporary Anglo-Saxon literary practice.[42]

Alfred's emending of these particular precepts, or lack thereof, evinces an understanding of their selective applicability to his social framework more than a means to introduce the idea of Christian mercy into Anglo-Saxon legislation. Such an editorial choice privileges cultural practice over

Christian ideals, fundamentally shifting the appraisal of the king's royal image. As Foucault argues, the law of the king is an embodiment of the king's person, a narrative body of the king.[43] Such narrative bodies are the real presence of the king and the source of his royal image "because *his* signs *are* the royal *reality*" (Marin 8). The primacy of *bot* in the *Domboc* forwards a representation of the king as a ruler whose royal image stems from that Anglo-Saxon cultural practice embedded in his law text. Through the management of his sources, Alfred appears as a king primarily defined by his representation of Anglo-Saxon legal practice. Two examples from the Mosaic preface especially clarify Alfred's approach of privileging *bot* over mercy: his translations of Exodus 23:1–5 and 21:12–14.

In Alfred's translation of Exodus 23:1–5, the passage that deals with justice for one's enemies and the wrongly accused, the king's changes to his exemplar in translation show a bending of Mosaic law to Germanic Anglo-Saxon legal and cultural practice. Exodus 23:1–2 provides injunctions against false testimony and corrupt judgment:

> …non suscipies vocem mendacii nec iunges manum tuam ut pro impio dicas falsum testimonium / non sequeris turbam ad faciendum malum nec in iudicio plurimorum adquiesces sententae ut a vero devies
>
> (Do not accept the word of a liar nor join your hand [to his] lest you should give false testimony for an impious man / You shall not follow the crowd to do evil nor agree to a sentence with the judgement of a crowd lest you turn away from the truth) [Exodus 23:1–2].

Alfred renders the text as follows:

> Leases monnes word ne rec ðu no þæs to gehieranne, ne his domas ne geðafa ðu, ne nane gewitnesse æfter him ne saga ðu.
>
> Ne wend ðu ðe no on þæs folces unræd 7 unryht gewill on hiora spræce 7 geclysp ofer ðin ryht, 7 ðæs unwisestan lare ne him ne geðafa.
>
> (Do not care to hear a false man's word, nor endure his judgments, nor say any testimony for him.
>
> Do not turn yourself towards the foolish and unrighteous will of people in their speech and clamor over your right, nor tolerate the advice of the unwise) [*Af. El.* 40–41].

While Alfred's translation of Exodus 23:1 can "[seem] intended to make an impression on the judicial reader," and that "Alfred saw the heart of [Exodus 23:2] as a warning against evil influence on judicial decisions" (Treschow 100–01), this does not necessarily mean the revisions were made to incorporate the concept of Christian mercy. A concern with the propriety of judges and their judgments was of paramount importance to secular Anglo-Saxon society, and could easily explain Alfred's emendations.[44]

More tellingly, Alfred makes a philosophically important omission in this section. The king dutifully translates Exodus 23:4:

> Si occurreris bovi inmici tui aut asino erranti reduc ad eum
>
> (If you meet the cattle or ass of your enemy wandering, return it to him) [Exodus 23:4].
>
> Gif ðe becume oðres mannes giemeleas fioh on hond þeah hit sie ðin feond, gecyðe hit him
>
> (If another man's stray cattle comes into your hand, even if it is of your enemy, make it known to him) [Af. El. 42].

However, Alfred omits the second part of the original injunction, "si videris asinum odientis te iacere sub onere non pertransibis sed sublevabis cum eo" (If you see the ass of him who hates you fall under its load, do not desert [it] but help with that) (Exodus 23:5). Treschow explains that Alfred omitted the passage because of its "repetitive" nature, and "because its specificity was irrelevant" (98). Repetition did not hamper Alfred's faithful translation of earlier Mosaic laws.[45] Moreover, Alfred's omission of the donkey on the basis that it was not "part of the Anglo-Saxon [pastoral] economy" is not the issue (Treschow 98). Alfred had no problem in rendering the Latin *asinus* as *feoh* elsewhere.[46] What appears to be at issue is what Exodus 23:5 asks of the audience.

In actuality, the demands of Exodus 23:5 on the audience would be too burdensome for an Anglo-Saxon audience, which accounts for Alfred's omission of the text in his translation. The text of Exodus 23:4 only requires the return of your enemy's tender if you should come upon it. The Anglo-Saxons could readily accept this idea, given their legal preoccupation with property and property rights: rightful ownership can be negotiated even in the face of enmity.[47] However, Exodus 23:5 goes further, asking the audience to actively help an enemy in need. The Judeo-Christian axiom to love one's enemy, especially in such concrete contexts that Exodus 23:5 supplies, would raise the kind of anxieties over the relationships between antagonists evidenced in such Old English literature as the Finnsburg episode in *Beowulf* or the tale of Cynewulf and Cyneheard. To assist a *feond* is to suffer potentially the same fate as Byrhtnoth at Maldon. [48] Both the *Anglo-Saxon Chronicle* and Asser's *Life* point out the perils of trying to make peace with one's enemies in Alfred's day.

Alfred's dealings with the Danish invaders in 876 is an instructive example of the dangers of providing succor to the enemy. The *Chronicle* records that Alfred made peace with the Danish raiding-army at Wareham, but "hie þa under þam hie nihtes bestelon" (then they stole away under the night). [49] Asser takes this treachery as a matter of course, in which the Danes "solita fallacia utens, et obsides et iuramentum atque fidem promissam non custodiens, nocte quadam, foedere disrupto, omnes [obsides], quos habebat, occidit, versusque inde ad alium locum" (practicing customary deception, and not preserving the hostages, the oath, or the promise of trustworthiness, that night, having broken the treaty, killed all those hostages they had, turning from there to another place). [50] As Alfred would well know from this encounter, in every extension of good will towards one's enemy lies the possibility of treachery.

Alfred's omission of Exodus 23:5, then, is perhaps more than just editorial tidiness. More likely, for an author as careful as Alfred, this omission evinces his understanding of the limits to which his Anglo-Saxon subjects were willing to go to accommodate the concept of Christian mercy. Although Alfred uses his legislation to shape his model of kingship and the character of his kingdom, the possibilities available are limited by the norms of his Anglo-Saxon culture. Alfred recognizes the cultural limitations of shaping a West Saxon national identity, as is implied in his translation of the apostolic letter to Antioch (Acts 15:28). Alfred translates: "þæt we nane byrðenne on eow settan noldon ofer þæt ðe eow nedðearf wæs to haldanne" (that we [the apostles] should not set any burden on you [the citizens of Antioch] beyond that which was a necessity for you to keep) (*Af El.* 49.5). His translation makes plain that he appreciates the delicate balance between sacred mandate and secular cultural practice. He uses this balance in crafting an identity for himself and his people that is built upon Anglo-Saxon cultural practices while accommodating Judeo-Christian mores.

On the one hand, Alfred affirms his subjects' need to adhere to the essential dictates of Scripture: "þæt ðe eow *nedþearf* wæs to healdanne" (that which was a *necessity* for you to keep [my emphasis]). On the other hand, he recognizes the practical limitations of demanding dogmatic obedience that would "byrðenne on eow settan" (set a burden on you). Anglo-Saxon culture, indebted to the compensatory *bot* system, could easily support the notion of rightful ownership as presented in Exodus 23:4, as it is concerned with appropriately distributing material goods. The imperative of Exodus 23:5 to aid one's enemy without material cause, a truly altruistic act, strains the boundaries of Anglo-Saxon law and cultural practice, and is thus omitted from Alfred's translation.

However, the most telling of Alfred's editorial choices in translation are those places in which the king augments the text with his own words, as in the case of his translation of Exodus 21:12–14, which clarifies the injunction not to murder in Exodus 20:13.[51] Alfred's changes to his source directly address the Anglo-Saxon feud-based *bot* system. Alfred translates the clarifying passage of Exodus 21:12–14 as follows:

> Se mon se ðe his gewealdas monnan ofslea, swelte se deaðe. Se ðe hine þonne nedes ofsloge oððe unwillum oððe ungewealdes swelce hine God swa sende on his honda, 7 he hine ne ymbsyrede, sie he feores wyrðe 7 folcryhte bote, gif he friðstowe gesece. Gif hwa þonne of giernesse 7 gewealdas ofslea his þone nehstan þurh searwe, aluc ðu hine from minum weofode, to þam þæt he deaðe swelte

> (He who kills a man of his own accord, let him suffer death. Yet he who kills him of necessity or unintentionally or unwillingly, as though God placed him in his hand, and he did not lay in wait for him, let him be worthy of the life and compensate the injury according to common law, if he seeks sanctuary. If someone then kills his neighbor [or kin] desirefully and intentionally through treachery, take him away from my altar, in order that he suffer death) [*Af El.* 13].

The only material changes to the text of Exodus 21:13 are Alfred's additions of the word "nedes" (of necessity) and the phrase "sie he feores wyrðe 7 *folcryhte bote*, gif he friðstowe gesece" (let him be worthy of the life and *compensate the injury according to common law*) [my emphasis] (*Af El.* 13).[52] These seemingly small changes remove the text from the realm of Christian mercy and place it in the world of monetary compensation.

In Alfred's translation of Exodus 21:13, not only is killing sometimes a necessity (*nied*), as it can be in resolving blood-feuds, but homicide is also "a deed that can be paid for by money" (Pollock and Maitland, vol. 2, 451).[53] Such feud-culture stipulations certainly stray from the dictates of Alfred's Old Testament source, and stray still farther from the sense of Christian mercy delineated in such contemporary texts as Alfred's translations of the *Consolation* or the *Regula pastoralis*.[54] According to Hyams, "The proper goal for a Christian is correction rather than the execution of justice that should be left to God" (Hyams, "Neither Unnatural" 214). The idea of a necessary killing flies in the face of such axioms as "lufie þone man 7 hatige his unþeawas" (love the man and hate his sin) or that a man "scolde oðrum monnum miltsian ðe he geðoht hu he wolde ðæt mon him miltsode gif he suelc wære" (should show mercy to other men when he thought how he wished that one would show mercy to him if he was such a one).[55] Rather, Alfred's stipulates the social processes already available to his audience in dealing with murder through deploying the *bot* system.

In examining Alfred's translation of Exodus 21:12–14, Treschow observes that the use of "the adverb *nedes* gives fairly broad licence" to the killer, and that "Germanic society [demands] compensation regardless of whether the slayer had acted in self-defence and without treacherous intent" (92). Yet the mechanics of the Anglo-Saxon *bot* system here actually supercede the Word of God. The biblical text of Exodus 21:12–14 does not allow for needful killing. Alfred's additions override the biblical tenet against permissible slaughter. The *bot* system's allowance of acceptable homicide receives preference over the restrictions of Scripture, which do not allow for monetary compensation to answer for murder. The case of Judas selling Jesus to his executioners for thirty pieces of silver is ample evidence of the poor light in which such an exchange is shown.[56]

Alfred moves beyond God's dictate to allow a feud-culture's pecuniary resolution. The king's approach to Judeo-Christianity adopted "those aspects of Latin-Christian culture which by general consensus could be grafted onto already well-established societal forms" (Byock 37).[57] Alfred is not engaging in a positivist reading of Mosaic law that utilizes a medieval allegorical approach to reading in order to "make the Old Testament safe for Christian readers or to make it consonant with the New Testament by discovering Christian doctrines [...] within it" (Godden, "Biblical" 208). Conversely, his translation accommodates Judeo-Christian textual culture to the norms of Anglo-Saxon cultural practice by his repeated use of the feud-based *bot* system.[58]

The argument for the significance of mercy in the Mosaic preface to the *Domboc*, and correspondingly the proof for Alfred's dependence upon Carolingian thought, actually shows the contrary: the fundamental importance of the indigenous *bot* system in Alfred's translation. While close readings of the *Domboc* can show that Alfred translated "the ancient law of Scripture [...] into an immediate authority" (Treschow 102), the claim that the Mosaic preface is most notable in that "it is harmonized with Alfred's own *Christian* culture [my emphasis]" perhaps goes too far (Treschow 102). Rather, the explicit changes that Alfred made to Scripture as he imported it into his law code are more noticeably and significantly attuned to the *bot* system. Both his editorial omissions and additions place Alfred's narrative presence in his translation of the Mosaic preface, and that presence is characterized by the preeminence of the feud-based, compensatory *bot* system. Alfred's forwarding of a royal presence defined by the cultural practice of *bot* provides a key to understanding the function of the *Domboc* and its secularizing effect on the character of his kingship and kingdom.

Bot, *the New Testament, and the Christian Diaspora*

Alfred uses the New Testament to make his primary reliance on secular Anglo-Saxon culture in his *Domboc* explicit. He chooses specific texts to justify his dependence on the *bot* system in legislation. Each of these choices accommodates Scripture to the social norms of his target audience. Ultimately, through his choice and adaptation of New Testament examples of lawgiving, Alfred justifies sublimating Christian tenets to the demands of the *bot* system.

The signal text for this process is Matthew 5:17, which Alfred employs to make the transition from the Old Testament to the New. The text justifies the refiguring of prior law to more effectively serve a new audience. Christ states, "nolite putare quoniam veni solvere legum aut prophetas non veni solvere sed adimplere" (do not think [I] come to destroy the laws of the prophets, [I] do not come to destroy, but to fulfill [them]) (Matthew 5:17). As Barker and Burdick note, "Jesus fulfilled the Law in the sense that he gave it full meaning. He emphasized its deep, underlying principles [...] rather than mere external acknowledgement and obedience" (1449, n. 5:17).

Alfred acknowledges the distinction between the literal word and underlying meaning in his preface to his translation of the *Regula pastoralis*. In translating, Alfred represents his exemplar "hwilum word be worde, hwilum andgit of andgi[e]te" (sometimes word by word, sometimes meaning for meaning).[59] For Alfred, it is more important "ðæt we ða on ðæt geðiode wenden ðe we ealle gecnawan mægen" (that we then translate [books] into that language which we all can understand) than adhering slavishly to the source text.[60] This understanding has both linguistic and cultural components. The audience needs to both understand the literal message of the text and be able to conceptually assimilate it into their worldview. The verse endorses incorporating feud-based customs into Mosaic law and lays the foundation for performing the same operation on the tenets of the New Testament.

Alfred further justifies his accommodation of holy law to secular cultural demands through his translation of Acts 15:28. Chapter 15 of Acts is concerned with the question of circumcision being a precursor to salvation for Gentiles.[61] The apostles agree that such a stringent requirement may keep some from the faith, and they write a letter setting forth a more culturally accommodating plan to the people of Antioch, Syria, and Cilicia.[62] As Alfred translates, the apostles assert "Þæm halgan Gaste wæs geðuht 7 us þæt we nane byrðenne on eow settan noldon ofer þæt ðe eow nedðearf was to healdanne" (It seemed good to the Holy Spirit and to us that we should not set any burden on you [the people of Antioch, Syria, and Cilicia] beyond that which was a necessary thing for you to hold) (*Af El.* 49.5).

Alfred here draws attention to the disjuncture between the ideals of heavenly law and the reality of human frailty. A key to effective leadership, in this model, is to steer a middle course and provide followers the kind and degree of law that is in keeping with God's dictates, but still attainable by the subjects of that law. As Alfred translates in the *Regula pastoralis*: "Þæm lareowe is to wietanne ðæt he huru nanum men mare ne beode ðonne he acuman mæge, ðylæs se rap his modes weorðe to swiðe aðened, oð he forberste" (The teacher is to know that, at all events, he command to no man more than he [that man] can endure, lest the rope of his mind becomes too exceedingly stretched out, until he bursts asunder).[63] Beginning with his translation of Matthew 5:15, and intensified by his translation of Acts 15: 22–29, Alfred repeatedly touches upon the theme of adapting holy law to new paradigms. Christ reinterprets Old Testament law in keeping with his teachings in Matthew 5:17. The apostles, in turn, adapt Christ's teaching to the limits of acceptance by the citizens of Antioch. Through these examples, Alfred lays the interpretive foundation for his own adaptation of law: a law that is flexible in regards to Scripture and accepting of secular Anglo-Saxon cultural practices.

Alfred makes this process explicit in his account of the synodic dissemination of holy law. He progresses from discussing Old and New Testaments dictates in terms of their acceptance and synodic dissemination "geond ealne middangeard" (throughout all middle-earth) to their more specific incarnation "geond Angelcyn" (throughout the English race).[64] He further refines his focus to his immediate subjects. He acknowledges that he is writing precisely for his own time, place, and kingdom "forðam me wæs uncuð, hwæt þæs ðam lician wolde ðe æfter us wæren" (because it was unknown to me what would please those who were after us) (*Af El.* 49.9). Alfred identifies "us" as referring to himself and his West Saxon subjects when he titles himself "Westseaxna cyning" (king of the West Saxons) (*Af El.* 49.10). He writes his law not only to suit himself, but also to suit his immediate culture. In this way, his laws reflect both his conceptions of his kingship and his kingdom.

The king affirms the functional principle of Holy Writ in its Anglo-Saxon incarnation through the endorsement of the *bot* system. He provides his royal legislative power and his specifically identified people with a past informed by Judeo-Christian tenets in order to build a sense of communal past and present unity. However, the king and his people only activate these beliefs in accordance with contemporary cultural norms. As Alfred writes:

> hie ða gesetton, for ðære mildheortnesse þe Crist lærde, æt mæstra hwelcre misdæd þætte ða weoruldshlafordas moston mid hiora leafan buton synne æt þam forman gylte þære fiohbote onfon, þe hie ða gesettan"

> (they [the bishops and *witan*] then set down, on account of their mercy, that Christ taught, that at almost every misdeed the secular lords would be allowed to, with their [the bishops' and *witan*'s] leave, without sin, at the first guilt, take their monetary compensation, which they had then set down) [*Af El.* 49.7].

Here a legitimizing link is forged between the Christian tenet of "mildheortnesse þe Crist lærde" (mercy that Christ taught) and the Germanic cultural practice of the *bot* "þe hie ða gesettan" (which they [the 'weoruldshlafordas'] had set down) (*Af El.* 49.7). In this section of the preface, Alfred authorizes the use of the feud-based *bot* system of compensation through a nebulous connection to Christ's teachings.[65] The result of this approval of the *bot* system is an "elaboration of the system of *bot* among Germanic peoples [which] is parallel to and connected with the contemporary elaboration of the ecclesiastical system of penance" (Pollock and Maitland 453).

The "parallel" nature of penance and compensation is the key issue. Christian penance allows for the contribution of alms and restitution as part of the act of contrition, but straight financial compensation is typically not permitted.[66] Frantzen shows just such a connection between compensation and penance in the eighth-century Irish penitentials: the *Hibernensis* and *The Old-Irish Penitential*.[67] Fragments of the *Hibernensis*, argues Frantzen, appear in English canons in the late tenth century, probably as a result of contacts with Brittany earlier in the century, establishing a textual link between England and the continent.[68] Frantzen posits that a continental connection to the penitential tradition has a direct influence on Alfred specifically through the person of Grimbald.[69] It is this connection to the penitential tradition, Frantzen maintains, that is an impetus for Alfred's "desire for a cooperation between native law and the penitential system new to English government" (*Literature* 126). However, in Alfred's laws, the punishments of the Church are carefully kept parallel and secondary to the demands of the *bot* system.

Alfred's Laws

Alfred's law code (*Af* 1–77) is the most telling portion of the *Domboc* as it is the expression of the king's authority personified. Here the law functions as the narrative body of the king. The suspended force of its conditional judgments is the power of the king contained within the text, and the content, focus, and juridical mechanics of the law are an immediate presence of the royal image. If the character of the nation is tied to the representation of its ruler, then the laws most closely linked to Alfred and his court provide an invaluable insight into the kind of kingship and kingdom he forwards through his *Domboc*.

The first of Alfred's laws, *Af.* 1–1.8, is of central importance in creating Alfred's royal image in the *Domboc*, given its possible direct attribution to Alfred and its pivotal placement. Although the great majority of Alfred's own laws are adapted from prior sources, there has been no clear attribution for the provenance of *Af.* 1.[70] As such, it may offer an example of Alfred's direct involvement in the crafting of new legislation and, by extension, an example of the development of his royal image.[71] Further, *Af.* 1–1.8 deserves special consideration due to its place as the first of the king's own laws. Structurally, *Af.* 1 marks the juncture between the law of his sacred and secular forbears in the *Domboc's* historical preface and the present law of Alfred's own legislation. Symbolically, the king's first law is the site where Alfred defines the character of his kingship over the West Saxons.

Although the king places himself on the continuum of lawgivers from God through Moses, Christ and the apostles; he ultimately invokes earlier secular rulers Æthelberht, Offa, and Ine to legitimize his authority in legislation.[72] The preeminence of the secular world is immediately apparent in the text of the Alfred's first law:

> Æt ærestan we læraõ, þæt mæst õearf is, õæt æghwelc mon his aõ 7 his wed wærlice healde. Gif hwa to hwæõrum þissa genied sie on woh, oõõe to hlafordsearwe oõõe to ængum unryhtum fultume, þæt is þonne ryhtre to aleoganne þonne to gelæstanne.

> (At first we instruct, that [which] is most necessary, that each man carefully keep his oath and his pledge. If anyone is wrongfully compelled to either of these, either to high treason or to any unlawful aid, then [it] is better to leave it [the oath] unfulfilled than to perform it) [*Af.* 1].

By choosing to start his law code with legislation regarding oaths, Alfred appeals to an element of secular Anglo-Saxon social life that is grounded in "ancient Germanic procedure" (Pollock and Maitland 39).[73] Oaths between men as a matter of securing surety in transactions are found among the laws of the Anglo-Saxons as early as the legislation of Wihtræd.[74] Both lexical choice and context herald the secular nature of Alfred's use of this injunction. Earlier language of giving one's word in a sacred context uses such words as *ciegan* (to call upon [God's] name) (*Af. El.* 2), *gewitnes* (testimony) (*Af. El.* 8), *swerian* (to swear) (*Af. El.* 28, 48), *wedd* (pledge) (*Af. El.* 36), *leasung* (false testimony) (*Af. El.* 44). Nowhere in the historical preface does the term *aõ* appear. Indeed, Eric Stanley argues that Alfred's particular word pair of *aõ* and *wedd* has its first appearance in English or any other cognate Germanic language in *Af.* 1.[75] Also, the primary definition of *aõ* in the Old English corpus is "an oath, *judicial* swearing" [my emphasis].[76] The additional qualification of *Af.* 1.1 specifically against *hlafordsearu* (literally "lord-treachery") is an oath to a secular lord (*hlaford*) and not a heavenly one (*Dryhten*).[77]

Therefore, the *aõ* and *wedd* of *Af.* 1–1.8 signify oaths and pledges between mortal men, not between man and God, and not in God's name.[78] Alfred's use of these terms signals his invoking the compensatory nature of the *bot* system, not the sacred covenant between man and God. The oath between a king and his lords, and between a lord and his retainers, guarantees the relationship between these parties which is based on exchange: the Germanic *comitatus* relationship between lord and thegn, which Alfred's code extends to the relationship between king and subject.[79] Simply stated, the lord or king provides lands, gifts, and protection in return for loyalty and service.[80]

The *að* of *Af.* 1–1.8, then, takes part in the *bot* system in the sense that "*bot* is a more general word, including compensation of any kind" (Pollock and Maitland 48). The *að* becomes a unit of exchange in the king-subject relationship. This compensatory nature of *að* is evident in Anglo-Saxon law through the comparable worth of oaths on a sliding scale keyed to social station.[81] Men of greater station can exculpate those of lesser station through adding their more valuable oaths to the proceedings.[82] Conversely, those of lower station can bolster the worth of their own oath through the recruiting of "oath-helpers" to improve their case. [83] Alfred thus sets the cornerstone of his legislation on Anglo-Saxon cultural practice.

This secular basis of his kingship calls upon the Church only insofar as its sanctions can bolster the punishments for secular transgression. This co-existence of lay and clerical punishments is not unusual in itself. Alfred's practice parallels a Frankish example as "in the ninth century, the demarcation between royal judicial powers and the episcopal prerogative of imposing public penance became increasingly blurred" (Smith 671).[84] Alfred's nod to public penance in his *Domboc* fits with Frantzen's argument that "it is highly unlikely that the machinery of private penance would have fared well during the ninth century invasions" (*Literature* 126).[85] Alfred sublimates the language of sacred penance to that of the secular compensation of the feud-based *bot* system in order to establish the primacy of secular cultural practice over sacred injunction.

The primary punishment for oath-breaking in *Af.* 1.2 illustrates the placing of secular justice before that of the Church in Alfred's law:

> Gif he þonne þæs weddige þe him riht sie to gelæstanne 7 þæt aleoge, selle mid eaðmedum his wæpn 7 his æhte his freondum to gehealdanne 7 beo feowertig nihta on carcerne on cyninges tune, ðrowige ðær swa biscep him scrife, 7 his mægas hine feden, gif he self mete næbbe

> (However, if he pledges what is lawful for him to perform and leaves it unfulfilled, with humility he shall give his weapons and his possessions to his friends to keep and be in prison forty nights in the king's dwelling, endure there the judgement the bishop gives to him, and his kinsmen shall feed him, if he has no food himself) [*Af.* 1.2].[86]

It is only after his secular incarceration that the violator is subject to the bishop's judgment. This pattern recurs throughout the law. If one flees his punishment and escapes, he is both "afliemed 7 sie amænsumod of eallum Cristes ciricum" (outlawed and is excommunicated from all of Christ's churches) (*Af.* 1.7). If the culprit is caught, he is liable for both the secular *borgbryce* (breach of surety) and the *scrif* (penance) due for his *wedbryce* (breach of pledge) (*Af.* 1.8).

Although these related crimes are all in violation of a secular dictate, the keeping of secular oaths, the king brings the Church into the process to add its clerical *scrif*, or penance, to the secular punishment. However, the defining and ultimate penalty comes from secular society. If the lawbreaker dies before receiving his secular and sacred penalties, the final punishment for the outlaw is "licgge he orgilde" (to lie without payment) (*Af.* 1.5), that is, to deny his kin of payment of his *wergild*. The king's and community's severest punishment is to deny the dead a place in the cultural exchange of compensation. Above all else, this system of payments defines Alfred's kingship and his kingdom.

Although Church punishments may be invoked in the service of upholding the secular oaths between men, the overriding strictures against Alfred's *ærest* (first) law in both importance and order originate from the dictates of the feud-based Anglo-Saxon culture of compensation. The king is authorized and able to strip the violator of both secular and sacred protection, placing the secular machinery of adjudication above the purview of ecclesiastic penance.

The Alfred represented by his first law, *Af.* 1–1.8, is a ruler operating primarily in the sphere of Anglo-Saxon cultural practice. The law is driven not by Old Testament severity nor by New Testament mercy, but by the secular Anglo-Saxon practice of *bot*. While Church penalties are employed in this law, they are invoked specifically to punish the secular crime of oath-breaking. The punitive machinery of the Church is employed in the service of enforcing secular dictates. Alfred's invocation of the Church in this crucial first law may point towards his aspiration to Christian kingship in the Carolingian model, but the actual machinery of jurisprudence he employed and the concomitant primary vision of rulership he projects via this law is based on Anglo-Saxon ideals of kingship. Thus Alfred's first law, one of the few reasonably attributable to the king himself, gives primacy to the king's image as a secular ruler in an Anglo-Saxon milieu. This law also highlights the defining nature of the compensatory *bot* system for his kingdom.

Conclusion

Alfred's appeals to various models of authority in his *Domboc* develops an image of the king and his kingdom significantly indebted to both Judeo-Christian and Anglo-Saxon ideals and traditions. However, while his devotion to Judeo-Christianity is an integral component of the king's lasting image, his *Domboc* highlights the importance of his image as an ideal secular Anglo-Saxon king over a specific people: the West Saxons. His choice of Moses as his primary legislative forebear, contemporaneously portrayed as an archetype of Anglo-Saxon leadership, and his bending of Mosaic law to Germanic Anglo-Saxon cultural practice, provide a model for understanding the importance of the king's contemporary culture to his legislative approach. His choice of Acts 15:23–29 to serve as his conceptual bridge from the Old Testament to the New, which allows one to follow God's law insofar as one is able to keep it (*Af. El.* 49.5), also allows for transmuting heavenly dictates so as to be relevant to Alfred's people. This is demonstrated in Alfred's harmonizing the feud-based Anglo-Saxon *bot* system with Judeo-Christian legal tradition (*Af. El.* 49.7).

Despite the Judeo-Christian nature of the preface, Alfred introduces his own lawmaking process in terms of secular Anglo-Saxon juridicial practice (*Af. El.* 49.9–10). Alfred directly ties his role in this history of lawgiving to the secular rulers whose good examples he invokes (*Af. El.* 49.9–10). Alfred's laws are adapted from earlier Anglo-Saxon secular sources (as in *Af.* 44–77) or crafted for the workings of secular Anglo-Saxon jurisprudence, implementing religious punishments insofar as they fit the secular practices of his West Saxon people (as in *Af.* 1–1.8). The cumulative effect of the *Domboc*, therefore, is to render an image of Alfred as mindful of Christian ideals, but the text is overwhelming presented in terms of the ideals and cultural practices of secular West Saxon kingship through the language of *bot*. As we shall see, future compilers would fasten upon Alfred's unique representation of West Saxon kingship and community as a source to further their own political and institutional ends.

CHAPTER 3

Eleventh and Twelfth Century Redeployments of the *Domboc*

The *Domboc*, like numerous medieval texts, survives its creators by many years. However, the discrete survivals of various manuscripts and texts tell individual stories. Each reproduction has its own set of generating factors, dependent upon its particular context. The context in which a text reappears can be instructive on at least two fronts. First, the manuscript survival of an early text can provide a window into the cultural ethos at the time of its reproduction. The texts a culture reproduces and preserves are direct indicators of what the culture values or finds useful as a means to a specific end. Second, and contingent upon the first point, the reproduction of a text can indicate its reception history. Examining the probable uses of a text, and the social and textual contexts in which it appears, suggests the copiers' appraisal of the reproduced text.

Thus, an examination of the *Domboc*'s reappearance in eleventh and twelfth centuries shows how its reproduction reflects the manifestation of a particular cultural ethos in a specific historical circumstance. The *Domboc* appears following the Danish conquest of the eleventh century and Norman conquest of the twelfth century, revealing the cultural currency the text carried in the aftermath of social and political upheaval. The text's contents, steeped in the familiar language of compensation through the *bot* system, assured the continuation of long-accepted cultural practices. Additionally, as an iconic Anglo-Saxon text, the *Domboc*'s very presence signaled cultural continuity amidst the transition of conquest. The negotiation between symbolic form and applicable content is the hallmark of the *Domboc*'s post-conquest role.

For example, when Cnut captured the Anglo-Saxon throne in 1016, he used specific content from the *Domboc* in the process of legitimizing his claim to kingship. One facet of Cnut's post-conquest attempts to validate his place on the Anglo-Saxon throne was the creation and promulgation of laws that embraced and expanded upon Anglo-Saxon legal precedent. Under the new king, the writing of royal legislation (*I–II Cnut*) that included excerpts from the *Domboc* indicated that Alfred's law-book was reproduced primarily for its link to an Anglo-Saxon past, a past readily identified through the use of the *bot* system. The connection to this past helps to establish a legitimizing post-conquest national identity as remaining fundamentally Anglo-Saxon in character.

While William the Conqueror (1066–87) did not officially re-release the *Domboc* in his name, the specific contents from the text did reappear following the Norman Conquest in various collections of legislation including the *Instituta Cnuti* and the *Quadripartitus*. The *Instituta* expands upon *I–II Cnut*, adding a third section of legislation taken primarily from the *Domboc*. Reissuing Cnut's legislation following the Norman Conquest creates an overt link between William's conquest and that of Cnut. The amount of new material imported from the *Domboc* into the *Instituta* recognizes the importance of Anglo-Saxon legislation in the process of post-conquest assimilation. Alfred's legislation taking part in the *bot* system forms the bulk of the new material in the *Instituta* and provides continuity with an Anglo-Saxon past.

While the content of the *Instituta* signals the desire for continuity with an authorizing Anglo-Saxon past, the overarching function of the *Quadripartitus* provides a similar function during the reign of Henry I (1100–1135). In the *Quadripartitus*, the *Domboc* appears in full as part of a line of legislation that creates the illusion of a seamless continuity of legislative authority from the Anglo-Saxon past to the Anglo-Norman present. However, another document of this time period reproduces the *Domboc* in full not to bolster the validity of the new regime, but to protect its creators' pre-conquest claims. The *Textus Roffensis* of the early twelfth century was compiled at Rochester Priory in an effort to substantiate its rights to its holdings following regime change. The compiler of the *Textus* recalls the *Domboc* in full to ensure continuity here as well, but a continuity of a very specific sort: the preservation of the priory's (legitimate and questionable) claims to specific rights and properties.

The *Domboc*, throughout the eleventh and twelfth centuries, resurfaces in times of social and political turmoil: following conquest by foreign powers. This resurfacing serves a double purpose as evidenced by the different ways in which the text is used. The *Domboc*'s text contains legislation specific to Anglo-Saxon cultural practice exemplified by the *bot* system. The continued acceptance and reinscription of these laws reduces the sting of conquest by allowing for the continuation of traditional practices. This approach to the *Domboc* occurs in the immediate aftermath of conquest during the reigns of Cnut and William I.

The *Domboc* also, as a whole work, provides a symbolic function of ensuring acceptance and continuity of culture that would reassure the conquered even as it legitimizes the rightful new rule of the conquerors. This approach to the *Domboc* occurs at a temporal remove from conquest, such as during the reign of Henry I, when the symbolic weight of the text is more important than its particular contents. However, regardless of the mode of reproduction, the *Domboc* consistently remains a link to an authorizing Anglo-Saxon past, providing continuity for new regimes.

Cnut and the Domboc

The success of Cnut's conquest of the Anglo-Saxons relies on this legitimization through administrative continuity, and the *Domboc* plays a significant part in its ultimate effectiveness. Shortly following the eleventh-century Danish conquest of England, Cnut issues a law code (*I–II Cnut*) that seeks to make peace through continuity with prior Anglo-Saxon law.[1] This continuity is apparent through the author's incorporation of earlier Anglo-Saxon laws into Cnut's new law code.[2] As for the content of the laws, Wormald argues, "Cnut's code was just what the word conventionally means: a codification of mostly pre-existent law"(*Making* 349). Within it are direct quotations, paraphrases, or indirect references from royal legislation from Æthelberht (560–616) to Æthelred II (978–1016). However, the individual codes and laws used in *I–II Cnut* carry some significance. The quotations and paraphrases from Alfred's *Domboc* in *I–II Cnut* are specifically dependent upon Alfred's function as a king. They exemplify the Anglo-Saxon cultural practices of feud and *bot*. As such, they reveal the *Domboc* as a text that was primarily useful to the author of Cnut's codes as a conduit to these practices, representative of a native, pre-conquest realm.

The use of Alfred's laws in the legislation of Cnut reveals a pattern of borrowing that focuses on laws representative of the *bot* system. Current evidence suggests Archbishop Wulfstan authored *I Cnut*.[3] The archbishop's use of *bot* language functions as a link to native practice, legitimizing the rule of his monarch Cnut. The first borrowing from Alfred's law code appears in *I Cnut* 19.1 as: "7 word 7 weorc freonda gehwylc fadige mid rihte, 7 að 7 wedd wærlice healde" (And let every friend guide his words and works properly, and carefully keep his oath and pledge).[4] Wulfstan's phrase "að 7 wedd wærlice healde" (*I Cn.* 19.1) can be traced to *Af.* 1: "his að 7 his wed wærlice healde" (carefully keep his oath and his pledge). Although Wulfstan relied on Alfred for a source, given Alfred's apparent coining of the word-pair *að* and *wedd*, he recontextualized the citation for Cnut's code.[5] Wulfstan modifies the context to suit his goals, but creates a connection to the most important of Alfred's laws: the ones that govern secular ruler-subject loyalty through oath. Even as he revises Alfred's law, Wulfstan makes an authorizing link to the past through native cultural practice.

Wulfstan specifically turns to Alfred's law code for its management of the *bot* system in statutes 47–47.1 and 57–59 of *II Cnut*.[6] The former pair of Cnut's statutes read as follows:

> Gif hwa openlice lengctenbryce gewyrce þurh feohtlac oððe þurh wiflac [oððe þurh reaflac] oððe þurh ænig healice misdæde, sy þæt twybete, swa on heahfreolse, be ðam þe seo dæd si.
>
> And gif man ætsace, ladige mid þryfealdre lade.
>
> (If anyone openly performs a breach of the Lenten fast through fighting or through fornication [or through robbery] or through any egregious misdeed, let that be subject to double compensation, as on a great festival, in accordance with the deed.
>
> And if one denies it, let him excuse himself with threefold exculpation) [*II Cn.* 47–47.1].[7]

Out of all the other law codes in Old English, the double-penalty for offenses during high holy days (such as Christmas, Easter, and Holy Thursday) only occurs in *Af.* 5.5. Here Alfred commands that "þara gehwelc we willað sie twybote, swa on Lenctenfæsten" (for each of those [days] we desire [the monetary penalty for the crime] to be twice-compensation, as during the Lenten feast). Later, in *Af.* 40.1, Alfred again asserts that the payment for crimes "in lenctenfæsten, hit sie twybote" (during the Lenten feast, let it be twice-compensation). This compensation participates in the *bot* system, as it assigns remuneration for transgression. Thus, Wulfstan's first direct use of Alfred's *Domboc* as a source employs the *bot* system through the stipulation of *twybete* for crimes during holy days. Wulfstan specifically invokes Alfred's law for its management of the system of culturally accepted compensations for wrongs.

The recurring compensatory formula within *II Cn.* 45.3–46 and *II Cn.* 48, immediately surrounding the Alfredian borrowing, recounts the payment for crimes as a "lahslit mid Denum, fullwite mid Englum" (fine for breach of law among the Danish, full payment to the king among the English) (*II Cn.* 48).[8] This legislative formula relies upon the comparison between Danish and Anglo-Saxon secular justice. Although the content of Alfred's *Af.* 5.5 deals with a religious subject–the Lenten feast–the actual function of the legislation is an operation of the *bot* system. Wulfstan shares Alfred's concern with the proper keeping of the Christian holy day, an interest the archbishop evinces in his homilies.[9] However, despite Wulfstan's pastoral interests, his invocation of Alfred's law underscores Alfred's role as a king whose primary identification is that of an arbiter of feud-based Anglo-Saxon culture.

The contents of *II Cnut* 57–59 illustrate the secular and compensatory nature of Wulfstan's borrowings from Alfred:

Gif hwa ymb cinigc oððe hlaford syrwe, si he his feores scyldig 7 ealles þæs ðe he age, butan he ga to þryfealdan ordale.

Gif hwa cinigces borh abrece, gebete þæt mid V pundan.

Gif hwa arcebisceopes borh oððe aþelingas abrece, gebete þæt mid þrim pundan.

Gif hwa leodbisceopes oððe ealdormannes borh abrece, gebete þæt mid II pundan.

Gif hwa on cinigces hirede gefeohte, þolige þæs lifes, butan se cingc him gearian wylle.

(If anyone plots against the king or a lord, he is liable of his life and all that he owns, unless he goes to three-fold ordeal.

If anyone breaks the king's surety, let him compensate for that with five pounds.

If anyone breaks the archbishop's or nobleman's surety, let him compensate for that with three pounds.

If anyone breaks the provincial bishop's or ealdorman's surety, let him compensate for that with two pounds.

If anyone fights in the king's household, he forfeits his life, unless the king desires to pardon him) [*II Cn.* 57–59].

Here Wulfstan appropriates *Af.* 4.2, in which Alfred stipulates the penalty against the life and possessions of one who would "ymb his hlafordes fiorh sierwe" (plot against his lord's life). Wulfstan follows with a close borrowing of *Af.* 3, where Alfred outlines the penalties for breaking the *borg*, or surety and protection, of king, archbishops, bishops, and ealdorman. Wulfstan's only substantial change to this section was to balance the secular and ecclesiastical examples with the addition of *æþeling*, or nobleman, to *II Cn.* 58.1. Finally, on fighting in the king's hall, Wulfstan draws upon *Af.* 7, in which Alfred commands that it is the king's decision to decide life or death for the perpetrator, "swa he him forgifan wille" (as he [the king] desires to grant to him [the accused]).

Wulfstan invokes Alfred's law only as it manages the regulation of feud-based Anglo-Saxon cultural practice.[10] The specific issues are treachery against one's earthly lord, the breaking of surety, and fighting in the king's household. Lord-treachery was an important concern for Alfred.[11] The law against breaking of surety participates in the compensatory function of the *bot* system, which lies at the heart of feud-based culture. Social transgressions are mitigated and atoned for by means of monetary compensation.[12] Finally, the stricture against fighting in the king's household serves the purely cultural function of promoting social harmony within a group. Each of Wulfstan's choices from Alfred's text concerns the managing of secular social violations by means of *bot*.

At first, Wulfstan's reproduction of Alfred's *bot*-based laws may seem out of keeping with the archbishop's larger legislative goal: to "smeage gelome, hwæt him sy to donne and hwæt to forganne after Godes rihte" (meditate frequently [on] what he is to do and what to forego according to God's law).[13] Indeed, Wulfstan's typical approach to secular rulership has been characterized as "the application of human society to the mandates of Heaven" (Wormald, *Making* 464). As Wormald argues, Wulfstan was "*par excellence* a Carolingian ideologue in his integrated view of a holy people whose kings and bishops worked together to realize the kingdom of God" (*Making* 465). It would seem that the aim of aspiring to heavenly ideals would necessarily sublimate earthly legislation to sacred dictates.

However, Wulfstan ultimately focuses more on integration than on sublimation of the secular to the sacred. As the archbishop states in his *Sermo Lupi ad Anglos*, the only way for the Anglo-Saxons to save their souls at Judgment is to both "Godes lagum fylgean" (follow God's laws) and "að 7 wed wærlice healdan" (carefully keep [earthly] oath and pledge).[14]

This combination requires balancing elements represented as recognizably distinct: the law of human society and the Law of God. Wulfstan's selection of Alfred's laws that manage the *bot* system aligns Alfred's law with earthly law. Although Alfred's *Domboc* may have invited a comparison to Mosaic law (*Af. El. Pro.*-49.10), Wulfstan represents Alfred's law only in its secular context. For Wulfstan and the legislative arm of Cnut's kingship, Alfred's laws represent the laws of secular Anglo-Saxon society.

Wulfstan's apparent intentions in the compilation of his law code have a significant bearing on later eleventh and twelfth-century reinscriptions of it. Wormald characterizes Cnut's law code as "above all a tribute to the legislative achievements of kings since Alfred" (*Making* 355). As Mary Richards argues, Cnut issues identifiably Anglo-Saxon "legislation as a means to establish his authority over all England" ("Anglo-Saxonism" 54–55). Such an ideological project corresponds with Wulfstan's homiletic concerns with social order and stability.[15] Cnut desired a stable and unified kingdom for ease and efficacy of rule; Wulfstan desired that human society mirror the order of God's law.[16] *I–II Cnut* served both ends in its continuation of native Anglo-Saxon law, identifiable by virtue of its conspicuous use of the *bot* system.

Cnut's kingdom, unified through legislation that relies on a conspicuous and ubiquitous Anglo-Saxon presence, forges a new Anglo-Danish national identity. This identity is at least partly the result of a textual connection to the past through legislation. Cnut forges a new vision of the Anglo-Saxon nation using its own texts, but reissuing them in his name, establishing his authority and marking the prior Anglo-Saxon nation as subsumed by his new Anglo-Danish administration. This model of conquest, by means of limited accommodation through legislation as a project of national revisioning, was successful enough to be seized upon by a later conqueror of the Anglo-Saxons: William of Normandy.

William I and the Domboc

Following the Norman Conquest, Alfred's *Domboc* reappears to again emphasize the continuity of rule under a new regime. According to Pauline Stafford, a fundamental difference between Cnut's Danish conquest of 1016 and William I's of 1066 is the way in which each military victory was officially confirmed. She argues that "conquest in one case [Cnut's] prompted comprehensive legal statement [*I–II Cnut*], in the other [William I's] a comprehensive survey of land and royal rights [the Domesday Book]" (Stafford 108). However, William I's reign was not without a "comprehensive legal statement." During this period Cnut's legislation (*I–II Cnut*) is bolstered with additional Anglo-Saxon legal material, including excerpts from the *Domboc*. The resulting text is unofficially re-issued as the *Instituta Cnuti* during William I's reign in an apparent effort to duplicate the Danish king's post-conquest success.[17]

Cnut based his post-conquest rule on a model of cultural accommodation through legislation. This legislation appears to serve as a model for a law collection issued under William I, the late-eleventh-century *Instituta Cnuti*. William I's Norman administration continued the earlier Anglo-Danish practice of mining Alfred's *Domboc* for language of compensation based on the *bot* system.[18] The compiler's strategy emphasizes the role of Alfred's legislation as a link to Anglo-Saxon cultural practices. The selective incorporation of *bot* language from the *Domboc* is the most tangible connection between the new administration and the pre-conquest, Anglo-Saxon past.

The provenance and contents of the *Instituta* provide clues to the motives behind its inscription relative to the role of the *Domboc* excerpts in the text. The text is a composite work with a tripartite structure. As Felix Liebermann identified them, "the first and second parts are in the main translations of Cnut's ecclesiastical and secular laws [*I* and *II Cnut*] respectively [...while...] the third part contains, besides a dozen chapters of which no Anglo-Saxon original exists, a variegated patchwork of Latinised excerpts from *Alfred-Ine*, *Merce* [*Mircna Laga*], *Ath* [*Að*], *Had* [*Hadbot*], *Grith* [*Grið*], *Northleod* [*Norðleoda Laga*], and *Gethingth* [*Geþyncðu*]" ("On the *Instituta*" 80–81).[19] In addition to *I–II Cnut*, Wulfstan is the author of *Grið* and the *Geþyncðu* group (which includes *Mircna Laga, Að, Hadbot, Norðleoda Laga,* and *Geþyncðu*).[20] Liebermann identifies the translator as a Francophone ecclesiastic of the "Dano-Mercian region" ("On the *Instituta*" 83–87). Wormald puts the date of compilation late in the Conqueror's reign and attaches it to the production of *Willelmi Articuli (X)*, or the "Ten Articles" of William I.[21]

The language and homeland of the *Instituta* compiler provide clues as to the function and relevance of his text and its Alfredian borrowings. The Francophone translator lived in an area of England with long-standing ties to the Danes. Under the rule of a foreign conqueror, returning to

Cnut's laws to ameliorate the uneasiness of conquest is a natural enough choice. The translator's language ties him to the present conquerors, and his location ties him to a site of previously successful conquest and integration. Integration is a watchword for the *Instituta*, as it is the primary effect of the translator's project. As opposed to simply reiterating *I–II Cnut* in a Latin translation, the compiler includes a third section of laws that come from Wulfstan's texts on social rank, *wergild*, and oath following the Danish conquest. Significantly, the only identifiable extra–Wulfstanian material comes from the *Domboc*. These excerpts are inserted into the text of *I–II Cnut* in Books I–II of the *Instituta* and comprise the bulk of the additional text in Book III. All of these choices tie the current administration to the past with the effect of emphasizing continuity of rule.

The attempt at continuity is expressed linguistically in the contents of the text. The translator's word choice signals his emphasis of the *bot* system. His choice for the translation of "bot" is the Latin verb *emendare*.[22] In a legal context, *emendare* carries the specific meaning of "fine [...] for offence against [a] person" (Latham and Howlett 771).[23] This word shows the translator's knowledge of the function of the term "bot" in Anglo-Saxon legislation issued under Alfred and, later, Cnut: monetary compensation for injury.[24] The translator is not mechanically reproducing the earlier texts for broad ideological effect, as in Wormald's model. Rather, he is reproducing and integrating his source texts for a specific outcome: to tie legislation issued during William I's rule to that of both Cnut and Alfred. Reproducing Cnut's legislation connects William I's rule to a prior successful conquest by a foreign-born ruler. Reproducing Alfred's legislation connects the new administration to a native, Anglo-Saxon authority and identity.

The translator's knowledge regarding his word choice also informs his choices of statutes in the *Instituta*. His selections show a preoccupation with laws that manage society by the secular machinery of justice. The common strand through the texts attributed to Wulfstan in the *Instituta* is a negotiation of the social order, including the relationship of the clergy to their secular equivalents within a framework of secular judgments.[25] This worldly law encompasses the ideals of holy law, even though its judgments operate in the compensatory feud-based *bot* system. The *Grið* and *Gepyncðu* laws are marked by the pairing of secular and ecclesiastical equivalents in describing the payment of fines or the *wergild* (man-price) of individuals. These pairings dominate what the *Instituta* translator includes from Wulfstan's *Grið* and *Geþyncðu*. Common formulas are "cyning 7 arce-biscop" (king and archbishop) (*Grið* 6), "arcebiscopes 7 æþelinges [...] Bis-copes 7 ealdormannes" (archbishops and members of royal household [...] bishops and high ranking leaders) (*Norðleoda* 2–3), "biscpe 7 cynge" (bishop and king) (*Geþyncðu* 8).[26] The translator chooses Wulfstanian laws that bring the two major sectors of society, clerical and lay, together under the purview of civil law.

The need for paring sacred and secular society under law is twofold. On the one hand, the effect of choosing legislative texts that consolidate lay and clerical society would be most welcome following the upheaval of conquest. Releasing a comprehensive legislative document like the *Instituta* provides the conquered with a sense of stability and continuity. After all, such was the case for Cnut. As Wulfstan writes in the introduction of *I Cnut*: "Cnut cyngc mid his wiena geþeahte frið 7 freonscip betweox Denum 7 Englum fullice gefæstnode 7 heora ærran saca ealle getwæmde" (King Cnut, with the counsel of his advisors, completely established peace and friend-ship between the Danes and the Anglo-Saxons and settled all their previous disputes). A key element of post-conquest legislation, then, is the estab-lishing of peace in the realm between former combatants. Legislation that addresses large social concerns establishes a sense of stability by delineating social norms. Reproducing Cnut's laws in the *Instituta* seeks the same end.

On the other hand, the civil laws of the *Domboc* appearing amid these Wulfstanian laws on the social order are a selection of Alfred's and Ine's laws most identifiably concerned with the *bot* system.[27] *Bot* operates as a key to ordering society, providing the *Instituta* with links to both Wulfstan's earlier legislation and to the accepted Anglo-Saxon cultural practices of the conquered people. These laws can be separated into two broad cate-gories: laws incorporated into the rewriting of *I–II Cnut*, and laws newly introduced in Book III of the *Instituta*.

The laws of the former category were apparently inserted into the text of *I–II Cnut* because of their relevance to the preceding text. Wormald delineates these relationships: "Af. 20 was inserted after I Cn 5:2d, clearly enough prompted by its content; [...] Af 15–17 and 38–39.2 came in after II Cn 58–59, which were themselves based on nearly related Alfred matter" (*Making* 404, n. 649). All these laws show the *bot* system at work. *Af.* 20 deals with the responsibility for lost property lent without *leafnes* (per-mission). The financial compensation for fighting "beforan ærcebiscepe" (before an archbishop) or "beforan oðrum biscepe oððe ealdormen" (before another bishop or ealdorman) is the subject of *Af.* 15. The next law requires a cattle thief to "forgielde scill" (pay a shilling) (*Af.* 16) for chasing off a foal or calf while stealing its mother. The adult animals are to be paid for "be hiora weorð" (according to their worth) (*Af.* 16). *Af.* 17 stipulates the responsibility of a foster parent to clear himself of guilt if his charge dies.[28] The larger significance of these additions to *I–II Cnut* is in the way each law manages social transgressions through assigning remuneration, the defining action of the *bot* system.

The compiler also imports Alfredian material into books I and II of the *Instituta* to bring lay and clerical citizens under the rule of law defined by the *bot* system. Specifically, inserting *Af.* 38–39.2 into Book II of the *Instituta* shows a concern with social rank and the incorporation of the clergy into the cultural machinery of the *bot* system. The penalty for fighting before an ealdorman, for instance, demands the perpetrator to "bete wer 7 wite" (pay wergild and fine) (*Af.* 38). The scope of this law is then enlarged to encompass matching penalties for such misbehavior before equivalent ranks of the clergy and secular authority: either before "cyninges ealdormonnes gingran oððe cyninges preoste" (an assistant of the king's ealdorman or a king's priest) (*Af.* 38.2). Finally, *Af.* 39–39.2 delineates escalating payments made for fighting in the house of a ceorl to that of a "twelfhyndum men" (a twelve-hide man) (*Af.* 39.2).[29] These inclusions serve as concrete examples of legislation that recognizes the proper ordering of society, and the place and authority of the clergy alongside their secular counterparts. The escalation of monetary penalties in keeping with the status of the aggrieved satisfied the cultural norm. The equation of penalties across clerical and secular lines satisfied the clerical community. Alfredian material in the *Instituta* reinforces the proper order of society explicitly through invoking the *bot* system.

That all the laws from the *Domboc* found in the *Instituta Cnuti* are directly involved in the management of the *bot* system is suggestive of the compiler's motives in choosing these specific texts. Although contemporary manuscripts carried *I–II Cnut* alongside the Mosaic preface to Alfred's laws, the compiler of the *Instituta Cnuti* chose only the most secular of Alfred's laws: those handling the payment of *bot, wer,* and *wite*.[30] This selective incorporation of overtly compensatory legal material indicates the *Instituta* compiler's idea of the most important Anglo-Saxon laws to preserve, those most closely connected to feud-based, compensatory Anglo-Saxon cultural practices.

For the compiler of the *Instituta*, Ine's legislation (as written in Alfred's *Domboc*) further serves as a bridge to an authorizing Anglo-Saxon past. Specifically, the laws from the *Domboc* introduced in Book III of the *Instituta Cnuti* are all indebted to the *bot* system. Book III opens with the following excerpts in the order as listed: *Ine* 9, 13.1–15; *Af.* 29–31.1, 44–77, 19–19.2, 23–23.2.[31] The laws of Ine cited speak of the penalties for renegades. *Ine* 9 (*In. Cn. III* 1) specifies the fine for "hwa wrace do, ærðon he him ryhtes bidde" (anyone who does punishment, before he asks for his rights), that is, seeking one's own justice before going through the official channels. Operating outside the law is also addressed by *Ine* 13.1–15 (*In. Cn. III* 2–4). This group of laws establishes the legal definition of such groups of renegades as "ðeofas," (thieves) a "hloð," (band), or a "here" (army), and then identifies the penalties for anyone acting with such groups.[32] This legislation establishes an explicit connection to earlier, identifiable Anglo-Saxon law.

Like the laws of Ine taken from the *Domboc* for the *Instituta*, the laws of Alfred that continue Book III carry on the topic of aiding a renegade, managing society through the *bot* system. *Af.* 29–31.1 (*In. Cn. III* 5–8) establishes the judgments against "mon unsynnigne mid hloðe ofslea" (one among a band [who] kills an innocent man) (*Af.* 29). Continuing the preoccupation with social order found in *I–II Cnut*, the following laws delineate the rising penalties for killing men with higher social status. Although released in an Anglo-Norman context, the *Instituta* relies on identifiably Anglo-Saxon practices, emphasizing the continuity between regimes.

Thus, Alfred's injury tariff (*Af.* 33–77) appears in the *Instituta* to provide one of the most explicit examples of the *bot* system in action. Prescribing the monetary compensation for injuries to nearly every part of the body, *In. Cn. III* 9–39 closely follows Alfred's catalogue, from *heafodwund* (head-wound) (*Af.* 44) (*In. Cn. III* 9) to the severing of the *lytle ta* (little toe) (*Af.* 64.4) (*In. Cn. III* 28). The final borrowing from Alfred deals with damage done to property. *Af.* 19–19.2 (*In. Cn. III* 40) presents the compensatory obligations of one who "his wæpnes oðrum onlæne" (loans his weapon to another), and whose arms are then used for murder. If one's dog causes injury or death, *Af.* 23–23.2 (*In. Cn. III* 41), the owner is liable for greater and greater fines after each offense, up to full wergild, if "he hine hæbbe" (he [the owner] keeps him [the dog]) (*Af.* 23.2). Following a large section of Wulfstanian legislation, Book III of the *Instituta Cnuti* concludes with a final, animal related, borrowing from *Ine*. *In. Cn.*

III 64–64.1 provides separate values for the horns, eyes, and tails of cows and oxen.[33] Once again, the compiler mines the *Domboc* for information of a purely compensatory nature.

The inclusion of Alfred's laws participates in the ideological practice in which, as Richards argues, "English legislation was recognized by the Normans as a repository of cultural information useful for governance in the post–Conquest era" ("Anglo-Saxonism" 56).[34] The appending of Book III to Books I and II of the *Instituta Cnuti* provides an interpretive context for the *Instituta Cnuti* as a whole: an exercise in legislative legitimization of the new Norman regime. The compiler apparently appreciated the ideological function of legislation as a tool of cultural assimilation. Such a use for Cnut's legislation already existed in the *Instituta Cnuti*'s most immediate source: *I–II Cnut*. Wulfstan, in his codification of Anglo-Saxon law under Cnut, used legislation as a means to reaffirm the continuity of royal authority between the Anglo-Saxon reign of Æthelred and the Anglo-Danish reign of Cnut.[35] This concern with proper order was only magnified in the face of the drastic social upheaval of foreign conquest.[36]

Consequently, the Danish conquest of the Anglo-Saxons serves as a ready context for the compiler of the *Instituta Cnuti*, a member of the conquering Norman regime.[37] If *I–II Cnut* "serve[s] as a fixed point amid the disruptions of the 1016 conquest," then the *Instituta Cnuti* serves the same function in the wake of the Norman Conquest of 1066: asserting a continuity of royal authority through legislation (Wormald, *Making* 481). Books I and II of the *Instituta Cnuti* rely on invoking Cnut's kingship as a legitimizing link to the pre-conquest past.[38] As Wormald puts it, *I–II Cnut* is "the staple of written law until the twelfth century" (*Making* 404). Book III of the *Instituta Cnuti* depends primarily on the invocation of Alfred's laws in the *Domboc* to further establish a validating link to the Anglo-Saxon past.

The compiler's effort to bridge the gap between pre-conquest and post-conquest cultures is evident in the very few editorial additions he makes in translation. For example, in Book III the compiler translates *Af.* 29, which begins, "Gif mon twyhyndne mon unsynnigne mid hloðe ofslea…" (If anyone kills an unsinning two-hide man with a band of robbers…). His translation reads as follows: "Si quis per hloth occiderit hominem, *quem quidam Angli dicunt* twihende…[my emphasis]" (If anyone should kill a man, by means of a band of robbers, *a certain man whom the Anglo-Saxons call* two-hide…). The explicit use of the term *Angli* is particularly meaningful.

On the one hand, the compiler is identifying the *Angli* as separate from himself and his audience. He identifies the term *twihende* as belonging to the vocabulary of the *Angli*, and not to his own. The *Angli* of Alfred's law are not the post-conquest Anglo-Normans of the compiler's world. On the other hand, the use of the term *Angli* to define the people targeted by Alfred's West Saxon legislation has a complicated history as defining a cohesive *Angelcynn* (race of the Angles) (*Af. El.* 49.7).[39] The translator of the *Instituta*'s use of *Angli* conflates the people of Ine's and Alfred's Wessex with those of Cnut's England.[40] He struggles with what Bhabha refers to as the ambivalence of language surrounding national discourse.[41] The compiler uses Alfred's legislation as a link to an earlier fundamental Anglo-Saxon identity and authority to which the current Norman regime asserts it is the rightful heir, even as he highlights its alterity. He uses the Alfredian laws based most concretely in the system of monetary compensation as a conduit to a stable legitimizing past that the Norman regime can subsume, while retaining its own identity. Ultimately, the compiler invokes the feud-based culture of the *bot* system in the *Domboc* to fulfill the ideological agenda of the *Instituta Cnuti* to co-opt Anglo-Saxon royal authority while establishing its own dominance.

Henry I and the Domboc

While the careful choice of Alfredian statutes marks the compilation of the *Instituta Cnuti*, the reproduction of the entire *Domboc* in the legal collection *Quadripartitus* signals an approach to Alfred's text that relies more on overall effect than the content of particular statutes.[42] The *Quadripartitus*, which has a complex manuscript history, was most likely originally compiled in the first decade of the twelfth century.[43] An encyclopedia of pre-conquest legislation, the *Quadripartitus* includes law codes ranging from the seventh-century Ine through the writs of Henry I.[44] The inclusion of the *Domboc* employs Alfred's work only as part of the heritage of Anglo-Saxon legislation. The substance of the laws is essentially unchanged in its translation into Latin, but the very acts of translation and codification are of great importance to the afterlife of Alfred's *Domboc*.[45]

Wormald argues that the two main purposes of the *Quadripartitus* were comprehensiveness and systemization.[46] Q (the unknown *Quadripartitus* author) regularizes the scattered and variegated legislative heritage the Normans inherited from their Anglo-Saxon and Anglo-Danish pred-ecessors.[47] Wormald further argues for the compilation of the *Quadripar-titus* as part of the ideological project in which the "intellectual community was at the monarchy's disposal" (*Making* 474). As such, perhaps most importantly, Wormald sees the *Quadripartitus* as "a serious attempt to transmit pre-conquest texts in a language which all who mattered might understand" (*Making* 244). Those who mattered at the time of the com-pilation of the *Quadripartitus* were the ecclesiastical and secular leaders of the Norman ruling classes.[48]

The translation of the *Quadripartitus* and the *Instituta Cnuti* into Latin identifies the audience as the Norman administration, providing the motive for the reinscription of the *Domboc*. The administrative language of these secular and clerical leaders was Latin.[49] The translation of the *Domboc* into Latin might not seem to be a radical break from the practice of Anglo-Saxon leadership. Latin was a language known to Anglo-Saxon rulers and ecclesiastics.[50] However, although Latin was commonly known to upper secular and clerical classes of Anglo-Saxon leadership, the language of Anglo-Saxon political administration was Old English. The translation of laws from Old English to Latin in the *Quadripartitus*, together with the Anglo-Saxon content, was therefore an overt and ideologically charged method of announcing that the Anglo-Saxon legal system was now under new management.

As Wormald argues, the project of the *Quadripartitus* "presupposed that the law of Norman kings flowed directly from their predecessors' [as] legal fact as well as political symbol"(*Making* 466). However, the ostensible purpose for this emphasis on symbolic continuity lies in the condition of transition. It is only because of the marked shift in power from the pre-conquest administration of Anglo-Saxon rule to the post-conquest rule of the Normans that requires a self-conscious affirmation of administrative continuity.[51] When, as the record of the *Domesday Book* attests, there were precious few Anglo-Saxons of any great political standing left after the Conquest, the new Norman regime had to "diminish the conquest *as con-quest*" (O'Brien 18).[52] Therefore, the translation of Old English legal texts into Latin continues a symbolic tie to Anglo-Saxon administrative legiti-macy in England, even as it signals a break from the previous Anglo-Saxon administrative structures, rather than an accommodation of them.

According to Bruce O'Brien, the preservation of English law "is not the result of some curiously fast assimilation that made [the Normans] the willing and ethnically sensitive custodians of the legal heritage of the English" (133–34). Rather, the reproduction of Anglo-Saxon law codes after the Conquest reflects an administrative practicality in which, as David Douglas and George Greenaway note, "the Norman aristocracy utilize[s] existing organs of local government [...] not only to respect local custom, but to develop the institutions of monarchy which [they] found existing in the land [they] conquered" (49). The Preface to the *Quadripartitus* shows this as it relates how a good king takes the "leges et uiuende iura" (laws and rules of living) (*Quadr.* II *Praef.* 9) and uses them as the basis of his new rule. Of course, Q gives the conquering monarch credit for the beneficence of his new legislation, despite the breadth of his borrowings. Specifically, Q claims that "Hoc enim est emendatio Willemi regis in legibus Anglicis, quicquid honestum et utile circumquaque probaueris" (Whatever you judge honorable and useful everywhere, this is the improvement of King William in the English laws). However, William I's success in rule is due, at least in part, to his recognition of what is good in the Anglo-Saxon laws and using them as the basis for his own rule.

Even so, William I's initial co-opting of Anglo-Saxon law, a project continued under his son Henry I, enacts a subtle negotiation of domination. The substance of the laws themselves is little changed, but their very linguistic form is altered to reflect the mode of administration of the dominant culture. If Wormald's equation that the ideological function of legislation supercedes that of its legislative contents is correct, then the translation of Anglo-Saxon law from the vernacular into the Norman administrative language of Latin is a clear exercise not of accommodation, but of subjugation.[53] The *Quadripartitus*, then, uses the translated *Domboc* only as a means of associating the current administration with an Anglo-Saxon legislative heritage. The purpose of this association is to foster a sense of continuity with earlier native administrations even as the current ruler establishes his own power over the conquered people.

Q explicitly negotiates the space between continuity and asserting power in the prefaces to the *Quadripartitus*. Although the title implies a four-part structure, the text was never completed as such.[54] It is extant only in two parts: the first book is a translation of Anglo-Saxon legislation through Cnut, and the second book is an abbreviated introduction to the laws of Henry I.[55] Three prefaces to the *Quadripartitus* exist: the *Dedicatio* and the *Argumentum* preface the first book of the *Quadripartitus*, and the *Praefatio* introduces the second book.[56] The *Dedicatio* occurs only in the earliest, incomplete manuscript, most likely an early draft of the *Quadri-partitus*.[57] This preface is a catalogue of the decline of law and civilization, characterized "cotidie malorum innouatione profusum exaggerationibus" (by the daily renewal of ever more frequent evils) (*Dedic.* § 4).[58] Q tallies social ills ranging from how "malitiæ detestanda creuit inprobitas" (the detestable wantoness of malice increased) (*Dedic.* § 10) to the "luxuriæ dissoluentis sordidiora genera" (filthier kinds of dissolute lechery) (*Dedic.* § 11). Ultimately, Q asserts that "Iusticia, fortitudo, prouidentia, temperantia uana uulgi comenta sunt" (Justice, fortitude, foresight, temperance are the empty imaginings of the common people) (*Dedic.* § 17). Wormald argues that the reason for such a dim view of the state of affairs in England is that this early preface was written while William II was still on the throne.[59] The kingship of William II is seen by contemporary sources as a low point in royal administration between the peaks of the reigns of William I and Henry I.[60] The *Anglo-Saxon Chronicle* entry for 1100, the year of his death, claims that William II "wæs forneah ealre his leode lað 7 Gode andsæte" (was hated by very nearly all his nation and repugnant to God). Since the *Dedicatio* is primarily absorbed in detailing the sorry state of Anglo-Norman England and its law, it is not until the later *Argumentum* that Q reveals his ideas on the relationship between current law and the law of the Anglo-Saxons.[61]

This second preface's tone is markedly different from that of the *Dedicatio*, revealing the connection between the state of the nation and its legislative connection to its past.[62] Thus, under the misrule of William II, Q laments in the *Dedicatio* that he lives in a time in which "cuncta flagitiorum genera, cuncta mali discrimina plena concretione redudundarunt" (all kinds of shameful acts, all perils of evils, [have become] consolidated together and overflowed) (*Dedic.* § 10). However, he rejoices in the *Argumentum*: "Regis tamen et Normannorum ducis, augusti domini nostri Cesaris Henrici, magni Willemi regis filii, serena tempora, fatigatis iam nobis et pene deficientibus, pacis ac felicitatis antique uotiua gaudia reduxerunt" (Yet when we were worn out and almost done for, the peaceful times of the king and duke of Normandy, our lord Augustus Caesar, Henry [I], son of King William the great, brought back the longed-for joys of peace and our former happiness) (*Arg.* § 16). The accession of Henry I has a dramatically positive impact on the author's worldview.

Q identifies the instrument for this happiness as Anglo-Saxon legislation, "illa pacis foedera, quo semper Angligenarum corda suspirant et modis optant omnibus" (those bonds of peace, for which the hearts of Englishmen sigh and long in every way) (*Arg.* § 11). Although Q tacitly refers to these laws as Edward the Confessor's, he pointedly cites their origin as Cnut's law.[63] Particularly, Q praises Cnut's skill as a kind conqueror who has a "sibi subditos ampliori dilectione" ([deep] love for those subject to him) (*Arg.* § 2) through conducting "memorabilem cum eis synodum, in secula successiua profuturum" (a memorable synod that would benefit successive ages) (*Arg.* § 3).[64] Q cites the substance of the laws generated from this synod as "ab antiquis accepimus" (received [...] from our ancestors) (*Arg.* § 1). More specifically, he acknowledges that these laws were assembled by the Anglo-Saxon *witan*.[65] What makes Henry I's law so just and successful for Q and his audience was its identification as legitimately "English" in regards to its heritage as identifiably Anglo-Saxon law.

Q's authorial position helps to illustrate the subtle negotiation of continuity and change surrounding the formation of national identity through legislation. According to Wormald, Q was probably a clerical scholar who believed in the righteousness of the Norman Conquest and the reigns of William I and Henry I. Moreover, Wormald sees Q as "among the earliest evidence there is for the 'Anglicization' of the new Francophone ascendancy" (*Making* 473). Q, therefore, stands at the confluence of continuity with an "English" identification with the Anglo-Saxon past and the change wrought by the Norman present. As such, his translation of Anglo-Saxon law into the administrative language of the Norman regime is likely in keeping with both his station and personal politics.

Q is *Anglo*-Norman insofar as his king's royal legitimization is based, at least in part, upon a continuity of Anglo-Saxon law. However, within that macro-context, he preserves legislation according to the conventions of a Latinate Norman administration. His methodology in the *Quadripartitus* mirrors that of the coronation charter of his king, Henry I. In that charter, Henry I promises, in Latin, to return the laws of Edward to his kingdom: "Lagam regis Edwardi vobis reddo cum illis emendationibus quibus pater meus eam emendavit consilio baronum suorum" (I restore to you the law of king Edward with these emendations which my father has improved with the advice of his barons) (*C Hn cor* 13).[66] Like Henry I, Q's linguistic identification, through the use of Latin, may be Anglo-Norman, but his political identification, through a legislative association with Edward the Confessor, is based on an Anglo-Saxon precedent.[67]

If this is the case, what matters most regarding the inclusion of Alfred's *Domboc* in the *Quadripartitus* is not primarily the substance of his law code. Indeed, much of the *Domboc* is derivative of other easily accessed documents, such as the Old and New Testaments of the Bible, or is duplicated in other laws gathered in the *Quadripartitus*. Parts of the *Domboc* turn up in the laws of Edward the Elder, Æthelstan, Edmund, Edgar, Æthelred, and Cnut, all of whose law codes are found in the *Quadripartitus*. Also, given the generally conservative nature of the content of Anglo-Saxon legislation, the substance of Alfred's laws that were not directly employed in these later codes were most likely echoed by them. Therefore, in keeping with Wormald's argument, Alfred's *Domboc* was included not primarily because of its content, but because of its place in the march of extant Anglo-Saxon legislation. Indeed, Q's only direct editorial reference to Alfred is in the rubric before the king's code: "Incipit lex Ælfredi regis cum capitulis suis" (Here begins the law of king Alfred with its headings) (*Ælfred Rubr.*).[68] As such, the role of the *Domboc* in this legislative encyclopedia is that of a politically identified piece of legislation, and nothing more.

Local Rights and the Domboc

In both the *Quadripartitus* and the *Instituta Cnuti*, Alfred's *Domboc* is reinscribed in the administrative language of the Norman conquerors as an ideological tool dependent upon its politically significant representation of Anglo-Saxon legislation. The contemporaneous reproduction of the *Domboc* in Old English in the manuscript known as the *Textus Roffensis* also includes the complete *Domboc* for its overarching effect of legitimization through connection to the Anglo-Saxon past.[69] The circumstances surrounding the compilation of the *Textus Roffensis* and the context of the *Domboc*'s inclusion in the text, shows the compiler's reliance on the *Domboc*'s function as an Anglo-Saxon legitimizing authority. The compiler of the *Textus Roffensis* simply used the same means as the *Quadripartitus* compiler to arrive at a different end: not to validate Anglo-Norman rule, but to preserve pre-conquest rights.

The contents of the manuscript reveal the compiler's intent to create a link to a validating Anglo-Saxon continuity of authority. Including Alfred's *Domboc* within the *Textus Roffensis*, the compiler assembled an impressive body of Anglo-Saxon materials. The manuscript contains Anglo-Saxon laws, genealogical records, and lists of ecclesiastical and secular rulers to link the cartulary eventually presented in the manuscript to these texts of Anglo-Saxon authority. The contents are as follows:

- The laws of Æthelberht (860–871), Hloðære and Eadric (673–685, 685–687; respectively), and Wihtræd (690–725).
- A West-Saxon genealogy from Cerdic (538–554), the customary progenitor of the West Saxons, up through Æthelred (978–1016).
- Alfred's *Domboc*, in its entirety.
- A mixture of the laws of Æthelstan (839–851) and the *Geþyncðu* group.
- The laws of Edward (899–924), Edmund (939–946), Æthelred (978–1016), and William I's *Asetnysse*.
- Latin texts on exorcism, the *Instituta Cnuti*, and the *Articles* of William.
- Another mixture of the laws of Æthelstan (839–851) and the *Geþyncðu* group.
- An Anglo-Saxon law on weddings.
- An Anglo-Saxon charm.
- A Latin text of Henry I's coronation charter and two tracts on excommunication.
- Genealogies of English kings and lists of sacred and lay leaders.
- A Latin list of popes.
- Latin and Old English texts of a cartulary of Rochester Cathedral Priory.
- Notes on masses to be recited. [70]

Like the compilers of the two Latin translations of the *Domboc*, the compiler of the *Textus Roffensis* reproduced the *Domboc* as part of a project of institutional legitimization through association with identifiably Anglo-Saxon legislation.[71] However, the compilers of the *Quadripartitus* and the *Instituta Cnuti* translated the *Domboc* into Latin to bolster the legitimacy of the regimes of William I and Henry I. Conversely, the compiler of the *Textus Roffensis* retained the vernacular of the *Domboc* as part of a narrowly defined institutional project to "guard its possessions" and "preserve the Anglo-Saxon heritage [of Rochester Cathedral Priory] in the face of Norman advances into every sphere of English civilization" (Richards, *Texts* 43). Thus, compilers once again invoke the *Domboc* as an ideological link to a legitimizing Anglo-Saxon past.

The selected appearances of Alfred's name in the text provide the most direct evidence for the motivation of institutional legitimization. Alfred's first appearance in the *Textus Roffensis* is in the West Saxon Regnal Table (7ᵛ-8ᵛ). The table traces the genealogy of the West Saxon royal line from the Norse god Woden to the reign of Æthelred (978–1016).[72] The table is prefaced by the Christian context of reckoning the accession of Cerdic, the founder of the West Saxon regime, in terms of the years passed "fram Cristes accennednesse" (from Christ's birth) (7ᵛ).[73] However, the table itself focuses exclusively on the rule of earthly lords whose lineage run back to pagan Nordic origins in the person of Woden. It is within that context that Alfred first appears in the *Textus Roffensis*: "Þa feng Alfred to west seaxanna rice 7 heold xxviii healf gear" (Then Alfred acceded to the throne of the West Saxons and held [it] twenty-eight and a half years) (8ᵛ). Alfred is only identified by his role as king and by his affiliation as West Saxon. The conventional presentation of Alfred's accession identifies him as simply another link in the chain of Anglo-Saxon royalty.

The next appearance of Alfred refers only to his role as secular lord, emphasizing the symbolic use of Alfredian material. Following the West Saxon Regnal Table is the complete text of the *Domboc* (9ʳ-31ᵛ), preceded by the editorial rubric "Þis syndon þa domas ðe Ælfred cyncg geceas" (These are the laws which king Alfred chose) (9ʳ). Here again, Alfred is identified by his role as king, but also in terms of a particular function of his kingship: the choosing of laws. The laws themselves, as in the *Quadripartitus*, are little changed.[74] What is of greater importance than the laws themselves is their symbolic service to "the overall theme of the project, namely, the continuing authority and viability of the Old English laws" (Richards, *Texts* 48). The key to realizing this project is to attach the laws to a socio-politically identified image of Alfred that embodies that authorizing and validating function of the Anglo-Saxon past for the compiler's Norman circumstances.

Alfred's symbolically significant final appearances occur in the lists of the West Saxon Genealogy (101ʳᵛ) and the Anglo-Saxon Royal Genealogies (102–104). The West Saxon Genealogy, which purports to list the "angelcynnes cynecynn" (royal lineage of the English people) (101ʳ), traces the lords of the English from the biblical Adam to Edward the Confessor.[75] Within this list Alfred is merely referred to as one in a sequence: "Þa wæs Alfred" (Then was Alfred) (101ᵛ). Similarly, in the Anglo-Saxon Royal Genealogies, Alfred is only mentioned as "Alfred Aþolfing" (Alfred, son of

Æthelwulf) (103ᵛ). In both cases, the compiler invokes Alfred's image only as a link in the chain of legitimizing Anglo-Saxon authorities. The cumulative effect of Alfred's appearances in the *Textus Roffensis* displays Alfred's image solely in terms of his political identification to the West Saxon royal house and in his social, legislative function as a king.

The context of the *Domboc* in relation to the other works included in the *Textus Roffensis* further illustrates this point. For texts traveling in conjunction with other works, as the *Domboc* does within the *Textus Roffensis*, the very nature of their collocation may speak volumes. Materialist philology, as expounded by Stephen Nichols and Siegfried Wenzel, moves beyond conventional textual criticism to argue "that the individual manuscript contextualizes the text(s) it contains in specific ways [and] seeks to analyze the consequences of this relationship on the way manuscripts may be read and interpreted"(2). Such an approach can lead to a fruitful critique of an individual manuscript as a distinct historical artifact. In the case of the *Textus Roffensis*, a codicological investigation can shed light on the *Domboc's* role in the larger manuscript context. The *Textus Roffensis* begins with three Kentish pieces of legislation, the law codes of Æthelberht, Hlothere and Eadric, and Wihtræd; as well as the anonymous *Hadbot*.[76] This initial quire concludes with the West Saxon Genealogical Regnal List. The Regnal List is in turn followed by the *Domboc*. This progression establishes a chain of validating authorities in which Alfred serves as a crucial link.

The early Kentish law establishes the seminal law of the land by the Kentish king who was the founder of the Rochester priory. Yet the foundation charter of the priory presented in the cartulary that completes the *Textus Roffensis* is a forgery.[77] Ironically, the fact of the foundation charter's dubious validity only confirms the *Domboc's* role in the *Textus Roffensis*. Medieval monastic charter forgeries flourished in "the century after the Norman Conquest, when the old houses of the Black monks had to convince the incomers of their ancient dignities and privileges" (Clanchy, *From Memory* 318). The *Domboc* certainly serves in this capacity. It functions as part of a manifest record of ancient native law, heritable rights from before the Conquest. Just as monastic "forgers re-created the past in an acceptable literate form [...] as experts entrenched at the centre of literary and intellectual culture in the twelfth century" (Clanchy, *From Memory* 319), so the inclusion of the *Domboc* re-creates a specific past for the priory. The compiler's inclusions of forgery in the *Textus Roffensis* prove the conscious manipulation of the manuscript's contents for a particular effect. The forgery does not necessarily discredit the entire work. Rather, it shows the mind of the compiler at work in an effort to "demonstrate the continuing validity of past agreements essential to the independence of Rochester Priory" (Richards, *Texts* 57).

The cartulary also mirrors the arrangements of the laws throughout the text, showing a progression of legitimizing authority from Kent, through Mercia to Wessex, and ultimately to the current administration. Both the laws and the charters start with Kentish texts (through the person of Æthelberht), and progress to the royal house of Wessex. The Kentish law is immediately followed by the royal line of Wessex, to whom William I (and, by extension, his son Henry I) claimed kinship.[78] Finally, the compiler cites Alfred's *Domboc*, which "links Æthelberht's laws with the establishment of Christianity in England [and also] give[s] authority, as it were, to claims of possessions dating from the establishment of the see and those same early Christian kings of Kent" (Richards, *Texts* 45). Alfred's *Domboc*, then, is instrumental in a project in which, as Richards posits, "the Rochester monks may have hoped to preserve Anglo-Saxon laws in such a way as to glorify the heritage of their own episcopal foundation"(*Texts* 44). The *Domboc* both mirrors and functions as part of the linking of the ancient past to the present.

Conclusion

The manuscript copies of all or part of Alfred's *Domboc* in the eleventh and twelfth centuries invoke the legislation's political identification as Anglo-Saxon for ideological ends. In some cases, closer in time to the anxieties of conquest, the content of the law provides specific examples of continuity. In other cases, further removed in time from the shock of regime-change, the text as a whole can serve a more general symbolic function as a bridge to validating precedent. As Elaine Treharne and Mary Swan argue, "late copies of Old English texts have their own identities as the products of a particular set of political, ecclesiastical and literary circumstances, and their study reveals much about the attitudes of twelfth-century composers and compilers towards earlier authors and traditions" (7). Thus, the eleventh and twelfth century compilers of legal texts selectively trade upon the Anglo-Saxon identity of the *Domboc* for the purposes of continuity as best suited their particular circumstances.

In the wake of the Danish conquest the laws are chosen selectively. Their language of *bot* creates an attachment to the pre-conquest world of the Anglo-Saxons. After the Norman Conquest, the translator of the *Instituta Cnuti* continues the tradition of selectively reproducing those parts of the *Domboc* that best link the Norman administration to that of the native Anglo-Saxons. The highlighting of those texts most representative of the *bot* system show the *Domboc* is a crucial text in accessing Anglo-Saxon identity. However, not all reinscriptions of the *Domboc* are that subtle. In the cases of the *Quadripartitus* and the *Textus Roffensis*, the *Domboc* is imported in its entirety. These compendiums of the royal inscription of law function as an ideological act of legitimization over that of legislation. This role of lawmaking certainly continued from the period of Anglo-Saxon regency to that of the Normans. As Bruce O'Brien argues, "while the Normans wanted legitimization, the English sought the stability and security offered by their age-old customs. Whether meant sincerely or merely as propaganda, this affirmation of older [Anglo-Saxon] customs had been the path recommended to eleventh-century English rulers" (18), rulers such as Cnut and his heirs.

Throughout the eleventh and twelfth centuries, Alfred's *Domboc* served as a means for institutional legitimization. It functions as an ideological tool of continuity and assimilation for the Danes and Normans following their respective conquests of England. This is apparent in the *Domboc*'s appearance in *I–II Cnut*, the *Instituta Cnuti*, and the *Quadripartitus*. However, the *Domboc* also serves an equally ideological use in the vernacular for the conquered Anglo-Saxons. While, as Wormald notes, the *Quadripartitus* and *Instituta Cnuti* both served at least partly as documents of royal legitimization to be utilized by the Norman vanquishers of the Anglo-Saxons, the *Textus Roffensis* survived as a vernacular confirmation of heritable rights and privileges.[79] The *Domboc*'s inclusion in the *Textus Roffensis* is evidence of its use as a source of authority and validation for Rochester Priory's institutional holdings. In all of these instances, Alfred's *Domboc* is invoked in the interests invoking a cultural identity for political or institutional ends. In this way, text producers simultaneously invoke the *Domboc* in the name of, and for the benefit of, both the conquered and the conquerors in eleventh- and twelfth-century England.

CHAPTER 4

The Parker Circle, the *Domboc*, and Reformation National Identity

The conditions following Elizabeth I's ascent to the throne in 1558 were especially amenable to the reintroduction of Anglo-Saxon texts, such as the *Domboc*, into the English discursive community. Early texts could be used as foundational documents in the troubled re-birth of Protestant England as power passed from the Catholic Mary I (1553–1558) to the Protestant Elizabeth I (1558–1603). The emerging sense of nationalism engendered by the Reformation was contingent upon a definition of the national self anchored in both sacred and secular realms. Elizabeth's England was defined as a nation whose identity was derived from both its English administration and its Protestant religion. These key elements of an English national identity gave early Anglo-Saxon manuscripts immediate importance as legal, historical, and religious texts. The early texts provided the raw material for establishing legal and religious precedent for current religious and administrative practice under Elizabeth's rule.

In the midst of this cultural and theological identity crisis, Anglo-Saxon language and literature found a new and appreciative audience. In both religion and law, practitioners and scholars struggled with the debate that pitted the primacy of native origins against the tradition of the continent. For example, throughout the sixteenth century English law was at the center of a debate that measured the value of ancestral English common law against the perceived civilized order of Roman law.[1] At a time when some legal scholars argued for the adoption of a Roman model of legal content and codification to regularize the law of the land, others turned to ancient Anglo-Saxon texts to prove the long-standing validity and utility of the current system of English law. Similarly, Protestants used Anglo-Saxon documents to demonstrate that they were not promoting a radical reconstruction of the church born of pure ideology. Rather, through the use of Anglo-Saxon texts, the Protestants sought to prove that they were returning to a religious independence that was the tradition of their native land. The *Domboc* was an important text for both of these projects in the sixteenth century. Alfred's law-book provides a validating native history for Reformation law and religion because the text presents an Anglo-Saxon representation of the early church coincident with a system of native law. In combining a religious history of the Anglo-Saxons with a codification of native law, the *Domboc* portrays a cohesive past that was useful to Reformation ideology, but not embarrassingly barbarous.[2]

The work of one legal scholar, William Lambarde (1536–1601), highlights the *Domboc*'s role in the Reformation connection between law, religion, and national identity. Lambarde's use of the *Domboc* in his 1568 *Archaionomia*, a collection of Anglo-Saxon law, shows how Alfred's law-book was a key text in the reformers' search for native legal and religious precedents in the forging of Elizabethan national identity. Despite his claims of scholarly altruism, Lambarde uses the *Domboc* to forward an ideological agenda that validates the primacy of English common law and establishes the early native roots of Protestantism.

However, before making such an argument, Lambarde's project needs to be situated within the larger context of ideological Reformation publishing. Alfred's law book came back into public circulation at the hands of Archbishop Matthew Parker (1504–75), an important figure in the Reformation movement's search for native origins. Parker was at the helm of a wide-ranging effort to collect, copy, edit, and disseminate early texts to bolster the Protestant cause.[3] By the time of Parker's death in 1575, over 500 manuscripts and books were in his library, and many others had at least passed through his hands.[4] To accomplish his preservationist, scholarly, and ideological projects, the archbishop undertook a widespread search for the manuscript detritus of Henry VIII's dissolution of the monasteries.[5] The Archbishop then helped to bring a number of these texts to print, and wider circulation.[6]

His project was endorsed because he was a well-trusted and loyal champion of the Tudor family's dedication to the Church of England.[7] One of Parker's roles as Archbishop was to strengthen the Anglican faith's legitimacy over that of Catholicism. One key to this strategy was to find links to a native Christianity that could connect Protestant values or practices to the early Anglo-Saxon Church. Such links would connect the current Anglican Church to an indigenous identity.[8] Parker's own publication, the *De Antiquitate Britannicae Ecclesiae* of 1572, uses Anglo-Saxon manuscripts to document the early history of the island. This history is the crowning effort of Parker's campaign for the Protestant character of the early Anglo-Saxon church. If Parker could create an ancient national history for his faith, the Church of England would be perceived as the primary and truly native Christian faith of England.

By using the early texts of the Anglo-Saxon church to support his Anglican beliefs, Parker participates in what Richard Helgerson describes as the Elizabethan "writing of England"(9). The formation of English national identity, in Helgerson's model, depends upon four elements: the kingdom/nation, the text/form, the individual author, and the discursive community.[9] Each of these elements relies upon the others in the formation of a national identity. Parker, in his role as Archbishop, is in a position to facilitate the transmission of texts from individual authors, such as Lambarde, to the larger discursive community in the service of his nation.

Printed texts are uniquely suited to the process of widespread dissemination and national image-making. Although Benedict Anderson undervalues the effectiveness of manuscript transmission, he argues that printed vernacular texts, as opposed to sacred spoken forms, are fundamental to the forging of national identity.[10] Printed texts homogenize discourse because they provide a fixed linguistic reference. Over time, the predominant print dialects emerge as the standard or official language form of a culture, shaping the identity of that culture. Archbishop Parker's project to introduce the "monumentes of antiquitie" (Aelfric 3) of early England into print is a direct effort to shape an Anglican English national identity. Parker participates in a process that "turned inward to find out and eliminate those practices and those images that failed to reflect back its own unitary image, and it turned outward to declare its defining difference" (Helgerson 71). Parker's printing of the laws as part of an effort to "encourage the study of the early English language [...] which might help thereby to provide a firm basis for the newly established 'Ecclesia Anglicana'" (Keynes, "Cult" 240) directly partakes of the cultural politics of unity and difference central to the mission of the reformers under Elizabeth I.

Parker recognized the important role the *Domboc* could play in this mission. The archbishop sponsored the 1566 publication of *The Testimonie of Antiquitie*, putting an excerpt of the *Domboc* into print for the first time. Parker's main project in the *Testimonie*, largely a collection of Anglo-Saxon religious texts, was to disseminate these documents in order to foster the study of early English history and language. Such study would connect current Protestant doctrine to the ancient texts, reinforcing the foundations of the recently re-established Church of England. The *Testimonie* includes only a small portion of the *Domboc*: Alfred's translation of the Decalogue (*Af El. Pro.*-9), but it serves an important function in the book.[11]

However, a complete understanding of the role of the *Domboc* in the *Testimonie* first requires an explanation of the text's authorship. The *Testimonie* was not executed by Parker himself, but by one of his "circle." Scholars identify Archbishop Parker's circle as a group of men, with various personal connections to the archbishop, who were committed to learning through the preservation and dissemination of old manuscripts and texts.[12] There was no direct individual institutional support for the various projects of this group. However, their work fell under the general umbrella of Parker's approval by the Privy Council to search out and access ancient documents.[13] Thus, the publication of the *Domboc* extract in the *Testimonie* was ultimately underwritten by the Protestant administration.

Of Parker's circle, his personal secretary John Joscelyn (1529–1603) was most likely the editor and translator of the text, as well as the author of the *Testimonie*'s preface and editorial comments.[14] Joscelyn's ties to Parker's circle were personal and professional. He was appointed the Archbishop's chaplain and Latin secretary, but was an able scholar of Anglo-Saxon as well. Joscelyn produced two major pieces of unpublished Anglo-Saxon scholarship, an Old English grammar and dictionary. The grammar is now lost, but the dictionary survives, and the Anglo-Saxon law codes were a source for it. In fact, Joscelyn specifically used a transcription of London, British Library Cotton Otho B.xi, containing Alfred's *Domboc*, in his lexicographic work.[15] This transcription of the manuscript, made by another "circle" member Laurence Nowell (c.1515–c.1570), became part of one of the most important resources for seventeenth-century Old English scholars due to Joscelyn's lexicography.[16] Joscelyn was an integral member of Parker's circle, and he executed the *Testimonie* in keeping with the Archbishop's agenda of commingling history, scholarship, and ideology in the service of the national church.

To understand the *Domboc*'s role in shaping national identity, we need to understand its context in Joscelyn's text of the *Testimonie*. Joscelyn fashioned a reformed national identity by focusing on three key Protestant doctrines: vernacular scriptures, symbolic elements in communion, and the ability of priests to marry. He sought to derive these factors from the early writings. Joscelyn devotes the most space to the issue of transubstantiation, although he does support priests' marriages and continuously emphasizes the origin of his texts as coming from the "Saxon tongue."[17] In the preface to the *Testimonie*, Joscelyn argues that Ælfric's homilies support the non-mystical nature of the Eucharist, citing Ælfric's teachings as reflective of the character of the entire English ecclesiastical community.

The preface opens with a dilemma at the heart of the Protestant movement and which brought Ælfric's text to publication in the first place: "Great Contention hath now been of long tyme about the most comfortable Sacrament of the Body and Bloud of Christ" (Aelfric 2). Joscelyn immediately makes a connection to a legitimizing historical precedent: "here is set forth unto thee a Testimonye of verye ancient tyme, wherein is plainly shewed what was the Judgement of Learned Men in this matter, in the days of the Saxons before the Conquest" (Aelfric 3). The *Testimonie* contains Ælfric's Easter Homily as its signature text. Counting Ælfric as one of the "learned Men" of the "Saxons," Joscelyn includes the Easter Homily as evidence to show how religious leaders of early Britain "denied the bodely presence" in the Eucharist (Aelfric 16). Here is the entire scope of Parker's plan writ small: invoking an authorizing past to legitimize his monarch's church and state.

Joscelyn's handling of sources for his argument against transubstantiation underlines its connection to the *Domboc*. The correct reading of the Easter Homily has been debated for centuries. The text is supple enough to allow interpretations for or against transubstantiation.[18] Joscelyn allows that much of Ælfric's theology was affected by Roman teachings or ignorance.[19] Yet this does not detract from Joscelyn's enthusiasm for his self-identified forebears. And when Ælfric can not supply him with examples for the rectitude of priests' marriages, as the learned man held the orthodox view on the subject, he easily turns to other sources that support his agenda.

In this way, Joscelyn's editorial strategy provides an interesting echo of Alfred's approach to choosing valid legislation: "Ic þa Ælfred cyning þas togædere gegaderode 7 awritan het, monege þara þe ure foregengan heoldon, ða ðe me licodon; 7 manege þara þe me ne licodon ic awearp mid minra witena geðeahte" (I, Alfred king, then gathered these [laws] together and commanded [my witan] to write down many of those [laws] that our predecessors held, which to me seemed good; and many that did not seem good to me I set aside with my wise men's counsel) (*AfEl.* 49.9). Alfred, as both monarch and chief editor of his *Domboc*, was the arbiter of which laws were to survive in writing. The power to choose which texts would survive as the official record of the kingdom was the power to shape ideology, to define the character of the realm. In his handling of the source material for his *Testimonie*, Joscelyn worked in much the same capacity as he had in Archbishop Parker's project. His choices would help to form an official record of the birth of Protestantism.

The strongest platform the reformers had in the Protestant effort was the tenth-century precedent of vernacular representation of religious texts in both sacred and secular contexts. The appearance of vernacular translations of the Exodus selections in Alfred's text makes the *Domboc* directly important to Parker's mission. Thus, Joscelyn includes Alfred's version of the Ten Commandments in the *Testimonie*.[20] While he does not substantively alter the text, he uses its perceived faults as an opportunity to instruct. Benedict Robinson argues that the editorial practices of Parker's circle systematically purged their texts of any evidence of Catholicism.[21] Alfred's text, on the contrary, is left intact despite the doctrinal problem it raises. Joscelyn uses this problem as an opening to proselytize.

The problem is Alfred's treatment of the second commandment, Exodus 20:4–6. These lines of the Old Testament instruct that God's followers not venerate any object, but God alone. Alfred removes this commandment completely, and only at the end of the Decalogue does he add a weaker version of the commandment from Exodus 20:23, not allowing the creation of gold or silver idols. This manipulation, allowing for a loophole for the veneration of objects, seems completely at odds with Parker's rationale for publishing the old texts. However, so effective are the Alfredian texts in promulgating the relationship between the Protestant church and its Anglo-Saxon forebears that Joscelyn values the connection to King Alfred's *Domboc* over the difficulties the content of the selection presents.

He chooses the *Domboc* Decalogue for two purposes, one didactic and one ideological. First, he uses the problem to instruct his readers about the misunderstandings engendered by Catholic dogma. Immediately following the excerpt, Joscelyn identifies Alfred's omission of Exodus 20:4–6. He provides the original Latin verses of Exodus 20:4 and part of 20:5, followed by their English translation:

> ...here is lefte out these wordes. (Non facies scultile neque; omnem similitudinem quae est in cœlo desuper, & quae est in terra deorsum,

nec eorum quæ sunt in aquis sub terra: non addorabis neq; coles, &c.
2. Thou shalt not make to thy selfe any grauen Image, nor the likenes
of any thing that is in heauen aboue, or in the earth beneath, or in the
water under the earth. Thou shalt not bowe downe to them nor worship them. For I thy Lord.&c.) [Aelfric 86–87].

He recognizes the source of this irregularity as "the Second Nicene councell,
wherein it was decreed [that] the worshipping of Images" was permissible
(Aelfric 87). The Second Nicene Council approved the veneration of sacred
objects in 787.[22] Joscelyn addresses Alfred's adherence to the Council's
decree as typical of texts "intreatyng the commaunementes, which were
written before the Conquest" (Aelfric 87). Thus, Joscelyn explains a
quandary faced by the text he presents.

However, Joscelyn does not end with mere explanation. He uses the
opportunity to denigrate Catholicism and reiterate the purpose of Parker's
publication of the text. Upon identifying the missing text, Joscelyn passes
judgment on those he sees as responsible for the omission: "See what followed of taking away from the worde of God contrareye to the express
comaundement of the same upon the ungodly decree of that councell"
(Aelfric 87). For Parker, betraying the Word of God is an egregious sin.
The reinstating of the original text is his primary concern and marks the
whole of his enterprise including both Joscelyn's and Lambarde's texts.

Consonant with this goal, Joscelyn uses this opportunity to reach
into the past for a "proper" precedent. As Joscelyn states: "But bicause we
have made mention of that Second Nicene councell […], we shall here
brieflye shewe what […] was thought of the same councell by the learned
of England" (Aelfric 87). He turns to a chronicle story about Alcuin.[23]
The entry demonstrates a contemporary opinion that the worship of idols
was that "which the Churche of God doth utterlye abharre" (Aelfric 88).
Joscelyn's choice of the ancient chronicle to refute Alfred's adherence to
the Second Nicene Council's allows him to stay constant to Parker's strategy
of reliance on early native texts even as he shows the depredations of
Catholic doctrine on what he takes to be the true faith. This faith has its
legitimate expression in the Protestantism of his church.

By citing the Anglo-Saxon church, reformers like Parker suggested a
Protestant precedent of scriptural interpretation on those issues that were
most relevant to the situation of the late sixteenth-century church. For the
reformers, the Anglo-Saxon church became an integral part of the history
of the Anglican Church. The Anglo-Saxons who resisted apostasy could

be seen as ancient counterparts to the Protestants in their struggles against what they perceived as the Catholic Church's deviance from the letter of the holy law.

Devotion to the letter of the law explains why Joscelyn kept this troubling passage from the *Domboc* in his text. The excerpt comes in a section of the *Testimonie* dedicated to presenting sacred texts "in the Englishe tounge whereby [men] mought the better serve their God" (Aelfric 79). A key element of Protestant doctrine was the acceptance of vernacular scripture. Promoting this mode of discourse was more important than the content of the text. When faced with presenting a Decalogue in the ancient vernacular, but flawed in light of Protestant doctrine, Joscelyn chose to editorialize about the doctrinal problem rather than omit the vernacular text.

The introduction to this section closes with a note that embodies Joscelyn's approach to his text under Parker's program:

> The tenne lawlyke wordes, that God himself taught Moyses, and wrote with hys finger in two tables of stone on the Mount Sinai for all mens chastisement, as well as for that olde people that was in tymes paste, as also for us that bee nowe: be here set out as they are yet seen in olde books of the Saxon tongue. But for better understanding of any word that may seeme hard unto the reader, we have thought good to place over the Saxon the familiar wordes of our own speeche [Aelfric 81].

Joscelyn explicitly makes the connection between the original people of God, the Anglo-Saxons of his national past, and his present people. The link to that authorizing past is the vernacular text. God inscribes the Ten Commandments for the Hebrews in Hebrew, the language of the people. The Anglo-Saxons follow this model and reproduce this text in Old English.[24] Although the *Testimonie* is not equivalent to a Bible, Joscelyn's text does bring an important, if relatively small, portion of that Christian scripture into the vernacular of Early Modern England by way of Alfred's *Domboc*. The written vernacular by God's original chosen people, then by the Anglo-Saxons, and finally by the Protestants is the mode and marker of valid doctrine.

Yet Joscelyn's *Testimonie* was not the only text to enlist the *Domboc* in Archbishop Parker's ideological editorial project. Lambarde, another member of Parker's circle, was a scholar, an antiquary, and a jurist who would eventually earn Elizabeth's royal appointment to Keeper of the Records in the Tower of London in 1601.[25] His 1568 *Archaionomia* serves as a locus for law, historical scholarship, and religious ideology. The contents of Lambarde's text show that the legal scholar actively and effectively participated in the national Protestant project under the direction of Archbishop Matthew Parker. Lambarde chooses to present the first complete printing of Alfred's *Domboc* in his *Archaionomia* because Alfred's law-book is a work concerned with the intersection of law, religion, and history.[26] These elements of Alfred's *Domboc* make it an ideal component of the archbishop's undertaking to forge a cohesive Protestant national identity for England through an explicitly textual connection to its past. The *Domboc* should be read as part of the archbishop's program to invoke Anglo-Saxon royal authority during a time when English national identity was being redefined.

Lambarde provides context for the *Domboc's* function in his text through the *Archaionomia's* preface. His preface, the "Epistola" (Letter), explains how the *Archaionomia* came about, to whom it was addressed, and the function he hoped it would serve. Investigating the "Epistola" illuminates the *Domboc's* role as a link to an Anglo-Saxon past that validates a Protestant Elizabethan present and traditional English law. This introductory letter also provides the necessary context of Lambarde's position in Parker's circle.

The *Archaionomia's* roots lie in the scholarly endeavors tied to Archbishop Parker's circle of nationalist antiquarians. As Lambarde relates:

> Obtulit mihi superiori anno Laurentius Noelus, diligentissimus inuestigator antiquitatis, mihique multa & iuncunda consuetudine coniunctus, ac qui me (quicunque in hoc genere sim) effecit, priscas Anglorum leges, antiquissima Saxonum lingua, et literis conscriptas, atque a me (quonium ei tu erat trans mare eundum) ut latinas facerem, ac per uulgarem vehementer flagitauit.

> Last year Laurence Nowell, a most diligent scholar of antiquity, and a close and much-loved friend of mine, who has made me what I am in this field, made a suggestion to me and strongly urged me to translate into Latin and the common tongue the ancient laws of the English, which are written down in the most ancient language and alphabet of the Saxons (since he had to go overseas at the time) [A.iii].[27]

Lambarde's relationship to Nowell provides a window into the birth of Anglo-Saxon studies in the sixteenth century. Although Nowell was older than Lambarde, the two appeared to work co-operatively on their antiquarian projects. Nowell, an antiquary and friend of Parker, worked under the auspices of his patron, Sir William Cecil (the eventual Lord Burghley). Cecil was Queen Elizabeth's personal secretary, and he had an abiding scholarly interest in history and geography. His interest in old books was the link between him and Archbishop Parker. They corresponded on the matter, and documents moved between the two men.[28] Thus, Nowell was connected to Parker through Cecil. Lambarde was also connected to Parker indirectly through association with Nowell, but he also had a direct relationship with Parker through the use of the archbishop's manuscripts.[29]

In fact, Nowell's work was to become very important to Lambarde's text and shows how the *Domboc* was involved in the relationships between these men.[30] In 1562, Nowell made a transcript of an Anglo-Saxon manuscript containing the *Domboc*: London, British Library Cotton Otho B.xi.[31] The significance of this act is twofold. First, Nowell's transcription is an important act of preservation. Over three-quarters of the medieval manuscript was destroyed in the Cotton Library fire of 1731.[32] Nowell's transcript remains the only record of the complete original manuscript. Second, Nowell's transcription of Otho B.xi provided an important source for Lambarde's text of the *Domboc*.[33] Lambarde had been transcribing ancient texts alongside Nowell since 1564.[34] While the *Archaionomia* was published in 1568, Nowell's suggestion dates to 1567. Nowell left for the continent in March of that year, leaving his possessions in Lambarde's care, but Lambarde was not called to the bar until the following June.[35] Thus, Lambarde accepts Nowell's charge on the cusp of his change in status from student to barrister, with Nowell's scholarly possessions, including the *Domboc* transcribed from Otho B.ix, at his disposal.

Subsequently, Lambarde describes his project as done at the urging of Nowell as "mihique multa & iuncunda consuetudine coniunctus" (a close and much-loved friend of mine), rather than at the behest of a teacher or social superior. Similarly, he speaks of Parker in terms of his scholarly pursuits: "quorum pleraque; in Reuerend, in Christo patris, atque optime de Antiquitate meriti, D. Matthei Cantuariensis Archiepiscopi" (that reverend Father in Christ, Matthew, Lord Archbishop of Canterbury, who has done so much for the study of antiquity) (A.iiii.–B.i.). Ultimately, he characterizes his task as follows:

> Habes nunc igitur, & institui mei rationem, & laboris consilium, in quibus ut pios & candidos lectores omnes æquiares me iudices habiturum confido, quod doctis hanc conuersionem qua se exerceant, in doctis

> qua se iuuent, utrisque autem qau se delectent exhibeo, ostendo
> omnibus, obtrudo autem nemini.

> So now you have the plan of my undertaking and my proposed method
> of dealing with the task; in these I trust that all my readers, being
> devout and honest, will prove fair-minded, because I am revealing this
> translation to scholars to exercise themselves upon, for the unlearned to
> improve themselves with, and for both to delight themselves with, and
> in displaying it to all I am thrusting it upon nobody [B.i.].

The transmission of the *Domboc* in the *Archaionomia*, then, would appear
to be primarily a scholarly enterprise. However, despite his claims of scholarly impartiality, Lambarde's description of his process frames his scholarly
endeavor both as an altruistic pursuit of knowledge among like-minded
scholars and as a vehicle for an ideological agenda.

Lambarde's dedication illuminates the intermingling of personal and
ideological motives for the text. The *Archaionomia* is dedicated to William
Cordell, "Equiti aurato, & Serenissimæ Reginæ Elizabetae ab Archivus"
(Knight Bachelor and Archivist to our most serene Queen Elizabeth)
(A.ii.). Lambarde knew Cordell as a bencher at Lincoln's Inn, where Lambarde was a student. He chose Cordell as his primary audience for the following reasons:

> Primum, quia in iuris & legum interpretatione florentissimus et es, et
> haberis: Diende ut singularis meæ ergate beneuolentiæ perpetui sint
> testes. Postremo, quo tu qui Serenissime reginæ Elizabetæ Tabulario
> præsis, veteres has clarissimorum Regum tabulas tuo fœlicissimo sapien-
> tissimoque patrocinio tuearis.

> First, because you both are and have the reputation of a most eminent
> authority in the interpretation of the legal code and laws; secondly, in
> order that these labors may be perpetual witness of my particular good-
> will towards you; and finally, in order that, as the chief archivist of our
> most serene Queen Elizabeth, you may keep safe these records of the
> most illustrious kings with your most happy and wise patronage [B.i.].

Here Lambarde acknowledges his personal attachment to Cordell, but does
so in conjunction with pointed reference to Cordell's official function as
"Tabulario præsis" (chief Archivist). Lambarde signals the double-purpose
of sixteenth-century Anglo-Saxon scholarship. On the one hand, it was
scholarship for scholarship's sake, an altruistic project. On the other hand,
this scholarship also became a matter of official record. As such, it performed
the administrative function of building a record of official ideology.

The *Domboc* is a deliberate choice for such a project because Alfred's text also builds a national identity tied to pre-conversion origins. His preface to the laws catalogues the "ærendgewrit" (written message) (*Af El.* 49.2) of the apostles that clarifies the gospels for the peoples of Antioch, Syria, and Cicilia. Alfred claims to use as his source the texts of "monega senoðbec" (many synod-books) in which wise men "writan, hwær anne dom hwær oþerne" (wrote here one law, there another) (*Af El.* 49.8). When his sources were collected, his wise men were "awritan het" (commanded to write) (*Af El.* 49.9) the chosen laws. Alfred knew the power of an official record. It is through the processes of cataloging and writing that Alfred establishes the new order. By choosing which texts survive in the official record, Alfred shapes and forwards his own ideology. Through connecting Mosaic and New Testament law to the laws of his time, he establishes a validating connection to the past.

Lambarde performs an analogous process with his *Archaionomia*. Using Heraclitus' conceit that "leges ciuitatis murum" (the laws of a state are its walls), Lambarde discourses on the importance of law to a civil society.[36] Most of his generic praise of law seems innocuously bland. Generally, he asserts that "salutem populorum, regnorum incolumitatem, vitamque omnium quietam & beatam conditas esse leges" (laws are established to promote the welfare of nations, the safety of kingdoms, and a peaceful life for all) (A.iii.). However, a close reading of Lambarde's "Epistola" provides clues to his position in a legal debate that continued throughout the sixteenth century.

The debate concerns the shape and role of English common law in Elizabethan England.[37] One model, following Thomas Starkey, argues for the Romanization of English law. Starkey argues that the messy and barbarous common law should be streamlined, ordered, and catalogued in the Justinian model of the *Corpus Juris Civilis*.[38] The will of the monarch under whom this project is enacted is the ultimate arbiter of the law. Alternately, Helgerson posits a model celebrating the essential difference of English common law from its continental counterparts, an ideal traceable back to John Wycliff's *De Officio Regis* of 1379. In this model, the very eclecticism of common law accounts for its Englishness, making it the hereditary law of the people.[39] Since the law arises from the ruling of magistrates, it directly reflects the native individual experiences of citizens with the law. The resulting statutes may be unevenly codified and distributed, but they represent an insular law created by and for those people specifically subject to that law.

Lambarde clearly favors the latter model. In his view, the laws are not to be dictated from without, but "assidua fuerint magistratuum vigilia conservatae" (are observed with the unceasing vigilance of the magistrates) (A.iii.). Management of the law, in his view, should be an insular operation. Lambarde designates the magistrates as the key agents in preserving and promoting traditional law. The magistrates are a telling choice because they are on the front lines of the judicial process. Their law has to be applicable to the circumstances of their immediate jurisdictions. A Roman, more hierarchical, law would make little sense in this context. The traditional law of the people is more fitting. Lambarde establishes an interrelation between the legal profession, ancient law, and nationality as he states the impetus for his *Archaionomia*. He claims that he was driven to the project because "non potui aut adeo in patriam ingratus, in antiquitatum inofficiosus, aut mei ordinis tam esse immemor" (it has been impossible for me to be so ungrateful to my native land, so undutiful to former times, or so forgetful of my own rank in society) (A.iii.) to do otherwise. As a legal professional, he has an obligation to the law. As a scholar, he has a duty to preserve and promulgate treasures from the past. As an Englishman, he has a responsibility to show fidelity towards his nation.

The *Domboc* is an ideal starting place for Lambarde's *Archaionomia* as its text depends upon a native legal history. In addition to the examples of Moses, Christ, and the apostles, Alfred credits some of the more worldly sources of his law as the writings of "halegra biscepa 7 eac oðerra geðungenra witena" (holy bishops, and also of other exalted wise men) (*Af El.* 49.7). More specifically, Alfred cites the laws of native rulers as precedents: "oððe on Ines dæge, mines mæge, oððe on Offan Mercna cyninges oððe on Æðelbryhtes, ðe ærest fulluhte onfeng on Angelcynne" (either in Ine's day, kinsman of mine, or in Offa's [time], king of Mercia, or in Æthelberht's [time], who first accepted baptism among the English race) (*Af. El.* 49.9). Lambarde echoes Alfred's methodology as he paraphrases the *Domboc* at the close of his "Epistola." He has included the ancient laws of English kings because

> Anglicarum legum memoria (quæ res una ad summam earum existimationem desyderanda videtur) ab Ethelberto rege, qui primus anglorum sacro tinctus est baptismate ad hoc nostrum tempus ætatis amplissimus literatum monimentis erit consignata.

> ...the history of English laws (which seems uniquely desirable in view of their very high reputation) from the time of King Ethelbert, who was

the first English king to receive the sacrament of baptism, up to our own time, may benefit from a very full literary record [B.ii.].

Thus, the inclusion of the *Domboc* in the *Archaionomia* allows Lambarde to satisfy his commitments to profession, scholarship, and country all in a single text.

Lambarde's professional rank (barrister by the time of publication) may compel him to keep these statutes current in legal intercourse since, despite their age, the laws "utilitatum faciant omnia" (all have the value of utility) (A.iii.). However, it is the association of these ancient laws to the national concern that garners most of Lambarde's attention. Throughout the text he connects the law to the nation. For example, he has accepted Nowell's request to translate the old laws "ut illi obsequendo, reipub. inseruirem" (in order to serve my country by obeying him [Nowell]) (A.iiii.). He also characterizes himself as working at Queen Elizabeth's behest. In the process of performing this task, he states that "adeo me satisidoneum profite or regiæ voluntatis internuntium" (I admit that I am an inadequate intermediary of the queen's wish) (A.iiii.). While he does not identify the queen's specific wish in his text, he most likely is referring to Archbishop Parker's endorsement by the Privy Council to gather and print old works.[40]

Lambarde's publishing of the *Domboc*, then, participates in a second great debate of his age: the conflict surrounding the Protestant Reformation. Lambarde's Protestant sympathies are clear through the very people he thanks and credits in his "Epistola": Queen Elizabeth, William Cordell, Archbishop Parker, and Laurence Nowell. Yet he goes further to comment upon the debate itself: "Cæterum, ut finem aliquem orationi nostræ faciamus, cum duo sint hac nostra tempestate hominum genera, qui summa inter se contentione digladiantur, vetusti nimirum erroris patroni, & renouatæ religionis vindices" (Yet, to bring my words to a close, there are in our time two kinds of men, who fight with each other with the greatest determination; these are of course the defenders of ancient error, and the champions of the reformed religion) (B.i.). Although he urges both sides of the conflict to moderation, his characterization of the Catholics as laboring under "ancient error" underlines his own politics.

The most telling evidence of Lambarde actively participating in the Reformation debate is in his single act of editorializing within his text. Echoing Joscelyn's invective against the Second Nicene Council in the *Testimonie*, Lambarde similarly states in the *Archionomia*:

> Admonendus es (amice lector) nulla aut nostra, aut librariorum incuria, prætermissum secundum hoc Decalogi de nonfigendis imaginibus præceptum, verum consulto ab ys qui primo has leges mandarunt litteris relictum. Post celebratum enim Anno salutis humanæ. 794. Secundum illud Nicea (quod simulachrorum confirmauit adorationem) concilium, quo maior hominum præceptis (quæ erat temporum illorum caligo) tribueretur autoritas, de sacrosanctis Dei scriptis aliquid detrahendum existimarunt. Neque vero (quod sciam) in ullo usquam Saxonice conscripto exemplari reperitur.

> I must warn you, dear reader, that it is not owing to any negligence of mine or the book-keepers that the second commandment of the Decalogue about not making graven images has been omitted, but was deliberately omitted by those who first wrote these laws down. For after the council held in the year of man's salvation 794 following on the Council of Nicaea (which confirmed the worship of images), in order that greater authority might be attributed to the commandments of men, such was the ignorance of the period that they considered something should be taken away from holy writings of God. Nor indeed is it to be found, as far as I know, in any copy written anywhere in Saxon [G.iiii.].[41]

For all of his calls to moderation and appeals to scholarship, Lambarde's *Archaionomia* participated in the widespread project of ideological publishing under Archbishop Parker as fully as Joscelyn's *Testimonie*.

The two texts display a unity of purpose. Both texts praise Parker's scholarly efforts. The preface to the *Testimonie* characterizes Parker's preservation of ancient texts as a "diligent search for such writings of historye, and other monumentes of antiquitie, as might reveale unto us what hath been the state of our church in England from tyme to tyme"(3).[42] Joscelyn's conceit of returning to ancient texts for knowledge is nothing new in English historical writing. Around the year 1137, for example, English historian Geoffrey of Monmouth used a "Britannici sermonis librum vetustissimum" (very ancient book in the British language) as a source text for his *Historia regum Britanniae*.[43] However, Lambarde's description of his Anglo-Saxon exemplars as "venerandæ vetustatis monumenta" (monuments of venerable antiquity) (A.iiii.) is uncannily similar to Joscelyn's wording. Lambarde is most likely following Joscelyn's example, which is not unusual since Parker is acknowledged as the impetus behind both texts. Lambarde provides an overview of the history of English law. Thus, both of these collections use the text as a source of both religious inspiration and nationalistic propaganda.

The *Domboc* is a potent text for the reformers not only due to its perceived legitimacy as a textual artifact, but also because of its content. Alfred's connection of the Anglo-Saxons to the ancient Hebrews dovetails perfectly with John Foxe's propagation of the idea of Reformation England as the Elect Nation, a nation chosen by God as His people, an idea surely to be attractive to Parker and his circle. Alfred implies the Elect Nation status of the West Saxons as he draws a direct line of legitimate sanctified authority from Moses, through Christ and the apostle, to the leaders of his forebears and own time.[44] Foxe similarly draws attention to the comparison between the English and the biblical Israelites in his *Acts and Monuments*.[45] As Elizabeth came to power, she was seen as a divine blessing on ordainedly deserving nation, "which the Lord of his mercy hath bestowed vpon this land during all the reigne hetherto of this our Souereigne and most happe Queene ELIZABETH, in such sort as the like example of Gods aboundant mercies are not to be seen in any nation about vs" (Foxe 20). If England were to be seen as God's chosen people, it is no surprise that such claims would foster a greater sense of national unity and patriotism.[46]

Patriotism in Reformation England also meant fidelity to the both the church and law of England. The development of a national church united the state and the church in a single entity. Likewise, the *Domboc*'s formula of kings who ruled "mid Godes gife" (by God's grace) (*Ine Pro.*) demonstrated the unity of church and state in legitimate rule. As the Protestant church and state, under Elizabeth's rule, used anti–Catholic rhetoric to distance itself from Catholics both at home and abroad, it consolidated a unifying identity for itself as non–Catholic. Where Alfred's text could not supply the reformers with such arguments, Joscelyn and Lambarde pointedly editorialized on the evils of Catholic doctrine, even as they depended upon Alfred's text for legitimizing authority elsewhere. Further, even in the theatre of English law, Edward Coke, one of the foremost barristers and jurists of his day, saw the process of the Reformation as one forwarding both a national Church and a particularly English legal model in his championing of English common law.[47] Alfred's law code, then, would have been a very attractive model to forward an ideological agenda combining law and religion in the definition of the nation. As Adrian Hastings notes, while "Elizabethan England was already becoming a genuinely national society, with tinges of nationalism strongly fed on Protestantism" (35), "the range and quantity of [Anglo-Saxon] vernacular literature appears quite remarkably rounded and functional for the needs of a nation" (41). Under Archbishop Parker's influence, Nowell, Lambarde, and Joscelyn seemed to recognize this affinity between their Elizabethan present and the Anglo-Saxon past. This recognition led to the variously transcribed and published the laws of the *Domboc* due in no small part to legislation's role in creating an English national identity. The *Domboc* was an important tool for reform not only as printed text and as religious precedent, but also as law.

The return of the *Domboc* to circulation during the 1560s was no accident of scholarship. During a period of great political and religious turmoil, the *Domboc*'s unique characteristic as the first Anglo-Saxon legislation to link a sense of kingdom to religious and legal history gave it especial import for lay and clerical leaders. The text's combination of sacred and political authority was consonant with Elizabeth's role in Reformation England. Its sense of continuity with the past aligned it with the historical projects of the reformers. Its comparison of the Anglo-Saxon experience with that of the biblical Israelites mirrored the English Protestant view of being the Elect Nation. Its presentation of vernacular scripture in writing was in keeping with Protestant doctrine. Finally, the text's melding of politics and religion in the context of law addressed a critical concern of Reformation England as it continued to define itself through its legislation.

The *Domboc*, in the mid-sixteenth century, operated as an extremely fertile location for the construction of national identity based on the textual preservation of legal and religious history. Parker and his circle recognized the relevance of the *Domboc* to their own time, even though Alfred's text was over four centuries old at the time of Nowell's transcription. As a locus for legal, religious, and national discourse, the *Domboc* was a seminal text for the Parker circle's efforts in reconstituting the identity of a Tudor, Anglican England.

Conclusion

King Alfred's *Domboc* is a crucial text in the ruler's canon for understanding the important function of legislation in forging royal and national identities. Comparatively neglected by literary and cultural scholars, the *Domboc* is significant in its portrayal of Alfred's administration in action. While leadership texts such as the king's translation of the *Regula pastoralis* define the more general precepts of good rule, the *Domboc* shows their direct application. In addition to demonstrating a contemporary conception of the practical guidelines of Alfred's justice system, the text provides insight into the culture that informs these practices. From the time of its inscription through the ensuing centuries, the *Domboc* serves as a cultural touchstone. Even as it codifies law, the text encodes culture. Ultimately, it is the *Domboc*'s connection to an identifiable Anglo-Saxon culture that makes it relevant to the English during the eleventh, twelfth and late sixteenth centuries.

The contexts for committing the *Domboc* to writing are similar across the centuries of the Medieval and Early Modern eras. In each instance, the monarch in charge faced a serious threat to kingdom or culture. Similarly, each appearance of the *Domboc* operates to ameliorate the anxieties fostered by such a threat. The menace of the Danish invaders is a source of both political and cultural anxiety for Alfred and his people. These invaders would subjugate his kingdom to both Danish rule and culture. In the face of possible invasion and conquest, the *Domboc* carries a soothing message: we are a unified and ordered people. The basis of this unity and order is the native *bot* system of compensation for misdeeds.

The repeated use of this method of dispensing justice has the cumulative effect of creating a metonymic relationship between the laws and the people they represent. Alfred presents a genealogy of law that follows a direct line of authoritative legislation from God through Moses, Jesus, the apostles, and synods that ultimately leads to him as an earthly ruler of a specifically identified people: the Anglo-Saxons. Just as early Jews and Christians were "people of the law," so are the Anglo-Saxons. Alfred's pairing of the Decalogue with his own law in the *Domboc* is no accident. The Anglo-Saxons are the people of the chosen people's law. They are also the people of a law necessarily reflecting their current cultural practices.

To reinscribe the *Domboc*, then, is not only to reference a set of legislation, but also to invoke its cultural connections. Given this function of the text, it is no surprise that conquerors of the Anglo-Saxons' descendants should reissue the text among their own laws. The Danish Cnut seized the Anglo-Saxon throne in 1016, subsequently including portions of the *Domboc* in the laws issued under his own name (*I–II Cnut*). After the throne later reverted to Anglo-Saxon rule, the Norman William I conquered the Anglo-Saxons in 1066. Like the legislation in Cnut's day, law collections promulgated during the post–Conquest reigns of William I and Henry I (the *Instituta Cnuti* and the *Quadripartitus*, respectively) faithfully include the *Domboc* among their texts. Recirculating the *Domboc* amid the laws of the conquerors smooths the transition of conquest. As the text embodies both native law and custom, to reissue its statutes sends a message to the conquered people: your prior way of life will be recognized and respected, even as you come under new rule. The *Domboc* acts as a cultural artifact that fosters a persistence of native identity even in the face of conquest.

The proof of this function of the text is its reinscription by the conquered as well as the conquerors. The monks of the priory at Rochester Cathedral created the manuscript *Textus Roffensis* in the wake of the Norman Conquest. This collection of charters, laws, and genealogies worked to establish the legitimacy of the priory's holdings. Including the *Domboc* in this manuscript illustrates the use of this text as a foundational document. By placing the records of their holdings among the ancient laws of the land, the monks suggest an authority to their claims that predates the current administration.

The connection to an authorizing ancient authority also was the impetus behind Archbishop Parker's ideological publication project. The reign of Elizabeth I shows the utility of the *Domboc* for the legitimization of both political and religious authority. Elizabeth I faced a country divided by religion: the Catholicism of pre–Tudor England and the Protestantism she reinstated. When William Lambarde translated and printed the entirety of the *Domboc* for the first time in his *Archaionomia* of 1568, it was a volley in the ideological war for the supremacy of Protestantism. Lambarde pointedly disseminated the text as an example of Protestantism's longstanding native roots. Not only was the *Domboc* relevant as native law, but as native religion. Thus, the text played an important role in the forging of an Elizabethan English national identity.

In all of these cases, the *Domboc* unifies the people under the monarch who presides over its production. From the Anglo-Saxons of Alfred's day to the English of Elizabeth's time, the *Domboc* functions as a source of identity. A defining aspect of this identity is the world presented through the preface and laws of the *Domboc*. The preface presents an ersatz history of the West Saxons, linking their culture to that of the early Jews and Christians. This history justifies the practices delineated throughout the laws, practices representative of the *bot* system. As a result, the text portrays the administrator and subjects of these laws as technically adhering to Christian mores, even as they live by rules based in non–Christian feud-based culture.

The *Domboc* is more than an aggregate of varied legal statutes, but a carefully constructed work engaged in a continuing negotiation between the legal and the literary, the commemorative and the culturally active. The law code looked back, preserving the extant legal codes of the day, "þe ure foregengan heoldon" (that our forgoers held) (*Af El.* 49.9). The code also looked forward, for example, in reaching across regional borders to Mercia (*Af El.* 49.9) and citing the existence of a nebulously inclusive "Angelcyn" (*Af El.* 49.7, 49.9). The law code ostensibly worked on a legislative level, as a gathering of "domas" or judgments/laws (*Af El.* 49.8– 9).

However, it also operates on a literary level, as "law and literature were never wholly disentangled" (Wormald, *Making* 416). The law code can be seen as a foundation narrative, tracing the origin of good English law from Moses through the early church and ultimately through the early English (albeit regional) kings. In examining Alfred's vernacular law code in terms of its social, political, cultural, and textual contexts, the law code emerges as a work engaged in a process of both cultural and political inscription and redefinition.

Lacking any mention of Alfred's law code in Asser's *Life*, the law code serves as the only extant contemporary means of establishing and disseminating Alfred's role as lawgiver. In pointed contrast to the nearly hagiographical *Life*, the law code turns on the axis of practical application and political reality: legislation relevant to the society it manages. The law code becomes a key instrument in the definition of Anglo-Saxon identity in terms of the proper means of conflict resolution and the maintenance of social accord. This evaluation highlights the particularly Anglo-Saxon aspects of Alfred's royal authority.

The *Domboc* both shapes and is shaped by the king who inscribes it, the people whom it governs, and those who would later re-inscribe or invoke it. The key element in this process is the language of feud compensation, which links the law-book to an Anglo-Saxon representation of kingship and national identity. As much as the rest of Alfred's canon is marked by its connection to Christian theology and philosophy, the *Domboc*'s essential mode of expression is that of feud-based culture. This gives us insight into how legislation functions as literature, both created by a culture and creating culture at the same time.

Scholarly estimation of the *Domboc* has undervalued the law-book's place as a crucial element of the king's canon. Indeed, the *Domboc* is an important and influential text for both Alfred's own time and throughout the early construction of first West Saxon, and ultimately English, national identity. Undervaluing the *Domboc* in the study of the king's canon unnecessarily elides the secular aspects of Alfred's Anglo-Saxon kingship, an element of his law code that was to prove so important throughout the Danish and Norman conquests and Protestant Reformation.

Alfred's *Domboc* should be read not only as a legislative instrument, but also as a foundation narrative that tells the story of the cultural heritage of the Anglo-Saxons and proscribes the appropriate societal behaviors and relationships within its specific, self-identified national culture. Further, this law code, as foundation narrative, is important to the study of later historical periods as it is strategically invoked to call upon Alfred's image as a specifically identifiable Anglo-Saxon king for the purpose of self-consciously shaping an inherently English national identity.

Appendix

Reading the Domboc

The following text is a diplomatic transcription and translation of the complete *Domboc* as found in Cambridge, Corpus Christi College 173 (CCCC 173, or the "Parker Chronicle"), which is both the earliest and one of the few complete manuscript witnesses of the text.[1] The Old English text is transcribed as a diplomatic edition from *The Parker Chronicle and Laws (Corpus Christi College, Cambridge MS. 173): A Facsimile*, edited by Robin Flower and Hugh Smith, and published for the Early English Text Society (Original Series, no. 208) by Oxford University Press in 1941 (reprinted in 1973). When in doubt as to interpreting the script, I relied upon what is still the baseline scholarly edition of the text, Felix Liebermann's *Die Gesetze der Angelsachsen* (Halle: Max Niemeyer Verlag, 1903-16), republished in 1960 by Scientia Verlag. The following is not intended to be an exhaustive scholarly edition of the *Domboc*, for which I would refer you to Liebermann and, as of the time of this writing, the as yet unpublished electronic edition of the text to be released by a joint venture between the Institute of Historical Research at the University of London and the Department of Digital Humanities at King's College London (www.earlyenglishlaws.ac.uk). Rather, this diplomatic edition of the *Domboc*, as found in CCCC 173, is only to provide ready reference to an English translation of the complete base text of Alfred's law code in a single source.

In navigating the text, some explanations are in order. The Old English text is represented on the left, with the corresponding modern translation on the right. As this is a diplomatic transcription, I endeavored to preserve the Old English word forms as they appear in CCCC 173, instead of regularizing any variations. The translation is my own, and in preparing it, I tried to stay as close to the original text as possible in both syntax and word choice. As a result, the translation can be somewhat stilted or awkward in parts, but should enable the modern reader to scan back and forth from Old English to modern English with greater facility. The foliation (pagination) of the manuscript is indicated by the bracketed abbreviation "Fol.", followed by the page (leaf) number, and finally the indication of page side: "a" (recto, the front or right-hand page) or "b" (verso, the back or left-hand page). The 120 rubrics (functionally, a table of contents) are presented with only the original Roman numeration from the manuscript. The introduction to the law code is listed with Liebermann's Arabic numeration, as is the scholarly norm. The laws themselves are enumerated with both the original Roman numeration from the manuscript and Liebermann's Arabic numeration.

The *Domboc* begins with 120 rubrics, outlining the main sections of Alfred's law code. The text begins with an Old English rendering of the Ten Commandments. This is followed by a prologue, in Alfred's voice, who traces a line of legitimate and divinely ordained lawgiving from Moses, through Christ and the apostles, and ultimately to the king, himself (Liebermann's *Af. El.* [Alfred's Introduction] 1-49.10,). The laws proper then commence: Alfred's laws number 1 to 77 (II to LXIII in the manuscript), followed by Ine's prologue and laws 1-76.3 (LXIIII to CXX in the manuscript).

King Alfred's Domboc: Text and Translation

[Fol. 33a]

[Rubrics of Alfred's Laws]

i. Be ðon þæt mon ne scyle oþrum deman buton swa he wille, þæt him mon deme.

ii. Be aþum 7 be weddum.

iii. Be circena socnum.

iiii. Be borgbryce.

v. Be hlafordsearwe.

vi. Be circena friðe.

vii. Be circan stale.

viii. Be ðon þe mon on cynges healle feohte.

[Rubrics of Alfred's Laws]

1. On one who shall not judge others except as he desires that a man would judge him.

2. On oaths and on pledges.

3. On the churches' sanctuaries.

4. On the breach of surety.

5. On lord-slaughter.

6. On the churches' peace.

7. On church theft.

8. On one who fights in the king's hall.

ix. Be nunnan hæmede.
x. Be bearneacnum wife ofslægenum.

xi. Be twelfhyndes monnes wife for-
legenum.
xii. Be cirliscre fæmnan onfenge.

xiii. Be wudubærnette.
xiiii. Be dumbera monna dædum.
xv. Be þam monnum þe beforan bis-
copum feohtað.
xvi. Be nunnena onfenge.
xvii. Be ðam monnum þe heora wæpen
to monslyhte lænað.
xviii. Be ðam þe munecum heora feoh
buton leafe befæstað.
xix. Be preosta gefeohte.
xx. Be eofetes andetlan.
xxi. Be hundes slite.
xxii. Be nietena misdædum.
xxiii. Be ceorles mennenes nied-
hæmede.
xiiii. Be twyhyndum men æt hloþ-
slyhte.
[Fol. 33b]
xxv. Be syxhyndum men.
xxvi. Be .xii. hyndum men.
xxvii. Be ungewintredes wifmonnes
nedhæmde.
xxviii. Be swa gerades monnes slege.

xxviii. Be folcleasunge gewyrhtum.
xxx. Be godborgum.
xxxi. Be ciepemonnum.
xxxii. Be cierlisces monnes byndellan.
xxxiii. Be speres gemeleasnesse.
xxxiiii. Be boldgetale.
xxxv. Be ðon ðe mon beforan ealdormen on gemote gefeohte.
xxxvi. Be cierlisces monnes fletge-
feohte.
xxxvii. Be boclondum.
xxxviii. Be fæhðe.
xxxviiii. Be mæssedaga freolse.

9. On cohabitation with nuns.
10. On the slaughter of a pregnant
woman.
11. On adultery with a twelve-hind
man's wife.
12. On taking hold of a churlish
woman.
13. On wood-burning.
14. On the deeds of a dumb one.
15. On those ones who fight before
bishops.
16. On taking hold of nuns.
17. On those ones who loan their
weapon for manslaughter.
18. On those who entrust their cattle
to monks without leave.
19. On the fighting of priests.
20. On the declaration of a crime.
21. On dog's bite.
22. On cattle's misdeeds.
23. On a churl's maidservant's rape.

24. On the murder of a 200-wergild-
man by a band of robbers.

25. On 600-wergild man.
26. On a 1200-wergild man.
27. On a young woman's rape.

28. On the reckoning for a man's slaying.
29. On slander regarding deeds.
30. On solemn pledges.
31. On merchants.
32. On a churlish man's binding.
33. On carelessness of spears.
34. On the political district.
35. On one who, before an ealdorman
in court, fights.
36. On a fighting in a churlish man's
house.
37. On bookland.
38. On vendetta.
39. On the immunity of mass-days.

xl. Be heafodwunde.

xli. Be feaxwunde.

xlii. Be earslege.

xliii. Be monnes eagwunde 7 oðerra missenlicra lima.

xliiii. Be Ines domum.

xlv. Be Godes ðeowa regole.

xlvi. Be cildum.

xlvii. Be sunnan dæges weorcum.

xlviii. Be ciricsceattum.

xlviiii. Be ciricsocnum.

l. Be gefeohtum.

[Fol. 34a]

li. Be stale.

lii. Be ryhtes bene.

liii. Be ðam wrecendan, ær he him ryhtes bidde.

liiii. Be reaflace.

lv. Be ðam monnum þe hiora gelondan bebycggað.

lvi. Be gefongenum ðeofum.

lvii. Be ðam ðe hiora gewitnessa beforan biscepe aleogað.

lviii. Be hloðe.

lviiii. Be herige.

lx. Be ðeofslege.

lxi. Be forstolenum flæsce.

lxii. Be cirliscum ðeofe gefongenum.

lxiii. Be cyninges geneate.

lxiiii. Be feorran cumenum men butan wege gemetton.

lxv. Be swa ofslegenes monnes were.

lxvi. Be ðon ðe monnes geneat stalige.

lxvii. Be elðeodies monnes slege.

lxviii. Be witeðeowes monnes slege.

lxviiii. Be ciepemonna fore uppe on londe.

lxx. Be fundenes cildes fostre.

lxxi. Be þon þe mon dearnenga bearn gestriene.

lxxii. Be ðeofes onfenge æt ðiefðe.

40. On a head-wound.

41. On a wound under the hair.

42. On striking off an ear.

43. On a man's wound in the eye and of other various limbs.

44. On Ine's laws.

45. On God's servant's law.

46. On children.

47. On Sunday's work.

48. On church-scot.

49. On church sanctuary.

50. On fighting.

51. On stealing.

52. On a just request.

53. On that avenger, before he asks justice from him.

54. On robbery.

55. On those men who sell their countryman.

56. On capturing a thief.

57. On those who bear false witness before a bishop.

58. On a band of robbers.

59. On a raiding army.

60. On thief-slaying.

61. On stolen meat.

62. On capturing a churlish thief.

63. On a member of the king's household.

64. On a foreign man met off of the path.

65. On a slain man's wergild.

66. On the stealing by one's member of the household.

67. On the slaying of a foreigner.

68. On the slaying of one legally enslaved.

69. On merchants up in the countryside.

70. On the provision of a foster child.

71. On one who secretly begets a child.

72. On a thief's capture with stolen goods.

lxxiii. Be ðon þe mon sweordes onlæne oðres ðeowe.

lxxiiii. Be ðon þe cierlisc mon flieman feormige.

lxxv. Be ðon þe mon wif bycgge, 7 þonne sio gift tostande.

lxxvi. Be Wilisces monnes londhæfene. [Fol. 34b]

lxxvii. Be cyninges horsweale.

lxxviii. Be monslihte.

lxxviiii. Be þeofslihte, þæt he mote aðe gecyðan.

lxxx. Be ðeofes onfenge, 7 hine ðonne forlæte.

lxxxi. Be cirlisces monnes ontygnesse æt ðiefðe.

lxxxii. Be þon ðe ryhtgesamhiwan bearn hæbben, 7 þonne se wer gewite.

lxxxiii. Be unalefedum fære from his hlaforde.

lxxxiiii. Be ceorles weorðige.

lxxxv. Be borges ondsæce.

lxxxvi. Be ceorles gærstune.

lxxxvii. Be wuda bærnette.

lxxxviii. Be wuda onfenge butan leafe.

lxxxviiii. Be burgbryce.

xc. Be stæltyhtlan.

xci. Be ðon þe mon forstolenne ceap befehð.

xcii. Be witeþeowum men.

xciii. Be unaliefedes mæstennes onfenge.

xciiii. Be gesiðcundes monnes geþinge.

xcv. Be ðon ðe gesiðcund mon fierd forsitte.

xcvi. Be diernum geðinge.

xcvii. Be forstolenes monnes forefonge.

xcviii. Be werfæhðe tyhtlan.

xcviii. Be ewes weorðe.

.c. Be gehwelces ceapes angelde.

.ci. Be cierlisces monnes stale.

73. On one who makes the loan of a sword to another's servant.

74. On. a churlish man who harbors a fugitive.

75. On one who buys a wife, and then her dowry is not paid.

76. On a Welshman's land.

77. On the king's horse-groom.

78. On man-slaughter.

79. On thief-slaughter, after which he must say an oath.

80. On a thief's capture, and then letting him go.

81. On a churlish man's accusation of theft.

82. On lawfully married persons who have a child, and then the man dies.

83. On unlawful journey from his lord.

84. On a churl's homestead.

85. On the denial of bail.

86. On a churl's meadow.

87. On the burning of wood.

88. On wood taken without permission.

89. On breaking into a dwelling.

90. On a charge of stealing.

91. On one who lays hold of stolen property.

92. On one legally enslaved.

93. On unlawful capture of swine pasture.

94. On a thane-rank man's intercession.

95. On a thane-rank man who neglects military service.

96. On secret compacts.

97. On a stolen one's seizure.

98. On feud instigation.

99. On ewes' worth.

100. On the fixed price of any cattle.

101. On a churlish man's theft.

.cii. Be oxan horne.
[Fol. 35a]
.ciii. Be cuus horne.
.ciiii. Be hyrgeohte.
cv. Be ciricsceatte.
cvi. Be þon þe mon to ceape fordræfe.
cvii. Be gesiðcundes monnes fære.

cviii. Be þon þe hæfð .xx. hida londes.
cviiii. Be .x. hidum.
cx. Be .iii. hidum.
cxi. Be gyrde londes.
cxii. Be gesiðcundes monnes dræfe of londe.
cxiii. Be sceapes gonge mid his fliese.
cxiiii. Be twyhyndum were.
cxv. Be wertyhtlan.
cxvi. Be wergeldðeofes forefonge.

cxvii. Be anre nihtes ðiefðe.
cxviii. Be ðon ðe ðeowwealh frione mon ofslea.
cxviii. Be forstolenes ceapes forefonge.
cxx. Be þon gif mon oðres godsunu slea oððe his godfæder.
[Fol. 36a]
[Alfred's Prologue]
Dryhten wæs sprecende ðas word to Moyse 7 þus cwæð: Ic eom dryhten ðin God. Ic ðe utgelædde of Egipta londe 7 of hiora ðeowdome.

1. Ne lufa ðu oþre fremde godas ofer me.
2. Ne minne noman ne cig ðu on idelnesse; forðon þe ðu ne bist unscyldig wið me, gif ðu on idelnesse cigst minne noman.
3. Gemyne þæt ðu gehalgige þone ræstedæg; wyrceað eow .vi. dagas 7 on þam siofoðan restað eow: forðam on .vi. dagum Crist geworhte heofonas 7 eorðan, sæs 7 ealle gesceafta þe on him sint, 7 hine gereste on

102. On an ox's horn.
103. On a cow's horn.
104. On a hired yoke of oxen.
105. On church-scot.
106. On one who drives cattle.
107. On a thane-rank man's movements.
108. On one who has 20 hides of land.
109. On 10 hides.
110. On 3 hides.
111. On an enclosure of land.
112. On a thane-rank man's driving from the land.
113. On sheep's going with its fleece.
114. On a 200-wegild man.
115. On homicide.
116. On the capture of a thief who may be redeemed with wergild.
117. On a one-night's-old theft.
118. On a Welsh slave who kills a free man.
119. On the seizure of stolen property.
120. Concerning if one kills another's godson or his godfather.

[Alfred's Prologue]
God was speaking these words to Moses and thus said: I am the Lord your god. I who led you out of the land of the Egyptians and from their slavery.

1. You will not love false gods over me.
2. Nor call you my name in idleness; because you are not unsinning against me, if you call my name in idleness.
3. Be mindful that you hallow the rest-day; Work you 6 days and on that seventh you rest: because in 6 days Christ made the heavens and the earth, the seas and all of the creatures which are in them, and he

þone siofoðan dæg, 7 forðon Dryhten hine gehalgode.

4. Ara ðinum fæder 7 þinre medder,
ða þe Dryhten sealde, þæt ðu sie þy
leng libbende on eorþan.

5. Ne sleah ðu.
6. Ne lige ðu dearnenga.
7. Ne stala ðu.
8. Ne sæge ðu lease gewitnesse.
9. Ne wilna ðu þines nehstan ierfes
mid unryhte.
10. Ne wyrc ðe gyldne godas oððe syl-
frene.
11. Þis sint ða domas þe ðu him settan
scealt: Gif hwa gebycgge cristenne
þeow, .vi. gear ðeowige he; ðy siofoðan beo he frioh orceapunga; mid
swelce hrægle he ineode, mid swelce
gange he ut. Gif he wif self hæbbe,
gange hio ut mid him. Gif se hlaford
him þonne wif sealde, sie hio 7 hire
bearn þæs hlafordes. Gif se þeowa
þonne [Fol. 36b] cweðe: Nelle ic
from minum hlaforde ne from
minum wife, ne from minum bearne
ne from minum ierfe, brenge hine
þonne his hlaford to ðære dura þæs
temples 7 þurhþyrlige his eare mid
æle, to tacne þæt he sie æfre siððan
þeow.

12. Ðeah hwa gebycgge his dohtor on
þeowenne, ne sie hio ealles swa
ðeowu swa oðru mennenu: nage he
hie ut on elðeodig folc to bebycg-
ganne. Ac gif he hire ne recce, se ðe
hie bohte, læte hie freo on elðeodig
folc. Gif he ðonne alefe his suna mid
to hæmanne, do hiere gyfta: locige
þæt hio hæbbe hrægl; 7 þæt weorð
sie hiere mægðhades, þæt is se weot-
uma, agife he hire þone. Gif he hire
þara nan ne do, þonne sie hio frioh.

rested on that seventh day, and for
that the Lord hallowed it.

4. Honor your father and your
mother, which the Lord gave, that
you might be the longer living on
earth.

5. You will not kill.
6. You will not lie secretly.
7. You will not steal.
8. You will not speak false witness.
9. You will not desire your neighbor's
property with injustice.
10. You will not create golden gods or
silvern.
11. These are the laws which you shall
set them. If anyone buys a Christian
slave, he shall be enslaved 6 years;
the seventh then be he free without
payment; with such clothing he en-
tered, with such he goes out. If he
have himself a wife, she goes out
with him. If the lord gave him that
wife, she and her children are that
lord's. If the slave then says, "I will
not go from my lord nor from my
wife, nor from my children nor from
my possessions," bring then his lord
to the doors of the temple and pierce
through his ear with an awl, to be-
token that he shall be a slave ever afterwards.

12. Although anyone may sell his
daughter into slavery, she is not quite
a slave as other women: he may not
pass her out among foreign folk for
the purpose of buying. But if he
cares not for her, he who bought her,
let her free among foreign folk. If he
then allows his son to marry her, give
marriage-gifts to her: look that she
has clothing; and what worth is her
virginity, that is the dowry, he gives
her that. If he gives none to her, then
she is free.

13. Se mon se ðe his gewealdes monnan ofslea, swelte se deaðe. Se ðe hine þonne nedes ofsloge oððe unwillum oððe ungewealdes, swelce hine God swa sende on his honda, 7 he hine ne ymbsyrede, sie he feores wyrðe 7 folcryhtre bote, gif he friðstowe gesece. Gif hwa ðonne of giernesse 7 gewealdes ofslea his þone nehstan þurh searwa, aluc ðu hine from minum weofode, to þam þæt he deaðe swelte.

14. Se ðe slea his fæder oððe his modor, se sceal deaðe sweltan.

15. Se ðe frione forstele 7 he hine bebycgge, 7 hit onbestæled sie, þæt he hine bereccean ne mæge, swelte se deaðe. Se ðe werge his fæder oððe his modor, swelte se deaðe.

16. Gif hwa slea [Fol. 37a] his ðone nehstan mid stane oððe mid fyste, 7 he þeah utgongan mæge bi stafe, begite him læce 7 wyrce his weorc ða hwile þe he self ne mæge.

17. Se ðe slea his agenne þeowne esne oððe his mennen, 7 he ne sie idæges dead, ðeah he libbe twa niht oððe ðreo, ne bið he ealles swa scyldig, forþon þe hit wæs his agen fioh. Gif he ðonne sie idæges dead, ðonne sitte sio scyld on him.

18. Gif hwa on cease eacniende wif gewerde, bete þone æwerdlan, swa him domeras gereccen. Gif hio dead sie, selle sawle wið sawle.

19. Gif hwa oðrum his eage oðdo, selle his agen fore: toð fore teð, honda wið honda, fet fore fet, bærning for bærninge, wund wið wunde, læl wið læle.

13. He who kills a man of his own accord, let him suffer death. Yet he who kills him of necessity or unintentionally or unwillingly, as though God placed him in his hand, and he did not lay in wait for him, let him be worthy of the life and compensate the injury according to common law, if he seeks sanctuary. If someone then kills his neighbor desirefully and intentionally through treachery, take him away from my altar, in order that he suffer death.

14. He who strikes his father or mother, he shall suffer death.

15. He who steals a free man and he sells him, and is convicted of it, so that he is not able to justify himself, he shall suffer death. He who curses his father or his mother, he shall suffer death.

16. If anyone strikes his neighbor with stone or with fist, and he is able to go about with a staff, get him a leech and do his work while he is not able to himself.

17. He who strikes his own slave or his woman, and he not be dead on that same day, yet he lives two nights or three, he will not be quite as guilty, because it was his own property. If he then is dead on that same day, then set the guilt upon him.

18. If anyone in quarrelling injure a ~~breeding woman, he then shall compensate the injury, as the judges instruct him.~~ If she is dead, give soul in return for soul.

19. If anyone puts out another's eye, he gives his eye in its place: tooth for tooth, hand in return for hand, foot for foot, burning for burning, wound in return for wound, stripe in return for stripe.

20. Gif hwa aslea his ðeowe oððe his ðeowenne þæt eage ut 7 he þonne hie gedo anigge gefreoge hie for þon. Gif he þonne ðone toð ofaslea, do þæt ilce.

21. Gif oxa ofhnite wer oððe wif, þæt hie dead sien, sie he mid stanum ofworpod, 7 ne sie his flæsc eten; se hlaford bið unscyldig. Gif se oxa hnitol wære twam dagum ær oððe ðrim, 7 se hlaford hit wisse 7 hine inne betynan nolde, 7 he ðonne wer oððe wif ofsloge, sie he mid stanum ofworpod, 7 sie se hlaford ofslegen oððe forgolden, swa ðæt witan to ryhte finden. Sunu oððe dohtor gif he ofstinge, ðæs ilcan domes sie he wyrðe. Gif he ðonne ðeow oððe ðeowmennen ofstinge, geselle þam hlaforde .xxx. scill. [Fol. 37b] seolfres, 7 se oxa mid stanum ofworpod.

22. Gif hwa adelfe wæterpyt oððe betynedne ontyne 7 hine eft ne betyne, gelde swelc neat swelc ðær on befealle, 7 hæbbe him ðæt deade.

23. Gif oxa oðres monnes oxan gewundige, 7 he ðonne dead sie, bebycggen þone oxan 7 hæbben him þæt weorð gemæne 7 eac ðæt flæsc swa ðæs deadan. Gif se hlaford þonne wisse, þæt se oxa hnitol wære, 7 hine healdan nolde, selle him oðerne oxan fore 7 hæbbe him eall ðæt flæsc.

24. Gif hwa forstele oðres oxan 7 hine ofslea oððe bebycgge, selle twegen wið 7 feower sceap wið anum. Gif he næbbe hwæt he selle, sie he self beboht wið ðam fio.

25. Gif ðeof brece mannes hus nihtes 7

20. If anyone strikes his slave or his maidservant so that the eye comes out and he then makes them one-eyed, free them on account of that. If he then strike out a tooth, do the same for that.

21. If an ox gores a man or woman, so that they are dead, let him be stoned to death with stones, and none of his flesh be eaten; the lord will be un-sinning. If the ox were addicted to butting two days or three, and the lord knew it and he would not shut it in, and he then killed a man or woman, let him be stoned to death with stones, and the lord be killed or [the person] paid for, just as the wise men find to be right. If he pierces a son or daughter, for this same judgment let him be worthy. If he then pierces a slave or slave-woman, the lord pays 30 shillings of silver, and the ox stoned to death with stones.

22. If anyone digs a water-pit or opens an enclosure and he afterwards does not shut it, let him pay for such cattle as fall in there, and have them that are dead.

23. If an ox wounds another man's ox, and he is then dead, they may sell that ox and have them that value jointly and also the flesh of the dead one in that way. If the lord then knows that the ox were goring, and would not hold him, let him give another ox for it and let him have all that flesh.

24. If anyone steals another's ox and slays or sells it, let him give twice in return and four sheep in return for one. If he does not have what he should give, let him himself be bought in return for that fee.

25. If a thief breaks into a man's house

he weorðe þær ofslegen, ne sie he na mansleges scyldig. Gif he siððan æfter sunnan upgonge þis deð, he bið mansleges scyldig 7 he ðonne self swelte, buton he nieddæda wære. Gif mid him cwicum sie funden þæt he ær stæl, be twyfealdum forgielde hit.

26. Gif hwa gewerde oðres monnes wingeard oððe his æcras oððe his landes awuht, gebete swa hit mon geeahtige.

27. Gif fyr sie ontended ryt to bærnanne, gebete þone æfwerdelsan se ðæt fyr ontent.

28. Gif hwa oðfæste his friend fioh, gif he hit self stæle, forgylde be twyfealdum. Gif he nyte, hwa hit stæle, geladige hine selfne, þæt he ðær nan facn ne gefremede. Gif hit ðonne [Fol. 38a] cucu feoh wære, 7 he secgge, þæt hit here name oððe hit self acwæle, 7 gewitnesse hæbbe, ne þearf he þæt geldan. Gif he ðonne gewitnesse næbbe, 7 he him ne getriewe, swerige he þonne.

29. Gif hwa fæmnan beswice unbeweddode 7 hire midslæpe, forgielde hie 7 hæbbe hi siððan him to wife. Gif ðære fæmnan fæder hie ðonne sellan nelle, agife he ðæt feoh æfter þam weotuman.

30. Ða fæmnan þe gewuniað onfon gealdorcræftigan 7 scinlæcan 7 wiccan, ne læt þu ða libban.

31. 7 se ðe hæme mid netene, swelte he deaðe.

32. 7 se ðe godgeldum onsecge ofer God anne, swelte se deaðe.

33. Utan cumene 7 elðeodige ne

at night and he gets slain there, he shall not be guilty of manslaughter. If he does this later after the sun rises, he is guilty of manslaughter and then he will die himself, unless , he were [doing] a deed of necessity. If what he previously stole is found with him while he lives, let him pay twofold for it.

26. If anyone harms another man's vineyard or his fields or his lands by any means, he shall compensate just as the man values it.

27. If a fire is kindled for burning underwood, he shall compensate that loss which the fire consumed.

28. If anyone entrusts a fee to his friend, if he steals it himself, payment shall be twofold.. If he does not know who stole it, he shall exculpate himself, in that he did no crime there. If it then were live cattle, and he says that an army took it or it perished by itself, and he has a witness, it is not necessary he pay for that. If he then has no witness, and he trust him not, then he may swear.

29. If anyone seduce an unwedded virgin and sleep with her, pay compensation for her and have her afterward as a wife for him. If there the maid's father will not then give her, he shall give that fee according to the wise men.

30. The women who are wont to receive wizards and magicians and witches, do not let them live.

31. And he who has intercourse with cattle, he shall suffer death.

32. And he who offer sacrifice to heathen idols over God alone, he shall suffer death.

33. Foreigners and strangers you shall

geswenc ðu no, forðon ðe ge wæron
giu elðeodige on Egipta londe.

34. Þa wuduwan 7 þa stiopcild ne
sceððað ge, ne hie nawer deriað. Gif
ge þonne elles doð, hie cleopiað to
me, 7 ic gehiere hie 7 ic eow þonne
slea mid minum sweorde 7 ic gedo,
þæt eowru wif beoð wydewan 7
eowru bearn beoð steopcild.

35. Gif ðu fioh to borge selle þinum
geferan, þe mid þe eardian wille, ne
niede ðu hine swa swa niedling 7 ne
gehene þu hine mid ðy eacan.

36. Gif mon næbbe buton anfeald
hrægl hine mid to wreonne 7 to
werianne, 7 he hit to wedde selle, ær
sunnan setlgonge sie hit agifen. Gif
ðu swa ne dest, þonne cleopað he to
me, 7 ic hine gehiere, forðon ðe ic
eom swiðe mildheort.

37. Ne tæl ðu [Fol. 38b] ðinne Dryht-
en, ne ðone hlaford þæs folces ne
werge þu.

38. Þine teoðan sceattas 7 þine
frumripan gongendes 7 weaxendes
agif þu Gode.

39. Eal ðæt flæsc þæt wildeor læfen ne
eten ge þæt, ac sellað hit hundum.

40. Leases monnes word ne rec ðu no
þæs to gehieranne, ne his domas ne
geðafa ðu, ne nane gewitnesse æfter
him ne saga ðu.

41. Ne wend ðu ðe no on þæs folces
unræd 7 unryht gewill on hiora
spræce 7 geclysp ofer ðin ryht, 7 ðæs
unwisestan lare ne him ne geðafa.

42. Gif ðe becume oðres mannes
giemeleas fioh on hond þeah hit sie
ðin feond, gecyðe hit him.

43. Dem ðu swiðe emne. Ne dem ðu

not trouble, because you were once
strangers in the land of Egypt.

34. The widows and the orphans you
shall not injure, nor never hurt
them. If you then do otherwise, they
shall cry to me, and I hear them and
I then slay you with my sword and I
do, so that your wives shall be widows and your children shall be orphans.

35. If you give property to your asso-
ciate for security, he who will dwell
with you, compel him not as a slave
and afflict him not with your usury.

36. If one does not have but a onefold
garment with which to clothe him
and to wear, and he gives it as a
pledge, before the sun set let it be re-
turned. If you do not do in this way,
he shall then cry to me, and I hear,
because I am very mild-hearted.

37. Do not reproach your Lord, nor
curse the lord of the people.

38. Your. tithe tributes and your first-
fruits of those going on foot and of
those growing you must give to
God.

39. All that flesh that the wild beast
leaves, do not eat that, but give it to
the hounds.

40. Do not care to hear a false man's
word, nor endure his judgments, nor
say any testimony for him.

41. Do not turn yourself towards the
foolish and unrighteous will of people in their speech and clamor over
your right, nor tolerate the advice of
the unwise.

42. If another man's stray cattle comes
into your hand, even if it is of your
enemy, make it known to him.

43. Judge very equally. Do not judge

oðerne dom þam welegan, oðerne
ðam earman; ne oðerne þam liofran
7 oðerne þam laðran ne dem ðu.

44. Onscuna ðu a leasunga.

45. Soðfæstne man 7 unscyldigne ne
acwele ðu þone næfre.

46. Ne onfoh ðu næfre medsceattum,
forðon hie ablendað ful oft wisra
monna geðoht 7 hiora word onwen-
dað.

47. Þam elðeodegan 7 utan cumenan
ne læt ðu no uncuðlice wið hine, ne
mid nanum unryhtum þu hine ne
drece.

48. Ne swergen ge næfre under hæðne
godas, ne on nanum ðingum ne
cleopien ge to him.

49. Þis sindan ða domas þe se
ælmihtega God self sprecende wæs
to Moyse 7 him bebead to healdanne. 7 siððan se ancenneda Dryhtnes sunu, ure God, þæt is hælend
Crist, on middangeard cwom, he
cwæð, [Fol. 39a] ðæt he ne come no
ðas bebodu to brecanne ne to forbeodanne, ac mid eallum godum to
ecanne; 7 mildheortnesse 7 eaðmodnesse he lærde.

49.1. Ða æfter his ðrowunge, ær þam
þe his apostolas tofarene wæron
geond ealle eorðan to læranne, 7 þa
giet ða hie ætgædere wæron, monega
hæðena ðeoda hie to Gode gecerdon.
Þa hie ealle ætsomne wæron, hie
sendan ærendwrecan to Antiohhia 7
to Syrie, Cristes æ to læranne.

49.2. Þa hie ða ongeaton, þæt him ne
speow, ða sendon hie ærendgewrit to
him. Þis is ðonne þæt ærendgewrit
þe ða apostolas sendon ealle to Antiohhia 7 to Syria 7 to Cilicia, ða sint
nu of hæðenum ðeodum to Criste
gecirde.

one judgment to the prosperous, another to the poor; nor one to the
beloved and judge another to the
hated.

44. Always shun false witness.

45. Never slay an honest and unsinning
man.

46. Nor ever take bribes, because they
very often shall deceive the thought
of wise men and shall pervert their
words.

47. Strangers and foreigners, do not
allow unkindness against them, nor
trouble them with any injustice.

48. Nor ever swear to heathen gods, nor
in any things call upon them.

49. These are the laws which almighty
God himself was speaking to Moses
and commanded him to hold. And
afterwards he brought forth the
Lord's son, our God, that is called
Christ, came to middle-earth, he
said, that he did not come to break
nor to annul these laws, but with all
goodness to bring [them] forth; and
he taught mercy and humility.

49.1. Then after his suffering, before
his apostles were scattered throughout all the world to teach, and then
yet when they were gathered, many
heathen people they turned to God.
When they all were united, they sent
messengers to Antioch and to Syrian,
to teach Christ's law.

49.2. When they then understood that
it did not help them, then they sent
written messages to them. This is then
that written message which the apostles all sent to Antioch and the Syria
and the Cilicia, which are now from
heathen people turned to Christ.

49.3. Ða apostolas 7 þa eldran broðor hælo eow wyscað; 7 we eow cyðað, þæt we geascodon, þæt ure geferan sume mid urum wordum to eow comon 7 eow hefigran wisan budon to healdanne þonne we him budon, 7 eow to swiðe gedwealdon mid ðam mannigfealdum gebodum, 7 eowra sawla ma forhwerfdon þonne hie geryhton. Ða gesomnodon we us ymb ðæt, 7 us eallum gelicode ða, þæt we sendon Paulus 7 Barnaban; ða men wilniað hiora sawla sellan for Dryhtnes naman.

49.4. Mid him we sendon Iudam 7 Silam, þæt eow þæt ilce seccgen.

49.5. Þæm halgan Gaste wæs geðuht 7 us, þæt we nane byrðenne on eow settan noldon ofer þæt ðe eow neððearf wæs to healdanne: þæt is ðonne, þæt ge forberen, þæt ge deofolgeld ne weorðien, ne blod ne ðicggen ne asmorod, 7 from [Fol. 39b] diernum geligerum; 7 þæt ge willen, þæt oðre men eow ne don, ne doð ge ðæt oþrum monnum.

49.6. .I. Of ðissum anum dome mon mæg geðencean, þæt he æghwelcne on ryht gedemeð; ne ðearf he nanra domboca oþerra. Geðence he, þæt he nanum men ne deme þæt he nolde ðæt he him demde, gif he ðone dom ofer hine sohte.

49.7. Siððan ðæt þa gelamp, þæt monega ðeoda Cristes geleafan onfengon, þa wurdon monega seonoðas geond ealne middangeard gegaderode, 7 eac swa geond Angelcyn, siððan hie Cristes geleafan onfengon, halegra biscepa 7 eac oðerra geðungenra

49.3. The apostles and the elder brothers wish you health; and we shall say to you, that we have learned that some of our fellow disciples have come to you with our words, and commanded you to keep more oppressive customs than we commanded them, and too exceedingly have led you astray with these manifold commands, and have more perverted your souls than they have set them right. Then we assembled us concerning that, and then it pleased all of us that we send Paul and Barnabus; the men who desire to give their souls in God's name.

49.4. With them we sent Judas and Silas, that they may say the same to you.

49.5. It seemed good to the Holy Spirit and to us that we should not set any burden on you beyond that which was a necessary thing for you to hold: that is then, that you forbear, that you do not celebrate devil-worship, nor consume blood nor the strangled, and keep from secret fornication, and that you desire, that other men not do to you, you will not do that to other men.

49.6. .I. Of this one law a man can think, that he must judge all in justice; he needs no other book-book. He thinks that he should not judge to any man that which he would not have judged to himself, if he then sought judgment over him.

49.7. When that occurred, many people accepted Christ's faith, then many synods throughout all middle-earth became assembled, and also throughout the English people, then they accepted Christ's faith, of the holy bishops and also of the distin-

witena. Hie ða gesetton, for ðære mildheortnesse þe Crist lærde, æt mæstra hwelcre misdæde þætte ða weoruldhlafordas moston mid hiora leafan buton synne æt þam forman gylte þære fiohbote onfon, þe hie ða gesettan. Buton æt hlafordsearwe hie nane mildheortnesse ne dorston gecweðan, forþam ðe God ælmihtig þam nane ne gedemde þe hine oferhogdon, ne Crist Godes sunu þam nane ne gedemde þe hine to deaðe sealde, 7 he bebead þone hlaford lufian swa hine.

49.8. Hie ða on monegum senoðum monegra menniscra misdæda bote gesetton, 7 on monega senoðbec hie writan, hwær anne dom hwær oþerne.

49.9. Ic ða Ælfred cyning þas togædere gegaderode 7 awritan het, monege þara þe ure foregengan heoldon, ða ðe me licodon; 7 manege þara þe me ne licodon ic awearp [Fol. 40a] mid minra witena geðeahte, 7 on oðre wisan bebead to healdanne. Forðam ic ne dorste geðristlæcan þara minra awuht fela on gewrit settan, forðam me wæs uncuð, hwæt þæs ðam lician wolde ðe æfter us wæren. Ac ða ðe ic gemette awðer oððe on Ines dæge, mines mæges, oððe on Offan Mercna cyninges oððe on Æþelbryhtes, þe ærest fulluhte onfeng on Angelcynne, þa ðe me ryhtoste ðuhton, ic þa heron gegaderode, 7 þa oðre forlet.

49.10. Ic ða Ælfred Westseaxna cyning eallum minum witum, þas geeowde, 7 hie ða cwædon, þæt him þæt licode eallum to healdanne.

guished wise men. They then set down, on account of their mercy that Christ taught, that at almost every misdeed the secular lords would be allowed to, with their leave, without sin, at the first guilt, take their monetary compensation, which they had then set down. Except at lord-treachery they dared not proclaim any mercy, because God almighty judged none for them who despised Him, nor Christ, God's son, judged none for them who betrayed him to death, and he commanded to love a lord as himself.

49.8. They then in many synods of many human misdeeds set compensation, and in many synod-books they wrote, here one judgment, there another.

49.9. I, Alfred king, then gathered these together and commanded to write down many of those that our predecessors held, which to me seemed good; and many that did not seem good to me I set aside with my wise men's counsel, and in other ways commanded to hold. Because I did not dare to presume to set much of my own at all in writing, because it was unknown to me what of this would be pleasing to those who were to come after us. But that which I found either in Ine's day, kinsman of mine, or in Offa's, king of Mercia, or in Æthelberht's, who first accepted baptism among the Angelcynn, that which seemed the most right to me, I then gathered together here, and the others let go.

49.10. I then, Alfred, king of the West Saxons, to all of my wise men showed these, and they said that it pleased them to keep all.

referring to witan (witan system) — a...

[Alfred's Laws]

1. .II. Æt ærestan we lærað, þæt mæst
ðearf is, þæt æghwelc mon his að 7
his wed wærlice healde.

1.1. Gif hwa to hwæðrum þissa genied
sie on woh, oððe to hlafordsearwe
oððe to ængum unryhtum fultume,
þæt is þonne ryhtre to aleoganne
þonne to gelæstanne.

1.2. Gif he þonne þæs weddige þe him
riht sie to gelæstanne 7 þæt aleoge,
selle mid eaðmedum his wæpn 7 his
æhta his freondum to gehealdanne 7
beo feowertig nihta on carcerne on
cyninges tune, ðrowige ðær swa biscep him scrife, 7 his mægas hine
feden, gif he self mete næbbe.

1.3. Gif he mægas næbbe oððe þone
mete næbbe, fede cyninges gerefa
hine.

1.4. Gif hine mon togenedan scyle, 7
he elles nylle, gif hine mon gebinde,
þolige his wæpna 7 his ierfes.

1.5. Gif hine mon ofslea, licgge he
orgilde.

1.6. Gif he ut oðfleo ær þam fierste, 7
hine mon gefo, sie he feowertig nihta
[Fol. 40b] on carcerne, swa he ær
sceolde.

1.7. Gif he losige, sie he afliemed 7 sie
amænsumod of eallum Cristes ciricum.

1.8. Gif þær ðonne oþer mennisc borg
sie, bete þone borgbryce swa him
ryht wisie, 7 ðone wedbryce swa him
his scrift scrife.

2. .III. Gif hwa þara mynsterhama
hwelcne for hwelcere scylde gesece,
þe cyninges feorm to belimpe, oþþe

[Alfred's Laws]

1. .II. At first we instruct, that which
is most necessary, that each man
carefully keep his oath and his
pledge.

1.1. If anyone is wrongfully compelled
to either of these, either to high trea-
son or to any unlawful aid, then it is
better to leave it unfulfilled than to
perform it.

1.2. If he then pledges what is lawful
for him to perform and leaves it unfulfilled, with humility he shall give
his weapons and his possessions to
his friends to keep and be in prison
forty nights in the king's dwelling,
endure there the judgment the
bishop gives to him, and his
kinsmen shall feed him, if he has no
food himself.

1.3. If he has no kinsmen or then has
no food, the king's reeve shall feed
him.

1.4. If one is obliged to restrain him,
and he will not otherwise, if one
binds him, he shall lose his weapons
and his property.

1.5. If one slays him, he shall lie without payment.

1.6. If he escapes out before that space
of time, and one catches him, he
shall be forty nights in jail, as he
should before.

1.7. If he escapes, he shall be banished
and excommunicated from all of
Christ's churches.

1.8. If there is then human surety over
him, he shall compensate that
surety-breaking as justice directs,
and that pledge-breaking as his confessor prescribes.

2. .III. If anyone should seek any of the
monasteries for any sin, to which the
king's rent belongs, or another noble

· counsel of wise men

oðerne frione hiered þe arwyrðe sie,
age he þreora nihta fierst him to
gebeorganne, buton he ðingian wille.

2.1. Gif hine mon on ðam fierste
geyflige mid slege oððe mid bende
oððe þurh wunde, bete þara æghwelc
mid ryhte ðeodscipe, ge mid were ge
mid wite, 7 þam hiwum
hundtwelftig scill. ciricfriðes to bote
7 næbbe his agne forfongen.

3. .IIII. Gif hwa cyninges borg abrece,
gebete þone tyht swa him ryht wisie,
7 þæs borges bryce mid .v. pundum
mærra pæninga. Ærcebiscepes
borges bryce oððe his mundbyrd gebete mid ðrim pundum. Oðres biscepes oððe ealdormonnes borges
bryce oððe mundbyrd gebete mid
twam pundum.

4. .V. Gif hwa ymb cyninges feorh
sierwe, ðurh hine oððe ðurh wrec-
cena feormunge oððe his manna, sie
he his feores scyldig 7 ealles þæs ðe
he age.
4.1. Gif he hine selfne triowan wille,
do þæt be cyninges wergelde.
4.2. [Fol. 41a] Swa we eac settað be eallum hadum, ge ceorle ge eorle: se ðe
ymb his hlafordes fiorh sierwe, sie he
wið ðone his feores scyldig 7 ealles
ðæs ðe he age, oððe be his hlafordes
were hine getriowe.

5. Eac we settað æghwelcere cirican, ðe
biscep gehalgode, ðis frið: gif hie
fahmon geierne oððe geærne, þæt
hine seofan nihtum nan mon ut ne
teo. Gif hit þonne hwa do, ðonne sie
he scyldig cyninges mundbyrde 7
þære cirican friðes mare, gif he ðær

household which is honorable, he
shall have respite for three nights to
defend himself, unless he desires to
conciliate.

2.1. If in that period of time he is hurt
with slaying or with binding or
through a wound, compensate each
of those with just discipline, both
with wergild and with a fine, and
pay to the household compensation
of one hundred and twenty shillings
of the penalty for the breach of the
right of sanctuary.

3. .IIII. If anyone should break the
king's surety, he shall compensate the
crime just as justice directs him, and
of that breach with 5 pounds of ster-
ling pennies. Breaking an archbishop's surety or his protection shall
be compensated with three pounds.
Breaking the surety or protection of
another bishop or ealdorman shall
be compensated with two pounds.

4. .V. If anyone plots against the king's
life, by himself or through the harboring of exiles or his men, let him
be liable of his life and all that he
owns.
4.1. If he desires to exculpate himself,
he may do that by the king's wergild.
4.2. In this manner we also ordain concerning all degrees, both churl and
earl: he who plots concerning his
lord's life, let him then, in return, be
liable of his life and all that which
he owns, or exculpate himself
through his lord's wergild.

5. .VI. Also, we set down for each
church, which a bishop has conse-
crated, this peace: if a foeman runs
or rides to it, that for seven nights
no man may take him out, if he is
able to live through the hunger, unless he fights out himself. If anyone

mare ofgefo, gif he for hungre libban mæge, buton he self utfeohte.

5.1. Gif hiwan hiora cirican maran þearfe hæbben, healde hine mon on oðrum ærne, 7 ðæt næbbe ðon ma dura þonne sio cirice.

5.2. Gewite ðære cirican ealdor, þæt him mon on þam fierste mete ne selle.

5.3. Gif he self his wæpno his gefan utræcan wille, gehealden hi hine .xxx. nihta 7 hie hine his mægum gebodien.

5.4. Eac cirican frið: gif hwelc mon cirican gesece for ðara gylta hwylcum, þara ðe ær geypped nære, 7 hine ðær on Godes naman geandette, sie hit healf forgifen.

5.5. Se ðe stalað on Sunnanniht oððe on Gehhol oððe on Eastron oððe on ðone halgan þunresdæg on Gangdagas: ðara gehwelc we willað sie twybote, swa on Lenctenfæsten.

6. .VII. Gif hwa on cirican hwæt geðeofige, forgylde þæt angylde, 7 ðæt wite swa to ðam angylde belimpan wille, 7 slea mon þa hond of ðe he hit mid gedyde.

6.1. Gif he [Fol. 41b] ða hand lesan wille, 7 him mon ðæt geðafian wille, gelde swa to his were belimpe.

7. .VIII. Gif hwa in cyninges healle gefeohte oððe his wæpn gebrede, 7 hine mon gefo, sie ðæt on cyninges dome, swa deað swa lif, swa he him forgifan wille.

7.1. Gif he losige, 7 hine mon eft gefo, forgielde he hine self a be his

then does it, then let him be liable of the king's protection and the church's surety in addition, if he takes away more there.

5.1. If the members of the religious house have more need of their church, he may be kept in another building, and that shall not have more doors than the church.

5.2. The church elder shall be aware of that, that no food shall be given to him in that period of time.

5.3.If. he himself desires to give out his weapons to his foes, they shall keep him 30 nights and they shall tell his kinsmen.

5.4. Likewise of the church's peace: if any man shall seek the church because of any crime, that which was never before disclosed, and he there in God's name confesses, let it be half forgiven.

5.5. He who steals on Sunday or on Christmas or on Easter or on the holy Thursday in Rogation days: we desire each of these shall be twice-compensated, just as in Lent.

6. .VII. If anyone in the church shall steal anything, he shall pay that price, and the fine that shall be desired to be in regard to that price, and strike the hand off with which he did it.

6.1. If he shall desire to redeem the hand, and they shall be willing to allow that to him, he shall pay in regard to his wergild.

7. .VIII. If anyone fights in the king's hall or draw his weapon, and he is seized, let that be in the king's judgment, whether death or life, just as he desires to grant to him.

7.1. If he should escape, and afterwards he is captured, he shall always pay

weregilde, 7 ðone gylt gebete, swa wer swa wite, swa he gewyrht age.

for himself in conformity with his wergild, and he shall compensate for that crime, whether the wergild or the fine, just as he owns the deed.

8. .VIIII. Gif hwa nunnan of mynstere ut alæde butan kyninges lefnesse oððe biscepes, geselle hundtwelftig scill., healf cyninge, healf biscepe 7 þære cirican hlaforde, ðe ðone munuc age.

8. .VIIII. If anyone leads a nun out of a monastery without the king's leave ot the bishop's, he shall pay one hundred and twenty shillings, half to the king, half to the bishop and the lord of the church, which owns that nun.

8.1. Gif hio leng libbe ðonne se ðe hie utlædde, nage hio his ierfes owiht.

8.1. If she lives longer than he who led her out, she has no right to his property at all.

8.2. Gif hio bearn gestriene, næbbe ðæt ðæs ierfes ðon mare ðe seo modor.

8.2. If she begets a child, it shall not have that property any more than the mother.

8.3. Gif hire bearn mon ofslea, gielde cyninge þara medrenmæga dæl; fædrenmægum hiora dæl mon agife.

8.3. If one slays her child, yield to the king the amount of the maternal kinsmen; one shall give the proper amount to the paternal kinsmen.

9. .X. Gif mon wif mid bearne ofslea, þonne þæt bearn in hire sie, forgielde ðone wifman fullan gielde, 7 þæt bearn be ðæs fædrencnosles were healfan gelde.

9. .X. If one slays a woman with child, when that child is in her, he shall pay the full price for that woman, and for that child by half the price of the father's kin's wergild.

9.1. A sie þæt wite .lx. scill., oð ðæt angylde arise to .xxx. scill.; siððan hit to ðam arise þæt angylde, siððan sie þæt wite .cxx. scill.

9.1. The fine shall always be 60 shillings, until the rate of compensation rises to 30 shillings, when that rate of compensation rises to such an extent, then that fine shall be 120 shillings.

9.2. Geo wæs goldðeofe 7 stodðeofe 7 beoðeofe, 7 manig witu maran ðonne oþru; nu sint eal gelic buton manðeofe: .cxx. scill.

9.2. Formerly there was the gold-thief and the stud-thief and the bee-thief, and many fines [were] more than others; now they are all alike except for the man-thief: 120 shillings.

10. .XI. Gif mon hæme mid twelfhyndes monnes wife, hund [Fol. 42a] twelftig scill. gebete ðam were; syxhyndum men hundteontig scill. gebete; cierliscum men feowertig scill. gebete.

10. .XI. If one has intercourse with a twelve-hind man's wife, he shall compensate that man with one hundred and twenty shillings; he shall compensate a six-hind man with one hundred shillings ; he shall compensate a churlish man with sixty shillings.

11. .XII. Gif mon on cirliscre fæmnan breost gefo, mid .v. scill. hire gebete.

11.1. Gif he hie oferweorpe 7 mid ne gehæme, mid .x. scill. gebete.

11.2. Gif he mid gehæme, mid .lx. scill. gebete.

11.3. Gif oðer mon mid hire læge ær, sie be healfum ðæm þonne sio bot.

11.4. Gif hie mon teo, geladiege hie be sixtegum hida, oððe ðolige be healfre þære bote.

11.5. Gif borenran wifmen ðis gelimpe, weaxe sio bot be ðam were.

12. .XIII. Gif mon oðres wudu bærneð oððe heaweð unaliefedne, forgielde ælc great treow mid .v. scill., 7 siððan æghwylc, sie swa fela swa hiora sie, mid .v. pæningum; 7 .xxx. scill. to wite.

13. Gif mon oðerne æt gemænan weorce offelle ungewealdes, agife mon þam mægum þæt treow, 7 hi hit hæbben ær .xxx. nihta of þam lande, oððe him fo se to se ðe ðone wudu age.

14. .XIIII. Gif mon sie dumb oððe deaf geboren, þæt he ne mæge synna onsecggan ne geandettan, bete se fæder his misdæda.

15. .XV. Gif mon beforan ærcebiscepe gefeohte oððe wæpne gebregde, mid L scill. 7 hundteontegum gebete; gif beforan oðrum biscepe oððe ealdormen ðis gelimpe, mid hundteontegum scill. gebete.

16. Gif mon cu oððe [Fol. 42b] stodmyran forstele 7 folan oððe cealf ofadrife, forgelde mid scill. 7 þa moder be hiora weorðe.

11. .XII. If one seizes a churlish woman's breast, he shall compensate her with 5 shillings.

11.1. If he assaults her and does not have intercourse with her, he shall compensate with 10 shillings.

11.2. If he has intercourse with her, he shall compensate with sixty shillings.

11.3. If another one lay with her before, let it be half that compensation.

11.4. If one accuse her, let her exculpate herself with sixty hides, or she shall lose half the compensation..

11.5. If to a noble woman this should happen, her compensation shall increase by the wergild.

12. .XIII. If one burns another's wood or cuts it down unlawfully, he shall pay for each great tree with 5 shillings, and then for every one, for as many as there might be, with 5 pennies and 30 shillings as a fine.

13. If one inadvertently fells another man at common work, one shall give that tree to his kinsmen, and they shall have it from that land before 30 nights, or take it to him who owns that wood.

14. .XIIII. If a man is born dumb or deaf, so that he can not renounce sins nor confess, the father shall compensate for his misdeeds.

15. .XV. If one fights before an archbishop or draws his weapon, he shall compensate with 50 shillings and a hundred; if this should happen before a bishop or an ealdorman, he shall compensate with a hundred shillings.

16. If one steals a cow or brood-mare and drives off a foal or a calf, he shall pay with a shilling and the mother by her worth.

Harding

17. Gif hwa oðrum his unmagan oðfæste, 7 he hine on ðære fæstinge forferie, getriowe hine facnes se ðe hine fede, gif hine hwa hwelces teo.

18. .XVI. Gif hwa nunnan mid hæmeðþinge oððe on hire hrægl oððe on hire breost butan hire leafe gefo, sie hit twybete swa we ær be læwdum men fundon.

18.1. Gif beweddodu fæmne hie for-licgge, gif hio sie cirlisc, mid .lx. scill. gebete þam byrgean, 7 þæt sie on cwicæhtum feogodum, 7 mon nænigne mon on ðæt ne selle.

18.2. Gif hio sie syxhyndu, hundteontig scill. geselle þam byrgean.

18.3. Gif hio sie twelfhyndu, .cxx. scill. gebete þam byrgean.

19. .XVII. Gif hwa his wæpnes oðrum onlæne, þæt he mon mid ofslea, hie moton hie gesomnian, gif hie willað, to þam were.

19.1. Gif hi hie ne gesamnien, gielde se ðæs wæpnes onlah þæs weres ðrid-dan dæl 7 þæs wites ðriddan dæl.

19.2. Gif he hine triewan wille, þæt he to ðære læne facn ne wiste, þæt he mot.

19.3. Gif sweordhwita oðres monnes wæpn to feormunge onfo, oððe smið monnes andweorc, hie hit gesund begen agifan, swa hit hwæðer hiora ær onfenge, buton hiora hwæðer ær þingode, þæt he hit angylde healdan ne ðorfte.

20. .XVIII. Gif mon oðres monnes munuce feoh oðfæste butan ðæs munuces hlafordes lefnesse, 7 hit him losige, þolige his se ðe hit ær ahte.

17. If anyone entrusts his dependant to another, and he in that guardianship lets him die, he shall exculpate him-self of evil, he who fostered him, if anyone accuses him of any.

18. .XVI. If anyone seizes a nun by means of coition or upon her clothes or upon her breast without her leave, let it be twice-compensation as we have arranged before for laymen.

18.1. If a married woman commits adultery, if she is churlish, she shall compensate for that surety with 60 shillings, and it shall be in cattle-property, and one shall not give any man in that.

18.2. If she is six-hind, she shall give a hundred shillings for that surety.

18.3. If she is twelve-hind, she shall give 120 shillings for that surety.

19. .XVII. If anyone should loan of his weapon to another, so that he kill with it, he may join him, if he wishes, in order for wergild.

19.1. If he does not join him, he who loaned the weapon shall pay a third part of the wergild and a third part of the fine.

19.2. If he desire to exculpate himself, in that he in that loan knew no evil, that he may do.

19.3. If a sword-furbisher takes another man's weapon for cleaning, or a smith takes a man's material, they are both to return it whole, just as either of them it received before, unless ei-ther of them asked that he not be re-quired to compensate for it.

20. .XVIII. If one entrusts property to another man's monk without the monk's lord's leave, and he loses it for him, it shall be his loss who owned it before.

21. .XVIIII. [Fol. 43a] Gif preost oðerne mon ofslea, weorpe mon to handa 7 eall ðæt he him hames bohte, 7 hine biscep onhadige, þonne hine mon of ðam mynstre agife, buton se hlaford þone wer forðingian wille.

22. .XX. Gif mon on folces gemote cyninges gerefan geyppe eofot, 7 his eft geswican wille, gestæle on ryhtran hand, gif he mæge; gif he ne mæge, ðolie his angyldes.

23. .XXI. Gif hund mon toslite oððe abite, æt forman misdæde geselle .vi. scill., gif he him mete selle, æt æfteran cerre .xii. scill., æt ðriddan .xxx. scill.

23.1. Gif æt ðissa misdæda hwelcere se hund losige, ga ðeos bot hwæðre forð.

23.2. Gif se hund ma misdæda gewyrce, 7 he hine hæbbe, bete be fullan were swa dolgbote swa he wyrce.

24. .XXII. Gif neat mon gewundige, weorpe ðæt neat to honda oððe foreðingie.

25. .XXIII. Gif mon ceorles mennen to nedhæmde geðreataõ, mid .v. scill. gebete þam ceorle; 7 .lx. scill. to wite.

25.1. Gif ðeowmon þeowne to nedhæmde genede, bete mid his eowende.

29. [.XXIIII.] Gif mon twyhyndne mon unsynnigne mid hloðe ofslea, gielde se ðæs sleges andetta sie wer 7 wite; 7 æghwelc mon ðe on siðe wære geselle .xxx. scill. to hloðbote.

21. .XVIIII. If a priest slays a man, hand over the man and all of the estate that he bought himself, and the bishop shall divest him of holy orders, when he is delivered from the minister, unless the lord of that man desires to arrange for the man's wergild.

22. .XX. If one reveals the crime in the people's assembly of the king's reeve, and afterwards desires to abandon his charge, he shall accuse [another] of the charge in a more just manner, if he can; if he can not he shall lose his compensation.

23. .XXI. If a hound shall rend or bite one, at the first misdeed he shall give 6 shillings, if he gives him food, at the time after 12 shillings, at the third 30 shillings.

23.1. If at any of these the hound is lost, the compensation still must go forth.

23.2. If the hound works more misdeeds, and he has him, the compensation shall be full wergild so far as the compensation for the injury as he does.

24. .XXII. If cattle should wound one, hand over that cattle or he shall arrange for the man's wergild.

25. .XXIII. If one should attack a churl's handmaiden in rape, he shall compensate that churl with 5 shillings; and 60 shillings in fine.

25.1. If a servant forces a female servant in rape, he shall compensate with his testicles.

29. .XXIIII. If one slays an unsinning two-hind man with a band of men, the one who confesses of the slaying shall pay wergild and fine; and each man who was in that undertaking shall give 30 shillings as a penalty

125

- rights of slaves
- monetary penalties
- eye for eye
- death

30. .XXV. Gif hit sie syxhynde mon, ælc mon to hloðbote .lx. scill. 7 se slaga wer 7 fulwite.

31. .XXVI. Gif he sie twelfhynde, ælc hiora hundtwelftig scill., [Fol. 43b] se slaga wer 7 wite.

31.1. Gif hloð ðis gedo 7 eft oðswerian wille, tio hie ealle; 7 þonne ealle forgielden þone wer gemænum hondum 7 ealle an wite, swa to ðam were belimpe.

26. .XXVII. Gif mon ungewintrædne wifmon to niedhæmde geðreatige, sie ðæt swa ðæs gewintredan monnes bot.

27. Gif fædrenmæga mægleas mon gefeohte 7 mon ofslea, 7 þonne gif medrenmægas hæbbe, gielden ða þæs weres ðriddan dæl 7 ðriddan dæl þa gegildan, for ðriddan dæl he fleo.

27.1. Gif he medrenmægas nage, gielden þa gegildan healfne, for healfne he fleo.

28. .XXVIII. Gif mon swa geradne mon ofslea, gif he mægas nage, gielde mon healfne cyninge, healfne þam gegildan.

32. .XXVIIII. Gif mon folcleasunge gewyrce, 7 hio on hine geresp weorðe, mid nanum leohtran ðinge gebete þonne him mon aceorfe þa tungon of, þæt hie mon na undeorran weorðe moste lesan, ðonne hie mon be þam were geeahtige.

33. .XXX. Gif hwa oðerne godborges oncunne 7 tion wille, þæt he

imposed on members of a band of malefactors.

30. .XXV. If it be a six-hind man, each man shall pay the band-penalty of 60 shillings and slayer the wergild and the full fine.

31. .XXVI. If it be a twelve-hind, each of them one hundred and twenty shillings, the slayer the wergild and the fine.

31.1. If the band does this and afterwards desires to deny it on oath, they all are accused; and then all pay the wergild they possess in common and all one fine, just as regards the wergild.

26. .XXVII. If one attacks a young woman in rape, let that be as the compensation of an adult woman.

27. If a man without relatives of paternal kinship should fight and kill a man, and then if he has maternal kinsmen, then those shall pay of that wergild a third portion and a third portion then by his brotherhood, for a third portion he may flee.

27.1. If he has no maternal kinsmen, his brotherhood pays half, for half he may flee.

28. .XXVIII. If one so circumstanced kills a man, if he possesses no kinsmen, he shall pay half to the king, half to the brotherhood.

32. .XXVIIII. If one should perform slander, and he becomes convicted in it, he shall compensate with not any lighter thing than that he shall have his tongue carved off, in order that one can no more cheaply lease it, than it shall be esteemed by that wergild.

33. .XXX. If anyone should reproach another's solemn pledge and desires

hwelcne ne gelæste ðara ðe he him gesealde, agife þone foreað on feower ciricum, 7 se oðer, gif he hine treowan wille in .xii. ciricum do he ðæt.

34. .XXXI. Eac is ciepemonnum gereht: ða men ðe hie up mid him læden, gebrengen beforan kyninges gerefan on folcgemote, 7 gerecce hu manige þara sien; 7 hie nimen þa men mid him þe hie mægen eft to folcgemote to ryhte brengan. 7 þonne him ðearf sie ma manna up mid him to habbanne on hiora fore, gecyðe symle, swa oft swa him ðearf sie, [Fol. 44a] in gemotes gewitnesse cyninges gerefan.

35. .XXXII. Gif mon cierliscne mon gebinde unsynnigne, gebete mid .x. scill.

35.1. Gif hine mon beswinge, mid .xx. scill. gebete.

35.2. Gif he hine on hengenne alecgge, mid .xxx. scill. gebete.

35.3. Gif he hine on bismor to homolan bescire, mid .x. scill. gebete.

35.4. Gif he hine to preoste bescire unbundenne, mid .xxx. scill. gebete.

35.5. Gif he ðone beard ofascire, mid .xx. scill. gebete.

35.6. Gif he hine gebinde 7 þonne to preoste bescire, mid .lx. scill. gebete.

36. .XXXIII. Eac is funden: gif mon hafað spere ofer eaxle, 7 hine mon on asnaseð, gielde þone wer butan wite.

to accuse, that he did not perform all that which he swore to him, he shall deliver that preliminary oath in four churches, and the other, if he desires to exculpate himself in 12 churches, he will do that.

34. .XXXI. Likewise is instructed to merchants: the men which they who they bring lead up country with them, they shall bring them before the king's reeve in the town meeting, and he shall decide how many there may be, and they shall take the men with them which they can afterwards bring to the town meeting for justice. And when it is necessary for them to have more men up country with them on their journey, they shall always tell, as often as is necessary to them, in witness of the assembly of the king's reeve.

35. .XXXII. If one binds an unsinning churlish man, he shall compensate with 10 shillings.

35.1. If one beats him, he shall compensate with 20 shillings.

35.2. If he puts him in imprisonment, he shall compensate with 30 shillings.

35.3. If he shaves his hair off in insult, he shall compensate with 10 shillings.

35.4. If he shaves his hair like a priest, without binding him, he shall compensate with 30 shillings.

35.5. If he then shaves off his beard, he shall compensate with 20 shillings.

35.6. If he binds him and then cuts his hair like a priest, he shall compensate with 60 shillings.

36. .XXXIII. Likewise it is found: if one has a spear over the shoulder, and a man is impaled on it, he shall pay the wergild without the fine.

36.1. Gif beforan eagum asnase, gielde þone wer; gif hine mon tio gewealdes on ðære dæde, getriowe hine be þam wite 7 mid ðy þæt wite afelle,

36.1. [Fol. 43a] If he is impaled in front of his eyes, he shall pay the wergild; if one accuses him of intentionality in that deed, he shall exculpate himself by that fine and by that overturn the fine

36.2. gif se ord sie ufor þonne hindeweard sceaft. Gif hie sien bu gelic, ord 7 hindeweard sceaft, þæt sie butan pleo.

36.2. if the spear-point is higher than the hindward shaft. If they are both equal, the spear-point and the hindward shaft, that is without responsibility.

37. .XXXIIII. Gif mon wille of boldgetale in oðer boldgetæl hlaford secan, do ðæt mid ðæs ealdormonnes gewitnesse, þe he ær in his scire folgode.

37. .XXXIIII. If one desires to seek a lord in another district, do that with the ealdorman's knowledge, who he served before in his shire.

37.1. Gif he hit butan his gewitnesse do, geselle se þe hine to men feormie .cxx. scill. to wite: dæle he hwæðre ðæt, healf cyninge in ða scire ðe he ær folgode, healf in þa ðe he oncymð.

37.1. If he does it without his knowledge, he who harbors him as vassal shall pay 120 shillings as a fine: he shall divide all that, half to the king in the shire where he served before, half in that which he arrives.

37.2. Gif he hwæt yfla gedon hæbbe ðær he ær wæs, bete ðæt se ðe hine ðonne to men onfo, 7 cyninge .cxx. scill. to wite.

37.2. If he has done any evil where he was before, he who receives him as vassal shall compensate that, and 120 shillings to the king as a fine.

38. .XXXV. [Fol. 44b] Gif mon beforan cyninges ealdormen on gemote gefeohte, bete wer 7 wite, swa hit ryht sie, 7 beforan þam .cxx. scill. ðam ealdormen to wite.

38. .XXXV. If on fights before the king's ealdorman in the assembly, he shall compensate wergild and fine, just as it is just, and before that 120 shillings to the ealdorman as a fine.

38.1. Gif he folcgemot mid wæpnes bryde arære, ðam ealdormen hundtwelftig scill. to wite.

38.1. If he disturbs the town meeting by the drawing of a weapon, to the ealdorman one hundred twenty shillings as a fine.

38.2. Gif ðises hwæt beforan cyninges ealdormonnes gingran gelimpe oððe cyninges preoste, .xxx. scill. to wite.

38.2. If any of this happens before the king's ealdorman's deputy or the king's priest, 30 shillings as a fine.

39. .XXXVI. Gif hwa on cierlisces monnes flette gefeohte, mid syx scill. gebete ðam ceorle.

39. .XXXVI. If anyone fights in a churlish man's dwelling, he shall compensate with six shillings to that churl.

39.1. Gif he wæpne gebrede 7 no feohte, sie be healfum ðam.

39.1. If he draws a weapon and does not fight, it shall be half that.

39.2. Gif syxhyndum þissa hwæðer gelimpe, ðriefealdlice arise be ðære
cierliscan bote, twelfhyndum men
twyfealdlice be þæs syxhyndan bote.

40. Cyninges burgbryce bið .cxx. scill.
ærcebiscepes hundnigontig scill.,
oðres biscepes 7 ealdormonnes .lx.
scill., twelfhyndes monnes .xxx. scill.
syxhyndes monnes .xv. scill.; ceorles
edorbryce .v. scill.

40.1. Gif ðisses hwæt gelimpe ðenden
fyrd ute sie, oððe in Lenctenfæsten,
hit sie twybote.

40.2. Gif mon in Lenctenne halig ryht
in folce butan leafe alecgge, gebete
mid .cxx. scill.

41. .XXXVII. Se mon se ðe bocland
hæbbe, 7 him his mægas læfden,
þonne setton we, þæt he hit ne moste
sellan of his mægburge, gif þær bið
gewrit oððe gewitnes, ðæt hit ðara
manna forbod wære þe hit on
fruman gestrindon 7 þara þe hit him
sealdon, þæt he swa ne mote. 7 þæt
þonne on cyninges 7 on biscopes gewitnesse gerecce beforan ·his
mægum.

42. .XXXVIII. Eac we beodað: se mon
se ðe his gefan hamsittendne wite,
þæt [Fol. 45a] he ne feohte, ær ðam
he him ryhtes bidde.

42.1. Gif he mægnes hæbbe, þæt he his
gefan beride 7 inne besitte, gehealde
hine .vii. niht inne 7 hine on ne
feohte, gif he inne geðolian wille; 7
þonne ymb .vii. niht, gif he wille on
hand gan 7 wæpenu sellan, gehealde
hine .xxx. nihta gesundne 7 hine his
mægum gebodie 7 his friondum.

39.2. If either of these happen to a six-
hind man, it shall rise threefold in
comparison with the churlish compensation, a twelve-hind man shall
rise by twofold in comparison with
the six-hind compensation.

40. The king's housebreaking shall be
120 shillings, the archbishop's ninety
shillings, other bishop's and ealdorman's 60 shillings, twelve-hind
man's 30 shillings, six-hind man's 15
shillings; churl's housebreaking 5
shillings.

40.1. If any of these happen while the
army is out, or in Lent, it is twice-
compensation.

40.2. If one in Lent abandons the holy
law among the people without leave,
he shall compensate with 120 shillings.

41. XXXVII. The man who has the
bookland, and his kinsmen left it to
him, then we set down, that he can
not sell it from his family, if there is
a document or a witness, so that it
was of the prohibitions of the men
who were in the original line of inheritance and that which to them it
was given, that he can not do so in
that way. And that is then in the
king's and in the bishop's witness
told before his kinsmen.

42. .XXXVIII. Likewise we command:
the man who knows his foe is living
at home, that he shall not fight, before he asks justice of him.

42.1. If he has enough of his kinsmen,
that he besiege and surround his foe
inside, he shall keep him 7 nights inside and not fight him, if he desires
to endure inside; and then after 7
nights, if he desires to go in hand
and to give weapons, keep him safe
30 nights and tell about him to his
kinsmen and his friends.

42.2. Gif he ðonne cirican geierne, sie ðonne be ðære cirican are, swa we ær bufan cwædon.

42.3. Gif he ðonne þæs mægenes ne hæbbe, þæt he hine inne besitte, ride to þam ealdormen, bidde hine fultumes; gif he him fultuman ne wille, ride to cyninge, ær he feohte.

42.4. Eac swelce, gif mon becume on his gefan, 7 he hine ær hamfæstne ne wite, gif he wille his wæpen sellan, hine mon gehealde .xxx. nihta 7 hine his freondum gecyðe; gif he ne wille his wæpenu sellan, þonne mot he feohtan on hine. Gif he wille on hond gan 7 his wæpenu sellan, 7 hwa ofer ðæt on him feohte, gielde swa wer swa wunde swa he gewyrce, 7 wite 7 hæbbe his mæg forworht.

42.5. Eac we cweðað, þæt mon mote mid his hlaforde feohtan orwige, gif mon on ðone hlaford fiohte; swa mot se hlaford mid þy men feohtan.

42.6. Æfter þære ilcan wisan mon mot feohtan mid his geborene mæge, gif hine mon on woh onfeohteð, buton wið his hlaforde: þæt we ne liefað.

42.7. 7 mon mot feohtan orwige, gif he gemeteð oþerne æt his æwum wife, betynedum durum oððe under anre reon, oððe æt his dehter æwum borenre oððe æt his swistær borenre oððe æt his medder ðe wære to æwum wife forgifen his fæder.

43. .XXXVIIII. [Fol. 45b] Eallum

42.2. If he then runs to a church, let it then be the privilege of the church, just as we previously said above.

42.3. If he then not have the power afterwards, so that he might besiege him inside, ride to the ealdorman, ask him of his help; if he does not wish to help him, ride to the king, before he should fight.

42.4. Likewise, if a man should come upon his foe, and he previously did not know him to be settled in his house, if he wishes to surrender his weapons, a man may hold him 30 nights and call his friends to him; if he does not wish to surrender his weapons, then he may fight against him. If he wishes to yield and surrender his weapons, and anyone fights against him beyond that, he shall pay the wergild in accordance with the wound he makes, and the fine and have his kinsmen condemned.

42.5. Also we say, that a man may fight in company with his lord without liability for wergild, if one should fight against that lord; just as the lord may fight in company with his man.

42.6. After the same manner a man may fight in company with his born kinsman, if a man should wrongly fight him, except against his lord: that we do not allow.

42.7. And a man may fight without liability for wergild, if he encounters another man with his lawful wife, shut indoors or under a single blanket, or with his lawful born daughter or with his born sister or with his mother who was as lawful wife given to his father.

43. .XXXVIIII. To all free men these

frioum monnum ðas dagas sien forgifene, butan þeowum monnum 7 esnewyrhtan: .xii. dagas on gehhol 7 ðone dæg þe Crist ðone deofol oferswiðde 7 sanctus Gregorius gemynddæg 7 .vii. dagas to eastron 7 .vii. ofer 7 an dæg æt sancte Petres tide 7 sancte Paules 7 on hærfeste ða fullan wican ær sancta Marian mæssan 7 æt Eallra haligra weorðunge anne dæg. 7 .iiii. Wodnesdagas on .iiii. ymbrenwicum ðeowum monnum eallum sien forgifen, þam þe him leofost sie to sellanne æghwæt ðæs ðe him ænig mon for Godes noman geselle oððe hie on ænegum hiora hwilsticcum geearnian mægen.

44. .XL. Heafodwunde to bote, gif ða ban beoð butu ðyrel, .xxx. scill. geselle him mon.

44.1. Gif ðæt uterre ban bið þyrel, geselle .xv. scill. to bote.

45. .XLI. Gif in feaxe bið wund inces lang, geselle anne scilling to bote.

45.1. Gif beforan feaxe bið wund inces lang, twegen scill. to bote.

46. .XLII. Gif him mon aslea oþer eare of, geselle .xxx. scill. to bote.

46.1. Gif se hlyst oðstande, þæt he ne mæge gehieran, geselle .lx. scill. to bote.

47. .XLIII. Gif mon men eage ofaslea, geselle him mon .lx. scill. 7 .vi. scill. 7 .vi. pæningas 7 ðriddan dæl pæninges to bote.

47.1. Gif hit in ðam heafde sie, 7 he noht geseon ne mæge mid, stande ðriddan dæl þære bote inne.

days are to be given, except to slave men and hirelings: 12 days at Christmas and the day which Christ overcame the devil and Saint Gregory's anniversary and 7 days at Easter and 7 beyond and one day at Saint Peter's feast-day and Saint Paul's and at harvest-time a full week before Saint Mary's mass-day and one day at All Saint's Day and 4 Wednesdays in the 4 Ember-weeks are given to the slave men, who may sell whatever is most pleasing to them, that which any man gives to them God's name or what they may earn in any of their odd moments.

44. .XL. In compensation for a head-wound, if the bones are both pierced, a man shall give 30 shillings to him.

44.1. If the outer bone is pierced, he shall give 15 shillings for compensation.

45. .XLI. If a wound in the hair is of an inch long, he shall give one shilling for compensation.

45.1. If before the hair is a wound of an inch long, two shillings for compensation.

46. .XLII. If a man strikes the ear off another, he shall give 30 shillings for compensation.

46.1. If the sense of hearing ceases, that he can not hear, he shall give 60 shillings for compensation.

47. .XLIII. If a man smites out a man's eye, the man shall give to him 60 shillings and 6 shillings and 6 pennies and a third portion of a penny for compensation.

47.1. If it is in the head, and he can not see with it, a third portion of the compensation shall stand in.

131

48. Gif mon oðrum þæt neb ofaslea, gebete him mid .lx. scill.

49. Gif mon oðrum ðone toð onforan heafde ofaslea, gebete þæt mid .viii. scill.

49.1. Gif hit sie se wongtoð, geselle .iii. scill. to bote.

49.2. Monnes tux bið [Fol. 46a] .xv. scill. weorð.

50. Gif monnes ceacan mon forslihð, þæt hie beoð forode, gebete mid .xv. scill.

50.1. Monnes cinban, gif hit bið to-clofen, geselle mon .xii. scill. to bote.

51. Gif monnes ðrotbolla bið þyrel, ge-bete mid .xii. scill.

52. Gif monnes tunge bið of heafde oþres monnes dædum don, þæt biþ gelic 7 eagan bot.

53. Gif mon bið on eaxle wund, þæt þæt liðseaw utflowe, gebete mid .xxx. scill.

54. Gif se earm bið forad bufan elm-bogan, þær sculon .xv. scill. to bote.

55. Gif ða earmscancan beoð begen forade, sio bot bið .xxx. scill.

56. Gif se ðuma bið ofaslægen, þam sceal .xxx. scill. to bote.

56.1. Gif se nægl bið ofaslegen, ðam sculon .v. scill. to bote.

57. Gif se scytefinger bið ofaslegen, sio bot bið .xv. scill.; his nægles bið .iii. scill.

58. Gif se midlesta finger sie ofaslegen, sio bot bið .xii. scill.; 7 his nægles bot bið .ii. scill.

59. Gif se goldfinger sie ofaslegen, to

48. If a man smites the nose off another, he shall compensate him with 60 shillings.

49. If a man smites out the tooth of an-other from in front of the head, he shall compensate that with 8 shillings.

49.1. If it is the molar, he shall give 3 shillings for compensation.

49.2. A man's canine is worth 15 shillings.

50. If a man strikes a man's cheeks, so that they are broken down, he shall compensate him with 15 shillings.

50.1. A man's chin-bone, if it is split, a man shall give 12 shillings for com-pensation.

51. If a man's windpipe is pierced, he shall compensate with 12 shillings.

52. If a man's tongue is done from the head by another man's deeds, that shall be like as if eye compensation.

53. If a man is wounded in the shoul-der, so that the joint-fluid flows out, he shall compensate with 30 shillings.

54. If the arm is broken above the elbow, then he is obliged 15 shillings for compensation.

55. If the arm-bones are both broken, the compensation shall be 30 shillings.

56. If the thumb is struck off, that must be 30 shillings for compensation.

56.1. If the nail is struck off, that must be 5 shillings for compensation.

57. If the forefinger is struck off, the compensation shall be 15 shillings, its nail's is 3 shillings.

58. If the middle finger is struck off, the compensation shall be 12 shillings, and its nail's compensation shall be 2 shillings.

59. If the ring-finger is struck off, for

þam sculon .xvii. scill. to bote; 7 his nægles .iiii. scill. to bote.

60. Gif se lytla finger bið ofaslegen, ðam sceal to bote .viiii. scill., 7 an scilling his nægles, gif se sie ofaslegen.
61. Gif mon bið on hrif wund, geselle him mon .xxx. scill. to bote.

61.1. Gif he ðurhwund bið, æt gehweðerum muðe .xx. scill.
62. Gif monnes ðeoh bið þyrel, geselle him mon .xxx. scill. to bote.

62.1. Gif hit forad sie, sio bot eac bið .xxx. scill.
63. Gif se sconca bið þyrel beneoðan cneowe, ðær sculon .xii. scill. to bote.
63.1. Gif he forad sie beneoðan cneowe, geselle him .xxx. scill. to bote.
64. Gif sio micle ta bið ofaslegen, geselle him .xx. scill. to bote.

64.1. Gif hit sie sio æfterre ta, .xv. scill. to bote geselle him mon.

64.2. Gif seo midleste ta [Fol. 46b] sie ofaslegen, þær sculon .viiii. scill. to bote.
64.3. Gif hit bið sio feorþe ta, ðær sculon .vi. scill. to bote.
64.4. Gif sio lytle ta sie ofaslegen, geselle him .v. scill.
65. Gif mon sie on þa herðan to ðam swiðe wund, þæt he ne mæge bearn gestrienan, gebete him ðæt mid .lxxx. scill.
66. Gif men sie se earm mid honda mid ealle ofacorfen beforan elmbogan, gebete ðæt mid .lxxx. scill.

that must be 17 shillings for compensation, and its nail's 4 shillings for compensation.

60. If the little finger is struck off, that must be 9 shillings for compensation, and one shilling for its nail, if it is struck off.
61. If a man is wounded in the belly, a man shall give to him 30 shillings for compensation.

61.1. If he is pierced through, to either opening that is 20 shillings.
62. If a man's thigh is pierced, a man shall give to him 30 shillings for compensation.

62.1. If it is broken, the compensation also is 30 shillings.
63. If the shin is pierced beneath the knee, there must be 12 shillings for compensation.
63.1. If he is broken beneath the knee, he shall give to him 30 shillings for compensation.
64. If the great toe is struck off, he shall give to him 20 shillings for compensation.

64.1. If it is the second toe, and man shall give 15 shillings for compensation to him.

64.2. If the middle toe is struck off, there must be 9 shillings for compensation.
64.3. If it is the fourth toe, there must be 6 shillings for compensation.
64.4. If the little toe is struck off, he shall give to him 5 shillings.
65. If a man is in the testicles severely wounded to such an extent, that he can not beget children, he shall compensate him for that with 80 shillings.
66. If to a man the arm with the hand is altogether cut off before the elbow, he shall compensate that with 80 shillings.

66.1. Æghwelcere wunde beforan feaxe 7 beforan sliefan 7 beneoðan cneowe sio bot bið twysceatte mare.

67. Gif sio lendenbræde bið forslegen, þær sceal .lx. scill. to bote.

67.1. Gif hio bið onbestungen, geselle .xv. scill. to bote.

67.2. Gif hio bið ðurhðyrel, ðonne sceal ðær .xxx. scill. to bote.

68. Gif mon bið in eaxle wund, gebete mid .lxxx. scill., gif se mon cwic sie.

69. Gif mon oðrum ða hond utan forslea, geselle him .xx. scill. to bote, gif hine mon gelacnian mæge.

69.1. Gif hio healf onweg fleoge, þonne sceal .xl. scill. to bote.

70. Gif mon oþrum rib forslea binnan gehaldre hyde, geselle .x. scill. to bote.

70.1. Gif sio hyd sie tobrocen, 7 mon ban ofado, geselle .xv. scill. to bote.

71. Gif monnes eage him mon ofaslea, oððe his hand oððe his fot, ðær gæð gelic bot to eallum: .vi. pæningas 7 .vi. scill. 7 .lx. scill. 7 ðriddan dæl pæninges.

72. Gif monnes sconca bið ofaslegen wið ðæt cneou, ðær sceal .lxxx. scill. to bote.

73. Gif mon oðrum ða sculdru forslea, geselle him mon .xx. scill. to bote.

74. Gif hie mon inbeslea 7 mon ban ofado, geselle mon ðæs to bote .xv. scill.

75. Gif mon ða greatan sinwe forslea, gif hie mon gelacnian mæge, þæt hio hal sie, geselle .xii. scill. to bote.

66.1. For any wound before the hair and before the sleeve and beneath the knee the compensation shall be twice-payment more.

67. If the loin-bone is broken, there must be 60 shillings for compensation.

67.1. If it is penetrated, he shall give 15 shillings for compensation.

67.2. If it is pierced through, then there must be 30 shillings for compensation.

68. If a man is wounded in the shoulder, he shall compensate with 80 shillings, if the man is alive.

69. If a man cuts through the outside of another's hand, he shall give him 20 shillings for compensation, if the man can heal him.

69.1. If it half flies off, then it must be 40 shillings for compensation.

70. If a man breaks another's rib within the skin, he shall give 10 shillings for compensation.

70.1. If the skin is broken, and the man's bone tears out, he shall give 15 shillings for compensation.

71. If a man strikes out a man's eye, or his hand or his foot, then goes the same compensation for all: 6 pennies and 6 shillings and 60 shillings and a third portion of a penny.

72. If a man's shin is struck off at the knee, there must be 80 shillings for compensation.

73. If a man breaks the shoulder of another, the man shall give to him 20 shillings for compensation.

74. If a man hacks into it and the man's bone tears out, the man shall give for this 15 shillings for compensation.

75. If a man then cuts through the great sinew, if the man can heal it, that it shall be whole, he shall give 7 shillings for compensation.

75.1. Gif se mon healt sie for þære sinwe wunde, 7 hine mon gelacnian ne mæge, geselle .xxx. scill. to bote.

76. Gif ða [Fol. 47a] smalan sinwe mon forslea, geselle him mon .vi. scill. to bote.

77. Gif mon oðrum ða geweald forslea uppe on þam sweoran 7 forwundie to þam swiðe, þæt he nage þære geweald, 7 hwæðre lifie swa gescended, geselle him mon .c. scill. to bote, buton him witan ryhtre 7 mare gereccan.

[Ine Prologue]

.XLIIII. Ic Ine, mid Godes gife Wesseaxna kyning, mid geðeahte 7 mid lare Cenredes mines fæder 7 Heddes mines biscepes 7 Eorcenwoldes mines biscepes, mid eallum minum ealdormonnum 7 þæm ieldstan witum minre ðeode 7 eac micelre gesomnunge Godes ðeowa, wæs smeagende be ðære hælo urra sawla 7 be ðam staþole ures rices, þætte ryht æw 7 ryhte cynedomas ðurh ure folc gefæstnode 7 getrymede wæron, þætte nænig ealdormonna ne us undergeðeodedra æfter þam wære awendende ðas ure domas.

[Ine's Laws]

1. .XLV. Ærest we bebeodað, þætte Godes ðeowas hiora ryhtregol on ryht healdan.

1.1. Æfter þam we bebeodað, þætte ealles folces æw 7 domas ðus sien gehealdene:

2. .XLVI. Cild binnan ðritegum nihta sie gefulwad; gif hit swa ne sie, .xxx. scill. gebete.

2.1. Gif hit ðonne sie dead butan fulwihte, gebete he hit mid eallum ðam ðe he age.

75.1. If the man is lame because of that sinew wound, and the man can not heal it, he shall give 300 shillings for compensation.

76. If a man cuts through the small sinew, the man shall give to him 6 shillings for compensation.

77. If a man strikes another upon the tendon of the neck and severely wounds him to such an extent, that he is unable to have control of it, and yet live so injured, the man shall give to him 100 shillings for compensation, unless the witan a more just and greater one to him.

[Ine's Prologue]

.XLIIII. I Ine, by God's grace king of the West-Saxons, with the counsel and with the teaching of Cenred my father and of Hædde my bishop and of Eorcenwald my bishop, with all of my ealdormen and the chief councillors of my people and also a great council of God's servants, were deliberating about the salvation of our souls, and about the condition of our kingdom, that just law and just royal ordinances were established and fortified, so that not any of the ealdormen nor any of us subjects later would turn from these our judgments.

[Ine's Laws]

1. .XLV. First we command, that God's servants hold their canon in correctness.

1.1. After that we command, that all of the law of the people and judgments are thus held:

2. .XLVI. A child within thirty nights shall be baptized, if it is not so, 30 shillings he shall compensate.

2.1. If it hen is dead without baptism, he shall compensate for it with all that he owns.

3. .XLVII. Gif ðeowmon wyrce on Sun-
nandæg be his hlafordes hæse, sie he
frioh, 7 se hlaford geselle .xxx. scill.
to wite.

3.1. Gif þonne se ðeowa butan his gewitnesse wyrce, þolie his hyde.

3.2. Gif ðonne se frigea ðy dæge wyrce
butan his hlafordes hæse, ðolie his
freotes.

4. .XLVIII. [Fol. 47b] Ciricsceattas sin
agifene be sancte Martines mæssan;
gif hwa ðæt ne gelæste, sie he scyldig
.lx. scill. be .xii.fealdum agife þone
ciricsceat.

5. .XLVIIII. Gif hwa sie deaðes scyldig
7 he cirican geierne, hæbbe his feorh
7 bete, swa him ryht wisige.

5.1. Gif hwa his hyde forwyrce 7
cirican geierne, sie him sio swingelle
forgifen.

6. .L. Gif hwa gefeohte on cyninges
huse, sie he scyldig ealles his ierfes,
7 sie on cyninges dome, hwæðer he
lif age þe nage.

6.1. Gif hwa on mynster gefeohte, .cxx.
scill. gebete.

6.2. Gif hwa on ealdormonnes huse
gefeohte oððe on oðres geðungenes
witan, .lx. scill. gebete he 7 oþer .lx.
geselle to wite.

6.3. Gif ðonne on gafolgeldan huse
oððe on gebures gefeohte, .cxx. scill.
to wite geselle 7 þam gebure .vi. scill.

6.4. 7 þeah hit sie on middum felda
gefohten, .cxx. scill. to wite sie a-
gifen.

6.5. Gif ðonne on gebeorscipe hie ge-
ciden, 7 oðer hiora mid geðylde hit

3. .XLVII. If a servant works on Sunday
at his lord's bidding, he shall be free,
and the lord shall pay 30 shillings for
a fine.

3.1. If then the servant works without
his knowledge, he shall suffer in his
skin.

3.2. If then a master works that day
without his lord's bidding, he shall
be reduced to slavery.

4. .XLVIII. Church-scot may be paid
at Saint Martin's mass; if anyone
does not pay that, he is to be liable
of 60 shillings by 12-fold he shall pay
that church-scot.

5. .XLVIIII. If anyone is guilty of death
and he runs to a church, he shall
have his life and shall compensate,
just as justice directs him.

5.1. If anyone is convicted in his skin
and runs to the church, the whip
shall be forgiven for him.

6. .L. If anyone should fight in the
king's house, he shall be liable of all
his property, and shall be in the
king's judgment, whether he shall
own his life or not.

6.1. If anyone should fight in the minister, he shall compensate 120
shillings.

6.2. If anyone should fight in the ealdorman's house or in that of another
distinguished councilor, he shall
compensate 60 shillings and he shall
give another 60 for a fine.

6.3. If he then should fight in a tenant's
house or in a free peasant's, he shall
give 120 for a fine and 6 shillings to
that free peasant.

6.4. And though the fighting is in the
middle of open fields, he is to pay
120 shillings for a fine.

6.5. If then in a feast they contend, and
one of the two of them with patience

forbere, geselle se oðer .xxx. scill. to
wite.

7. .LI. Gif hwa stalie, swa his wif nyte
7 his bearn, geselle .lx. scill. to wite.

7.1. Gif he ðonne stalie on gewitnesse
ealles his hiredes, gongen hie ealle on
ðeowot.

7.2. .x. wintre cniht mæg bion ðiefðe
gewita.

8. .LII. Gif hwa him ryhtes bidde beforan hwelcum scirmen oððe oþrum
deman 7 abiddan ne mæge, 7 him
wedd sellan nelle, gebete .xxx. scill.
7 binnan .vii. nihton gedo hine
ryhtes wierðne.

9. .LIII. Gif hwa wrace do, ærðon he
him ryhtes bidde, þæt he him
on[Fol. 48a]nime agife 7 forgielde 7
gebete mid .xxx. scill.

10. .LIIII. Gif hwa binnan þam
gemærum ures rices reaflac 7 nied-
næme do, agife he ðone reaflac 7
geselle .lx. scill. to wite.

11. .LV. Gif hwa his agenne geleod bebycgge, ðeowne oððe frigne, ðeah he
scyldig sie, ofer sæ, forgielde hine his
were.

12. .LVI. Gif ðeof sie gefongen, swelte
he deaðe, oððe his lif be his were
man aliese.

13. .LVII. Gif hwa beforan biscepe his
gewitnesse 7 his wed aleoge, gebete
mid .cxx. scill.

13.1. Ðeofas we hatað oð .vii. men;
from .vii. hloð oð .xxxv.; siððan bið
here.

14. .LVIII. Se ðe hloþe betygen sie,
geswicne se hine be .cxx. hida oððe
swa bete.

15. .LVIIII. Se ðe hereteama betygen

7. .LI. If anyone steals without his wife
and children knowing, he pays 60
shillings for a fine.

7.1. If he then steals with his whole
household knowing, they all go into
slavery.

7.2. A 10-year-old boy may be blamed
for a theft.

8. .LII. If anyone asks for justice for
himself before any shireman or other
judge and can not obtain it, and will
not give his pledge to him, he shall
compensate 30 shillings and within
7 nights make him worthy of justice.

9. .LIII. If anyone enacts a penalty, before he asks him for justice, he shall
give back what he received from him
and he shall pay for it and he shall
compensate with 30 shillings.

10. .LIIII. If anyone within the borders
of our kingdom does robbery and
seizure, he shall repay what he plun-
dered and give 60 shillings for a fine.

11. .LV. If anyone should sell his own
fellow-countryman, servant or free,
though he be guilty, over the sea, he
shall pay his wergild for him.

12. .LVI. If a thief is caught, he shall
suffer death, or his life shall be redeemed by his wergild.

13. .LVII. If anyone is false in his witness and his pledge before a bishop,
he shall compensate with 120
shillings.

13.1. Up to 7 men we call thieves; from
7 up to 35 a band; afterwards it is an
army.

14. .LVIII. He who is accused with a
band, he shall clear himself with 120
hides or he shall compensate in such
wise.

15. .LVIIII. He who is accused in a

sie, he hine be his wergilde aliese
oððe be his were geswicne.

15.1. Se að sceal bion healf be
huslgengum.

15.2. Þeof, siððan he bið on cyninges
bende, nah he þa swicne.

16. .LX. Se ðe ðeof ofslihð, se mot
gecyðan mid aðe, þæt he hine synnigne ofsloge, nalles ða gegildan.

17. .LXI. Se ðe forstolen flæsc findeð 7
gedyrneð, gif he dear, he mot mid
aðe gecyðan, þæt he hit age; se ðe hit
ofspyreð, he ah ðæt meldfeoh.

18. .LXII. Cierlisc mon gif he oft betygen wære, gif he æt siðestan sie gefongen, slea mon hond oððe fot.

19. .LXIII. Cyninges geneat, gif his wer
bið twelfhund scill., he mot swerian
for syxtig hida, gif he bið
huslgengea.

20. .LXIIII. [Fol. 48b] Gif feorcund
mon oððe fremde butan wege geond
wudu gonge 7 ne hrieme ne horn
blawe, for ðeof he bið to profianne:
oððe to sleanne oððe to aliesanne.

21. .LXV. Gif mon ðonne þæs ofslæg-
enan weres bidde, he mot gecyþan,
þæt he hine for ðeof ofsloge, nalles
þæs ofslegenan gegildan ne his
hlaford.

21.1. Gif he hit ðonne dierneð, 7 weorð-
eð ymb long yppe, ðonne rymeð he
ðam deadan to ðam aðe, þæt hine
moton his mægas unsyngian.

22. .LXVI. Gif ðin geneat stalie 7 losie
ðe, gif ðu hæbbe byrgean, mana
þone þæs angyldes; gif he næbbe,
gyld ðu þæt angylde, 7 ne sie him
no ðy ðingodre.

23. .LXVII. Gif mon elðeodigne ofslea,

predatory excursion, he shall redeem
himself with his wergild or he shall
clear himself with his wergild.

15.1. The oath shall be half with com-
municants.

15.2. A thief, after he is in the king's
bond, he may not then clear himself.

16. .LX. He who kills a thief, he may
declare with an oath, that he killed
him as a criminal, not at all the
brotherhood.

17. .LXI. He who finds stolen meat and
keeps it secret, if he dares, he may
declare with an oath, that he owns
it; he who traces it out, he owns that
informer's reward.

18. .LXII. A churlish man, if he were
often accused, if he at last is caught,
strike off his hand or foot.

19. .LXIII. The king's vassal, if his
wergild is 1200 shillings, he may
swear equivalent to 60 hides, if he is
a communicant.

20. .LXIIII. If a foreign man or stranger
goes through the woods off the track
and neither cries out nor blows a
horn, he shall be taken for a thief:
either to be killed or to be redeemed.

21. .LXV. If a man should then ask for
the wergild of the slain, he may declare, that he killed him as a thief,
not at all the slain man's
brotherhood nor his lord.

21.1. If he then hides it, and it becomes
revealed long after, then he opens up
that dead man for the oath, so that
his kinsmen may exculpate him.

22. .LXVI. If your vassal steals and escapes you, if you have surety, demand then that compensation; if he
does not have it, you pay that compensation, and not for him is there
settlement on that account.

23. .LXVII. If a man kills a foreigner,

se cyning ah twædne dæl weres, þrid-
dan dæl sunu oððe mægas.

23.1. Gif he ðonne mægleas sie, healf
kyninge, healf se gesið.

23.2. Gif hit ðonne abbod sie oððe ab-
bodesse, dælen on þa ilcan wisan wið
þone kyning.

23.3. Wealh gafolgelda .cxx. scill. his
sunu .c., ðeowne .lx., somhwelcne
fiftegum; Weales hyd twelfum.

24. .LXVIII. Gif witeðeow Engliscmon
hine forstalie, ho hine mon 7 ne
gylde his hlaforde.

24.1. Gif hine mon ofslea, ne gylde
hine mon his mægum, gif hie hine
on .xii. monðum ne aliesden.

24.2. Wealh, gif he hafað .v. hida, he
bið syxhynde.

25. .LXVIIII. Gif ciepemon uppe on
folce ceapie, do þæt beforan gewit-
nessum.

25.1. Gif ðiefefioh mon æt ciepan befo,
7 he hit næbbe beforan godum weot-
um geceapod, gecyðe hit be wite,
þæt he ne gewita ne gestala nære,
oððe gielde to wite .vi. 7 .xxx. scill.

26. [Fol. 49a] .LXX. To fundes cildes
fostre, ðy forman geare geselle .vi.
scill., ðy æfterran .xii., ðy ðriddan
.xxx., siððan be his wlite.

27. .LXXI. Se ðe dearnenga bearn
gestrieneð 7 gehileð, nah se his
deaðes wer, ac his hlaford 7 se cyning.

28. .LXXII. Se ðeof gefehð, ah .x. scill.,
7 se cyning ðone ðeof; 7 þa mægas
him swerian aðas unfæhða.

28.1. Gif he ðonne oðierne 7 orige
weorðe, þonne bið he wites scyldig.

28.2. Gif he onsacan wille, do he ðæt
be ðam feo 7 be ðam wite.

the king takes charge of a two-thirds
portion of the wergild, the son or
kinsmen the third portion.

23.1. If he then is kinless, half by the
king, half the thane.

23.2. If it then is an abbot or abbess,
divide in the same way with the
king.

23.3. A Welsh tenant 120 shillings, his
son 100, a servant 60, some with
fifty; a Welshman's hide with twelve.

24. .LXVIII. If an Englishman enslaved
by law steals away, hang him and do
not pay his lord.

24.1. If a man kills him, do not pay his
kin, if they do not redeem him in 12
months.

24.2. A Welshman, if he has 5 hides,
he is a six-hind man.

25. .LXVIIII. If a trader trades inland
with the people, do that before witnesses.

25.1. If a man includes stolen property
with goods, and he has not traded it
before good witnesses, he may declare
it by the fine, that he was not accom-
plice nor was he accessory to theft.

26. .LXX. For tending to a foster-child,
the first year give 6 shillings, the next
12, the third 30, afterwards by its appearance.

27. .LXXI. He who secretly begets a
child and conceals it, is not allowed
the wergild at his death, but his lord
and the king.

28. .LXXII. He who catches thief ob-
tains 10 shillings, and the king the
thief; and his kinsmen to swear oaths
of peace in regards to him.

28.1. If he then runs away and becomes
out of sight, then he shall be responsible for the fine.

28.2. If he desires to dispute, he may do
that by the property or by the fine.

29. .LXXIII. Gif mon sweordes onlæne oðres esne, 7 he losie, gielde he hine ðriddan dæle; gif mon spere selle, healfne; gif he horses onlæne, ealne he hine gylde.

30. .LXXIIII. Gif mon cierliscne monnan fliemanfeorme teo, be his agnum were geladige he hine; gif he ne mæge, gielde hine his agne were; 7 se gesiðmon swa be his were.

31. .LXXV. Gif mon wif gebyccge, 7 sio gyft forð ne cume, agife þæt feoh 7 forgielde 7 gebete þam byrgean, swa his borgbryce sie.

32. .LXXVI. Gif Wilisc mon hæbbe hide londes, his wer bið .cxx. scill.; gif he þonne healfes hæbbe, .lxxx. scill.; gif he nænig hæbbe, .lx. scill.

33. .LXXVII. Cyninges horswealh, se ðe him mæge geærendian, ðæs wergield bið .cc. scill.

34. .LXXVIII. Se ðe on ðære fore wære, þæt mon monnan ofsloge, getriewe hine ðæs sleges 7 ða fore gebete be ðæs ofslegenan wergielde:

34.1. Gif his wergield sie .cc. scill., gebete mid L scill., 7 ðy ilcan [Fol. 49b] ryhte do man be ðam deorborenran.

35. .LXXVIIII. Se ðe ðeof slihð, he mot aðe gecyðan, þæt he hine fleondne for ðeof sloge, 7 þæs deadan mægas him swerian unceases að. Gif he hit þonne dierne, 7 sie eft yppe, þonne forgielde he hine.

35.1. Gif mon to þam men feoh geteme, ðe his ær oðswaren hæfde 7

29. .LXXIII. If a man lends his sword to another's servant, and he runs away, he shall pay him a third portion; if a man gives a spear, half; if he lends a horse, he shall pay him for all.

30. .LXXIIII. If a man accuses a churlish man of harboring fugitives, by his own wergild he may exculpate himself; if he has no kinsmen, he may pay for him with his own wergild; and the thane thus by his wergild.

31. .LXXV. If a man buys a wife, and the nuptials do not happen, return that property and pay double and compensate for that surety, for the same as is his breach of surety.

32. .LXXVI. If a Welshman has a hide of land, his wergild shall be 120 shillings; if he then has half, 80 shillings; if he has none, 60 shillings.

33. .LXXVII. Of the king's groom, he who can carry messages for him, the wergild shall be 200 shillings.

34. .LXXVIII. He who was on the journey, of a man who kills a man, he may exculpate himself of that killing and the journey by compensation in conformity with the wergild of the slain man.

34.1. If his wergild is 200 shillings, he shall compensate with 50 shillings, and do a man the same justice in consideration of nobler birth.

35. .LXXVIIII. He who kills a thief, he must declare an oath, that he killed him fleeing as a thief, and the kinsmen of the dead are to swear an oath of reconciliation for him. If he then hides, and is afterwards discovered, then he shall pay for himself.

35.1. If a man, moreover, vouch to warranty property for a man, which

eft oðswerian wille, oðswerige be ðam wite 7 be ðæs feos weorðe; gif he oðswerian nylle, gebete þone mænan að twybote.

he had before denied on oath, and desires to deny on oath again, he shall deny on oath in conformity with the fine and by the worth of the property; if he desires no the deny on oath, he shall compensate that false oath twice-compensation.

36. .LXXX. Se ðe ðeof gefehð, oðða him mon gefongenne agifð, 7 he hine þonne alæte, oðða þa ðiefðe gedierne, forgielde þone þeof his were.

36.1. Gif he ealdormon sie, ðolie his scire, buton him kyning arian wille.

36. .LXXX. He who catches a thief, or captured one is given to him, and he then loses him, or then hides the theft, he shall pay for that thief with his wergild.

36.1. If he is an ealdorman, he shall lose his office, unless the king desires to pardon him.

37. .LXXXI. Se cirlisca mon, se ðe oft betygen wære ðiefðe, 7 þonne æt siðestan synnigne gefo in ceape oðða elles æt openre scylde, slea him mon hond of oðða fot.

37. .LXXXI. The churlish man, he who often was accused with theft, and then at last is taken guilty in trade or otherwise exposed in crime, strike a hand off him or a foot.

38. .LXXXII. Gif ceorl 7 his wif bearn hæbben gemæne, 7 fere se ceorl forð, hæbbe sio modor hire bearn 7 fede: agife hire mon .vi. scill. to fostre, cu on sumera, oxan on wintra; healden þa mægas þone frumstol, oð ðæt hit gewintred sie.

38. .LXXXII. If a churl and his wife have a child in common, and the churl dies, the mother shall have her child and bring it up: one shall give to her 6 shillings for maintenance, a cow in summer, an ox in winter; the kinsmen shall keep the homestead, until it is an adult.

39. [.LXXXIII.] Gif hwa fare unaliefed fram his hlaforde oðða on oðre scire hine bestele, 7 hine mon geahsige, fare þær he ær wæs 7 geselle his hlaforde .lx. scill.

39. [.LXXXIII.] If anyone travels without permission from his lord or into another shire steals himself away, and one discovers him, he shall go to where he was before and give his lord 60 shillings.

40. .LXXXIIII. Ceorles worðig sceal beon wintres 7 sumeres betyned; gif he bið untyned, 7 recð his neahge-bures ceap in on his agen geat, nah he æt þam ceape nan wuht: adrife hine ut [Fol. 50a] 7 ðolie æfwerd-lan.

40. .LXXXIIII. A churl's farm shall be enclosed winter and summer; if he is unfenced, and his neighbor's cattle go in through his own opening, he has no right at all to that cattle: he shall drive them out and suffer the damage.

41. .LXXXV. Borges mon mot oðsacan, gif he wat, þæt he ryht deð.

41. .LXXXV. A man may deny a pledge, if he knows that he does right.

42. .LXXXVI. Gif ceorlas gærstun hæbben gemænne oððe oþer gedalland to tynanne, 7 hæbben sume getyned hiora dæl, sume næbben, 7 etten hiora gemænan æceras oððe gærs, gan þa þonne, þe ðæt geat agan, 7 gebete þam oðrum þe hiora dæl getynedne hæbben, þone æ-werdlan þe ðær gedon sie. Abidden him æt þam ceape swylc ryht swylce hit kyn sie.

42.1. Gif þonne hryðera hwelc sie þe hegas brece 7 ga in gehwær, 7 se hit nolde gehealdan, se hit age oððe ne mæge, nime se hit on his æcere mete 7 ofslea; 7 nime se agenfrigea his fel 7 flæsc 7 þolie þæs oðres.

43. .LXXXVII. Ðonne mon beam on wuda forbærne, 7 weorðe yppe on þone ðe hit dyde, gielde he fulwite: geselle .lx. scill.; forþamþe fyr bið þeof.

43.1. Gif mon afelle on wuda wel monega treowa, 7 wyrð eft undierne, forgielde .iii. treowu ælc mid .xxx. scill.; ne ðearf he hiora ma geldan, wære hiora swa fela swa hiora wære: forþon sio æsc bið melda, nalles ðeof.

44. .LXXXVIII. Gif mon þonne aceorfe an treow, þæt mæge .xxx. swina undergestandan, 7 wyrð undierne, geselle .lx. scill.

44.1. Gafolhwitel sceal bion æt hiwisce .vi. pæninga weorð.

45. .LXXXVIIII. Burgbryce mon sceal betan .cxx. scill. kyninges 7 biscepes, þær his rice bið; ealdormonnes .lxxx. scill.; cyninges ðegnes .lx. scill.; gesiðcundes monnes landhæbbendes .xxxv.; 7 bi ðon ansacan.

42. .LXXXVI. If churls have a meadow in common or another common land to enclose, and some have their portion enclosed, some have not, and their common acres or grass is grazed, then go henceforth, who owns that opening, and compensate those others who have their portion enclosed, for the damage that was done there. Require from them in respect to that cattle so much justice as it is proper.

42.1. If then it is any of the cattle which break the hedges and go everywhere in there, and he would not restrain it, he who owns it, or he could not, he who finds it on his acreage may take it and kill it; and the owner takes his hide and flesh and forfeits the rest.

43. When a man burns up a tree of the woods, and the one who did it becomes known, he shall pay the full fine: he shall give 60 shillings; because fire is a thief.

43.1. If a man fells in the woods very many trees, and afterwards it is becomes known, he shall pay for 3 trees with 30 shillings each; he does not need to pay for more of them, were there as many as of them as there was: because the axe is the informer, by no means the thief.

44. .LXXXVIII. If a man then cuts down a tree, that 30 swine could stand under, and it becomes known, he shall give 60 shillings.

44.1. The tribute-blanket shall be a hide worth 6 pennies.

45. .LXXXVIIII. A man breaking into the house of the king and bishop shall compensate 120 shillings, where his kingdom is; of an ealdorman's 80 shillings; of a king's thane 60 shillings; of a land-owning man's 35; and then dispute it accordingly.

46. .XC. Ðonne mon monnan betyhð, þæt he ceap forstele oððe for[Fol. 50b]stolenne gefeormie, þonne sceal he be .lx. hida onsacan þære þiefðe, gif he aðwyrðe bið.

46.1. Gif ðonne Englisc onstal ga forð, onsace þonne be twyfealdum; gif hit ðonne bið Wilisc onstal, ne bið se að na ðy mara.

46.2. Ælc mon mot onsacan frymþe 7 werfæhðe, gif he mæg oððe dear.

47. .XCI. Gif mon forstolenne ceap befehð, ne mot hine mon tieman to ðeowum men.

48. .XCII. Gif hwelc mon bið witeðeow niwan geðeowad, 7 hine mon betyhð, þæt he hæbbe ær geðiefed, ær hine mon geðeowode, þonne ah se teond ane swingellan æt him: bedrife hine to swingum be his ceape.

49. .XCII[I]. Gif mon on his mæstenne unaliefed swin gemete, genime þonne .vi. scill. weorð wed.

49.1. Gif hie þonne þær næren oftor þonne æne, geselle scilling se agenfrigea 7 gecyðe, þæt hie þær oftor ne comen, be þæs ceapes weorðe.

49.2. Gif hi ðær tuwa wæren, geselle twegen scill.

49.3. Gif mon nime æfesne on swynum: æt þryfingrum þæt ðridde, æt twyfingrum þæt feorðe, æt þymelum þæt fifte.

50. .XCIIII. Gif gesiðcund mon þingað wið cyning oððe wið kyninges ealdormonnan for his inhiwan oððe wið his hlaford for ðeowe oððe for frige, nah he þær nane witerædenne, se gesið, forðon he him nolde ær yfles gestieran æt ham.

46. .XC. When a man accuses a man, that he stole cattle or harbors stolen goods, then he shall by 60 hides dispute that theft, if he is oath-worthy.

46.1. If then an English charge goes forth, he may dispute by twofold; if it then is a charge by the Welsh, the oath is no more by that account.

46.2. Every man may dispute harboring and feud , if he can or dare.

47. .XCI. If a man lays hold of stolen cattle, the man may not vouch to warranty his servant man.

48. .XCII. If any man is newly enslaved by law, and he is accused that he has stolen before, before the man was legally enslaved, then the accuser is owed one whipping on him: he may drive him to the whipping on penalty of his property.

49. .XCII[I]. If a man finds swine in his mast-pasture without permission, he shall then take a pledge worth 6 shillings.

49.1. If they then were not there more often than once, he shall give a shilling to the owner and declare that they did not come there more often, on penalty of the livestock's worth.

49.2. If they were there twice, he shall give two shillings.

49.3. If a man takes pay for pastorage in swine: by three fingers broad at the third, by two fingers more at the fourth, by a thumb-width more at the fifth.

50. .XCIIII. If a thane-kin man intercedes with the king or with the king's ealdorman for the sake of members of his household or with his lord for the sake of a servant or for the sake of a freeman, he, the

51. .XCV. Gif gesiðcund mon land-
agende forsitte fierd, geselle .cxx.
scill. 7 ðolie his landes; unlanda-
gende .lx. scill.; cierlisc .xxx. scill. to
fierdwite.

52. .XCVI. Se ðe diernum geðingum
betygen sie, geswicne hine be .cxx.
[Fol. 51a] hida þara geðingea oððe
.cxx. scill. geselle.

53. .XCVII. Gif mon forstolenne man
befo æt oþrum, 7 sie sio hand oð-
cwolen, sio hine sealde þam men þe
hine mon ætbefeng, tieme þonne
þone mon to þæs deadan byrgelse,
swa oðer fioh swa hit sie, 7 cyðe on
þam aðe be .lx. hida, þæt sio deade
hond hine him sealde. Þonne hæfð
he þæt wite afylled mid þy aðe, agife
þam agendfrio þone monnan.

53.1. Gif he þonne wite, hwa ðæs
deadan ierfe hæbbe, tieme þonne to
þam ierfe 7 bidde ða hond þe þæt
ierfe hafað, þæt he him gedo þone
ceap unbeceasne oþþe gecyðe, þæt sc
deada næfre þæt ierfe ahte.

54. .XCVIII. Se þe bið werfæhðe be-
togen 7 he onsacan wille þæs sleges
mid aðe, þonne sceal bion on þære
hyndenne an kyningæde be .xxx.
hida, swa be gesiðcundum men swa
be cierliscum, swa hwæþer swa hit
sie.

54.1. Gif hine mon gilt, þonne mot he
gesellan on þara hyndenna gehwelc-
ere monnan 7 byrnan 7 sweord on
þæt wergild, gif he ðyrfe.

thane-kin man, has no right there to
any fine, because he would not previously restrain them from evil at
home.

51. .XCV. If a land-owning thane-kin
man neglects military service, he
shall give 120 shillings and lose his
lands; a landless man 60 shillings; a
churlish man 30 shillings as a military service fine.

52. .XCVI. He who is accused of secret
meetings, he may clear himself of
those meetings with 120 hides or he
may give 120 shillings.

53. .XCVII. If a man attaches at law a
man stolen from another, and the
possessor is dead, he who sold that
man who himself attached the man
at law, he shall then vouch to warranty that man by the dead's tomb,
either for other property or what it
might be, and declare in that oath
by 60 hides, that the dead possessor
sold him to him. Then he has
satisfied that fine with the oath, he
shall return that man to the owner.

53.1. If he then knows who has the
dead's inheritance, he shall then
vouch to warranty by that inheritance and ask the possessor who has
that inheritance the he make that
property incontestable by him or declare that the dead never owned that.

54. .XCVIII. He who is accused breach
of peace and he desires to dispute
those killings with an oath, then
there shall be in a community of
hundred men one entitled to take
oath as a king's thane by 30 hides,
either by a thane-kin man or by a
churlish man, whichever it may be.

54.1. If the man is guilty himself, then
he must give to each in the community of a hundred men a servant and

54.2. Witeðeowne monnan Wyliscne mon sceal bedrifan be .xii. hidum swa ðeowne to swingum, Engliscne be feower 7 .xxx. hida.

55. .XCVIIII. Ewo bið mid hire giunge sceape scilling weorð oþþæt .xii. niht ofer Eastran.

56. .C. Gif mon hwelcne ceap gebygð 7 he ðonne onfinde him hwelc un-hælo on binnan .xxx. nihta, þonne weorpe þone ceap to honda; oððe swerie, þæt he him nan facn on nyste, þa he hine him sealde.

57. .CI. [Fol. 51b] Gif ceorl ceap forstilð 7 bireð into his ærne, 7 befehð þærinne mon, þonne bið se his dæl synnig butan þam wife anum, forðon hio sceal hire ealdore hieran: gif hio dear mid aðe gecyðan, þæt hio þæs forstolenan ne onbite, nime hire ðriddan sceat.

58. .CII. Oxan horn bið .x. pæninga weorð.

59. .CIII. Cuuhorn bið twegea pæninga; oxan tægl bið scill. weorð, cus bið fifa; oxan eage bið .v. pæninga weorð, cus bið scilling weorþ

59.1. Mon sceal simle to beregafole a-gifan æt anum wyrhtan .vi. wæga.

60. .CIIII. Se ceorl se ðe hæfð oðres geoht ahyrod, gif he hæbbe ealle on foðre to agifanne, gesceawige mon, agife ealle; gif he næbbe, agife healf on fodre, healfe on oþrum ceape.

61. .CV. Ciricsceat mon sceal agifan to þam healme 7 to þam heorðe, þe se mon on bið to middum wintra.

a byrnie and a sword for that wergild, if he is required.

54.2. A legally enslaved Welshman shall driven as a slave to a whipping by 12 hides, an Englishman by four and 30 hides.

55. .XCVIII. A ewe with her young sheep is worth a shilling until 12 nights after Easter.

56. .C. If a man buys any cattle and he then finds them unhealthy within 30 nights, then hand that cattle over; or he shall swear that he knew of no fraud to him when he sold it to him.

57. .CI. If a churl steals cattle and bears it into his house , and a man seizes it therein, then he is guilty for his portion alone, without his wife, be-cause she must obey her master: if she dares to declare an oath, that she did not partake of the stolen cattle, she shall take for herself a third of the property.

58. .CII. An ox's horn is worth 10 pen-nies.

59. .CIII. A cow-horn is two pennies; an ox's tail is worth a shilling, a cow's is five pennies; an ox's eye is worth 5 pennies, a cow's is worth a shilling.

59.1. A man shall always pay to one la-borer a 6 weight of rent paid in bar-ley.

60. .CIIII. The churl who has hired an-other's yoke, if he has enough in fod-der to pay for all, one shall see he shall pay for all; if he does not have it, he shall pay half in fodder, half in other property.

61. .CV. A man must pay church-scot from the field-stubble and from the hearth, where the man is in the mid-dle of winter.

62. .CVI. Þonne mon bið tyhtlan betygen, 7 hine mon bedrifeð to ceape,
nah þonne self nane wiht to gesel-
lanne beforan ceape. Þonne gæð oðer
mon, seleð his ceap fore, swa he
þonne geþingian mæge, on ða ræd-
enne, þe he him ga to honda, oð ðæt
he his ceap him geinnian mæge.
Þonne betyhð hine mon eft oþre siðe
7 bedrifð to ceape. Gif hine forð
nele forstandan se ðe him ær ceap
foresealde, 7 he hine þonne forfehð,
þolige þonne his ceapes se, ðe he him
ær foresealde.

62. .CVI. When a man is accused of a
charge, and the man himself is
driven to a bargain, then does not
own anything to give in the presence
of the bargain. Then goes another
man, gives his goods for his sake, just
as he then may intercede, on the resolution that he yields to him until he
may restore his goods to him. Then
a man accuses him again another
time and drives him to a bargain. If
he who lost goods to him before does
not desire to help him further, and
he then forfeits himself, he shall then
lose his property, he who lost to him
before.

63. .CVII. Gif gesiðcund mon fare,
þonne mot he habban his gerefan
mid him 7 his smið 7 his cildfestran.

63. .CVII. If a thane-kin man sets
forth, then he may have his steward
with him and his smith and his
nurse.

64. .CVIII. Se ðe hæfð .xx. hida, se
sceal tæcnan .xii. hida gesettes
landes, þonne he faran wille.

64. .CVIII. He who has 20 hides, he
shall show 12 hides of sown land
when he desires to set forth.

65. .CVIIII. [Fol. 52a] Se ðe hæfð .x.
hida, se sceal tæcnan .vi. hida
gesettes landes.

65. .CVIIII. He who has 10 hides, he
shall show 6 hides of sown land.

66. .CX. Se ðe hæbbe þreora hida,
tæcne oþres healfes.

66. .CX. He who has three hides, he
shall show one and a half.

67. .CXI. Gif mon geþingað gyrde
landes oþþe mare to rædegafole 7
geereð, gif se hlaford him wile þæt
land aræran to weorce 7 to gafole, ne
þearf he him onfon, gif he him nan
botl ne selð, 7 þolie þara æcra.

67. .CXI. If a man makes an agreement
to rent a quarter of a hide or more
and plows it, if the lord desires to
raise [the rent of] that land for him
through work and through rent, he
need not accept it from him, if he
does not give a house to him, and
shall lose those crops.

68. .CXII. Gif mon gesiðcundne monnan adrife, fordrife þy botle, næs
þære setene.

68. .CXII. If a thane-kin man is driven
out, he shall be driven away from the
dwelling, not from the plantation
there.

69. .CXIII. Sceap sceal gongan mid his
fliese oð midnesumor; oððe gilde
þæt flies mid twam pæningum.

69. .CXIII. Sheep shall go with his
fleece until the middle of summer; or
pay for that fleece with two pennies.

70. .CXIIII. Æt twyhyndum were mon

70. .CXIIII. For a man with a two—

sceal sellan to monbote .xxx. scill.,
æt .vi. hyndum .lxxx. scill., æt .xii.
hyndum .cxx. scill.

70.1. Æt .x. hidum to fostre .x. fata
hunies, .ccc. hlafa, .xii. ambra Wilisc
ealað, .xxx. hluttres, tu eald hriðeru
oððe .x. weðeras, .x. gees, .xx.
henna, .x. cesas, amber fulne
buteran, .v. leaxas, .xx. pundwæga
foðres 7 hundteontig æla.

71. .CXV. Gif mon sie wertyhtlan be-
togen 7 he hit þonne geondette beforan aðe 7 onsace ær, bide mon mid
þære witerædenne, oð ðæt se wer
gegolden sie.

72. .CXVI. Gif mon wergildðeof
gefehð, 7 he losige ðy dæge þam
monnum ðe hine gefoð, þeah hine
mon gefo ymb niht, nah him mon
mare æt ðonne fulwite.

73. .CXVII. Gif hit bið niht eald þiefð,
gebeten þa þone gylt þe hine gefeng-
on, swa hie geþingian mægen wið
cyning 7 his gerefan.

74. .CXVIII. Gif ðeowwealh Engliscne
monnan ofslihð, þonne sceal se ðe
hine ah weorpan hine to honda
hlaforde 7 mægum [Fol. 52b] oððe
.lx. scill. gesellan wið his feore.

74.1. Gif he þonne þone ceap nelle
foregesellan, þonne mot hine se
hlaford gefreogean; gielden siððan
his mægas þone wer, gif he mægburg
hæbbe freo; gif he næbbe, heden his
þa gefan.

74.2. Ne þearf se frige mid þam
þeowan mæg gieldan, buton he him
wille fæhðe of aceapian, ne se þeowa
mid þy frigean.

hind wergild a man shall give for a
fine paid to his lord 30 shillings, for
a 6-hind man 80 shillings, for a 12-
hind man 120 shillings.

70.1. For the maintenance for 10
hides:10 vats of honey, 300 loaves, 12
vessels Welsh ale, 30 of the clear
[ale], two old cattle or 10 sheep, 10
geese, 20 hens, 10 cheeses, a vessel
full of butter, 5 salmon, 20 pound-
weight of fodder and a hundred eels.

71. .CXV. If a man is accused of a
charge invoking the payment of
wergild and he then confesses it
before the oath, the man shall wait
for the fine, until the wergild is paid.

72. .CXVI. If a man who is a thief who
might be redeemed by payment of
his wergild is caught, and he escapes
that day from the men who caught
him, yet a man catches him [again]
around night, the man has a right to
no more than the full fine.

73. .CXVII. If the theft is a night old,
they shall then compensate for their
fault who [first] caught him, just as
they may determine with the king
and his reeve.

74. .CXVIII. If a Welsh servant kills
and English man, then he who owns
him shall hand him over to the lord
and kinsmen or he shall give 60
shillings against his life.

74.1. If he then for that property will
not pay, then the lord may set him
free; then his kinsmen pay for that
wergild, if he has a free family; if he
does not have [one], his enemies may
then seize him.

74.2. There is no need for a freeman to
pay for a kinsman together with a
servant, unless he desires to buy him
out of a vendetta, nor the servant
with the freeman.

75. .CXVIIII. Gif mon ceap befehþ forstolenne, 7 sio hond tiemð þonne, sio hine mon ætbefehþ, to oþrum men, gif se mon hine þonne onfon ne wille 7 sægþ, þæt he him næfre þæt ne sealde, ac sealde oþer, þonne mot se gecyðan, se ðe hit tiemþ to þære honda, þæt he him nan oðer ne sealde buton þæt ilce.

76. .CXX. Gif hwa oðres godsunu slea oððe his godfæder, sie sio mægbot 7 sio manbot gelic; weaxe sio bot be ðam were, swa ilce swa sio manbot deð þe þam hlaforde sceal.

76.1. Gif hit þonne kyninges godsunu sie, bete be his were þam cyninge swa ilce swa þære mægþe.

76.2. Gif he þonne on þone geonbyrde þe hine slog, þonne ætfealle sio bot þæm godfæder, swa ilce swa þæt wite þam hlaforde deð.

76.3. Gif hit biscepsunu sie, sie be healfum þam.

75. .CXVIIII. If a man attaches stolen property at law, and the receiver then vouches for warranty, the man who attached [it] at law, to another man; if the man then does not take it and says that he never gave it to him, but gave [something] other, then he may declare, he who vouches it for warranty to the receiver, that he gave to him none other but that same thing.

76. .CXX. If anyone kills another's godson or his godfather, the compensation to the slain's kin and the compensation to the slain's lord is the same; the compensation is to increase in conformity with the wergild, just as the price of compensation to the lord does, so shall that [payment] to the lord.

76.1. If it is then the king's godson, he shall compensate to the king in accordance with his wergild just as the same as for the kinsmen.

76.2. If he then was striving against him whom he killed in that [conflict], then the compensation to the godfather shall be reduced, just the same as the fine to the lord does.

76.3. If it is a bishop's son, it is by half of that.

Notes

Introduction

1. The letter dates to the first quarter of the tenth century, and is addressed to King Edward the Elder, Alfred's son. The letter transmits ealdorman Ordlaf's defense of his godson Helmstan's claim to five hides of land at Fonthill in Wiltshire. The amount of a "hide" of land was variable, but typically amounted to about 120 acres. For the full text and translation of the letter, along with commentary, see Simon Keynes, "The Fonthill Letter," *Words, Texts, and Manuscripts: Studies in Anglo-Saxon Culture Presented to Helmut Gneuss on the Occasion of his Sixty-Fifth Birthday*, eds. Michael Korhammer, Karl Reichl, and Hans Sauer (Cambridge: Brewer, 1992) 53–97.

2. See Keynes, "Fonthill" 73. The Old English is Keynes's transcription; the translation is my own.

3. See, for example, Janet Bately, *The Literary Prose of King Alfred's Reign: Translation or Transformation?*, Old English Newsletter Subsidia, vol. 10 (Binghamton: CEMERS SUNY-Binghamton, 1984); Allen J. Frantzen, *King Alfred*, Twayne's English Authors Series, ed. George Economou (Boston: Twayne, 1986); Dorothy Whitelock, "The Prose of Alfred's Reign," *Continuations and Beginnings: Studies in Old English Literature*, ed. Eric Gerald Stanley (London: Nelson, 1966) 67–103.

4. Literally meaning "judgement-book," the term *domboc* first appears in Alfred's preface to the laws in reference to The Golden Rule. According to Alfred, if one follows this basic principle, "ne ðearf he nanra domboca oþerra" (he needs no other judgment-book) (*Af El.* 49.6). The first time this term is used in reference to Alfred's law code outside of the king's own text is in the prologue to the law code of Edward I (Alfred's son, reigned 900–924), and apparently refers to the joint codes of Alfred (including the historical preface) and Ine. See F. L. Attenborough, ed., *The Laws of the Earliest English Kings* (Cambridge: Cambridge University Press, 1922) 112; Patrick Wormald, *The Making of English Law: King Alfred to the Twelfth Century* (Oxford: Blackwell, 1999) 286. The historical preface of Alfred's code is a selective retelling of Exodus 20–23. Alfred's own code follows, combining selections from the earlier codes of Æthelberht (560–616) and Offa (758–96). Finally, a selected, but possibly unemended, portion of Ine's code is appended. On Alfred's sources, see Dorothy Whitelock, ed., *English Historical Documents c. 500–1042*, 2nd ed., vol. 1 (Oxford: Oxford University Press, 1979) 358; Wormald, 277–85. For the standard scholarly edition of the *Domboc*, see Felix Liebermann, ed., *Die Gesetze der Angelsachsen*, 3 vols. (Aalen: Scientia, 1960) I. 15–123.

5. On the date, see Liebermann, *Gesetze* III. 34; Frantzen, *King Alfred* 11; Keynes and Lapidge, 39, 163; Whitelock, *English Historical Documents* 407; Wormald, *Making* 112, 276–77; David Pratt, *The Political Thought of King Alfred the Great* (Cambridge: Cambridge University Press, 2007) 219.

6. That is, a model of kingship following the example of Charlemagne (800–814) and his descendants: an imperial kingship of the Roman stamp, yet adherent to a Christian ethos. See below, Chapter 1, n. 3.

7. The compound term "native/indigenous" as well as the use of "Germanic" here carry special significance. They point to an acknowledgment of a specifically Anglo-Saxon definition of royal authority as distinct from a Frankish model of kingship. Writ large, the Frankish model, in its Carolingian incarnation, fundamentally depends upon the development and promulgation of a dynastic Christian empire. Anglo-Saxon kingship, in contrast, emphasizes the culturally proper actions of a king in reference to *comitatus* relationships (that is, the reciprocal relationship between service-giving followers and reward-giving leaders) and the approbation of his rule by the *witan* (or wise men/councillors) of the community. See D. P. Kirby, *The Earliest English Kings*, rev. ed. (London: Routledge, 2000) 1–9.

8. See Frantzen, *King Alfred* 17–18; Wormald, *Making* 282–84.

9. See Wormald, *Making* 285.

10. "Complete codes" in this instance, are taken to be those that seem to appear in their manuscript context in their entirety. For example, the *Parker Chronicle* (CCCC 173) contains a table of contents to the law code, the preface to the code, and the code itself as represented in the table of contents. That the total number of laws is 120, symbolic of the fullness of "the relationship between Mosaic law and the new dispensation" is also a marker of its completeness. See Wormald, *Making* 417–18.

11. See Whitelock, *English Historical Documents* 357–62.

12. This, of course, is to say nothing of any number of other problems inherent in examining early English law. See, for example, Robert D. Fulk on the linguistic difficulties attendant in studying such a diverse group of texts: Robert D. Fulk, "Localizing and Dating Old English Anonymous Prose, and How Inherent Problems Relate to Anglo-Saxon Legislation," *English Law Before the Magna Carta*, eds. Stefan Juranski, Lisi Oliver, and Andrew Rabin, Medieval Law and Its Practice 8 (Leiden: Brill, 2010) 59–79. For a summary of some of the other difficulties specific to the *Domboc*, see Pratt, *Political Thought* 214, 216–18.

13. See, respectively, N. R. Ker, *Catalogue of Manuscripts Containing Anglo-Saxon*, rev. ed. (Oxford: Oxford University Press, 1990) 57–59, 110–13, 71–72, 211–15, 30–34, 443–47.

14. Excerpts from Alfred's *Domboc* (roughly sections 29–77) appear in the first 42 statutes of the *Instituta*. Additional, fragmentary manuscripts of the *Instituta* are detailed in Liebermann. See Felix Liebermann, "On the *Instituta Cnuti Aliorumque Regum Anglorum*," *Transactions of the Royal Historical Society* 7 (1893) 105–06.

15. The *Domboc* appears in the *Quadripartitus* in its entirety.

16. See Wormald, *Making* 237–38.

17. See Ker 57–59; Wormald, *Making* 163–72.

18. See Ker 443–47.

19. See Raymond J. Grant, *Laurence Nowell, William Lambarde, and the Laws of the Anglo-Saxons*, Costerus New Series, ed. Erik Kooper, vol. 108 (Amsterdam: Rodopi, 1996) 9–17; Ker 230–34; Rebecca Brackmann, "Laurence Nowell's Old English Legal Glossary and his Study of the *Quadripartitus*," *English Law Before the Magna Carta*, eds. Stefan Juranski, Lisi Oliver, and Andrew Rabin, Medieval Law and Its Practice 8 (Leiden: Brill, 2010) 251–72.

20. See Ker 211–15.

21. See Ker 110–13.

22. See Ker 171–72.

23. Quotations from Alfred's law code follow Liebermann's transcription of CCCC 173; the translations are my own. I have chosen CCCC 173 as it is the earliest, and a complete, manuscript of the *Domboc*.

24. As Allen Frantzen succinctly notes, Alfred's "role in the texts attributed to him is difficult to distinguish from that of his helpers. [...] 'Authorship' may therefore belong to the actual writer of a text, or to one who dictated the text to a scribe, or simply to one who oversaw translations of Latin texts rather than produced them himself" (*King Alfred* 9). Given that the author of the law code himself attests to the creation of law as a collective effort between the king and his *witan* (49.9), it seems advisable to question the law code as the unmediated voice of a single historical person. Finally, this uncertainty of authorship is compounded by the possibility of an individual scribe who "gives his own 'rendition' of what he copied" or even the possible variety of influences rendered by the "collaborative effort in the scriptorium" (Frantzen, *King Alfred* 9). See also Fred C. Robinson, *The Editing of Old English* (Cambridge: Blackwell, 1994) 38. On the possibility of Alfred's personal authorship and the composition of the *Domboc*, see Wormald, *Making* 272–77; Pratt, *Political Thought* 218–22.

25. See Wormald, *Making* 236–44.

Chapter 1

1. In the context of this study, ideology is taken to mean the implicitly held systematic scheme of ideas that is used to define and shape culture.

2. Within my text, *Exodus* in italics indicates the Old English poem, while plaintext Exodus refers to the biblical book.

3. On the relationship between Alfredian and Carolingian models of kingship, see Richard Philip Abels, *Alfred the Great: War, Kingship and Culture in Anglo-Saxon England*, The Medieval World (New York: Longman, 1998) 219–57, *passim*; Janet Nelson, "The Political Ideas of Alfred of Wessex," *Kings and Kingship in Medieval Europe*, ed. Anne Duggan (London: King's College London Centre for Late Antique and Medieval Studies, 1993) 125–36; Janet Nelson, "'A King Across the Sea': Alfred in Continental Perspective," *Transactions of the Royal Historical Society* 5th ser. 36 (1986) 45–68; Wallace-Hadrill 124–51; Wormald, *Making* 109–25; David Pratt, "Written Law and the Communication of Authority," *England and the Continent in the Tenth Century: Studies in Honor of Wilhelm Levison (1876–1947)*, eds. David Rollason, Conrad Leyser, and Hannah Williams, Studies in the Early Middle Ages 37 (Turnhout: Brepols, 2011) 333–34; Pratt, *Political Thought* esp. 4–5, 63–66, 71–78, 87–90, 128–29, 216, 223–27, 233–34, 340. For an excellent recent overview of the varieties of contact between early medieval England and the continent, see David Rollason, Conrad Leyser, and Hannah Williams, eds., *England and the Continent in the Tenth Century: Studies in Honor of Wilhelm Levison (1876–1947)*, Studies in the Early Middle Ages 37 (Turnhout: Brepols, 2011).

4. Evelyn Scherabon Firchow and Edwin H. Zeydel, eds., *Einhard: Vita Karoli Magni* (Coral Gables: University of Miami Press, 1972) 98.

5. Firchow and Zeydel 100.

6. Curiously, although Asser relies on Einhard's *Vita* as a model for parts of his text, there is no mention of Alfred's law code in Asser's biography of the king. On Asser's reliance on Einhard, see Simon Keynes and Michael Lapidge, eds., *Alfred the Great, Asser's Life of King Alfred and Other Contemporary Sources* (Harmondsworth: Penguin, 1983) 53–55; Marie Schütt, "The Literary Form of Asser's *Vita Alfredi*," *English Historical Review* 62 (1957) 209–20.

7. *Af El.* 49.9.

8. On this reading of Alfred's *Domboc*, see Wormald, *Making* 277–85, 416–29.

9. See Patrick Wormald, "*Lex Scripta and Verbum Regis*: Legislation and Germanic Kingship, from Euric to Cnut," *Early Medieval Kingship*, ed. I. N. Wood (Leeds: University Leeds, 1977) 134–38; Wormald, *Making* 429.

10. See also, Wormald, *"Lex"* 105–07, 35–38; Wallace-Hadrill 36–37, 43–46, 148–50.

11. See Wormald, *Making* 283–85. Paul Hyams has recently questioned Wormald's assumption of the centrality of royal government in the life of the late Anglo-Saxons. See Paul Hyams, "Feud and the State in Late Anglo-Saxon England," *Journal of British Studies* 40 (2001) 1–43.

12. On the possible shortcomings of Wormald's view on the role of written law, see Pratt, *Political Thought* 217.

13. Alfred cites his knowledge of earlier law in the *Domboc*'s preface. He lists his sources as coming from "oððe on Ines dæge, mines mæge, oððe on Offan Mercna cyninges oððe on Æðelbryhtes" (either in Ine's day, kinsman of mine, or in Offa's [time] [reigned 758–96], king of Mercia, or in Æthelberht's [time] [reigned 560–616]) (*Af. El.* 49.9).

14. On the dates of these early rulers, see Kirby 24, 103–04, 12.

15. See Nicholas Howe, *Migration and Mythmaking in Anglo-Saxon England* (New Haven: Yale University Press, 1989) 72–107; Peter Lucas, ed., *Exodus* (Exeter: University of Exeter Press, 1994) 63–65.

16. See Malcolm Godden, "Biblical Literature: The Old Testament," *The Cambridge Companion to Old English Literature*, ed. Michael Lapidge (Cambridge: Cambridge University Press, 1991) 206–9, 16–18.

17. See Kenneth L. Barker and Donald W. Burdick, eds., *The NIV Study Bible, New International Version* (Grand Rapids: Zondervan, 1985) 19, 115, 271.

18. See Barker and Burdick 19. As an example, Exodus 19:5 relates God's conditional covenant to the Isrealites: "si ergo audieritis vocem meam et custodieritis pactum meum eritis mihi in peculium de cunctis populis mea est enim omnis terra" (if, therefore, you will indeed hear my voice and keep my covenant, you will be my own possession above all people, for all the earth is mine). All biblical text is taken from the Latin Vulgate. The translations are my own.

19. Although the law is general in scope, scholars typically assume it covers the oath of loyalty to one's lord. See, for example, Richard Philip Abels, *Lordship and Military Obligation in Anglo-Saxon England* (Berkeley: University of California Press, 1988) 83–84; Keynes and Lapidge 306 n.6; Eric Gerald Stanley, "On the Laws of King Alfred: The End of the Preface and the Beginning of the Laws," *Alfred the Wise: Studies in Honour of Janet Bately on the Occasion of Her Sixty-Fifth Birthday*, eds. Jane Roberts, Janet Nelson and Malcolm Godden (Rochester: Brewer, 1997) 211–21.

20. See Howe, *Migration* 72–107.

21. Alfred tailors Mosaic law to suit his ideological purposes through the invocation of the language of the *bot* system. See Chapter 2 for this investigation.

22. Although his exact exemplar is unknown, Alfred may have been translating from a Vulgate Bible, the *Liber ex lege Moysi*, or the *Collatio legum Romanarum et Mosaicarum*. See Wormald, *Making* 418–27.

23. See especially Felix Liebermann, "King Alfred and Mosaic Law," *Transactions of the Jewish Historical Society* 6 (1912) 21–31; Michael Treschow, "The Prologue to Alfred's Law Code: Instruction in the Spirit of Mercy," *Florilegium* 13 (1994); Wormald, *Making* 418–27.

24. The date and provenance of the poem allows for Alfred's knowledge of it. The OE *Exodus* manuscript (Oxford, Bodleian Library MS Junius 11) roughly dates to the year 1000. See Ker 406–08; Lucas 1–2. Of course, how long this Old English alliterative verse version of the book of Exodus was circulating before it was committed to the manuscript is a matter of conjecture. Lucas cites an accumulation of internal evidence that suggests an original composition date of within the eighth century. Lucas's evidence consists of a combination of stylistic, syntactic, and grammatical elements cumulatively suggesting his eighth-century date. On the date of the *Exodus*, see Lucas 69–72. Further, the provenance of the

OE *Exodus* manuscript has been traced to Malmesbury: see Lucas 2–4. Prior to and through-out Alfred's reign, Malmesbury was a major center for learning attached to the Wessex administration: see, Barbara Yorke, *Wessex in the Early Middle Ages*, Studies in the Early History of Britain (London: Leicester University Press, 1995) 196. As such, it is not unlikely that the portrayal of Moses originating from the Benedictine Abbey of the Blessed Virgin Mary and St. Aldhelm at Malmesbury would be in general agreement with the predominant portrayals of Moses throughout Wessex (including the royal city of Winchester) during the ninth and tenth centuries. Malmesbury functioned as a base for continental missionaries, but it also was a religious house of Wessex and likely participated in the relatively local cir-culation of common texts in the region. See Yorke 106–203.

25. Henry Sweet, ed., *King Alfred's West Saxon Version of Gregory's Pastoral Care*, 2 vols. (London: Oxford University Press, 1871) 3.

26. For the Germanic style of the *Exodus*, see Howe, *Migration* 72–107; Lucas 63–65.

27. For the text of "The Dream of the Rood," see John C. Pope, ed., *Eight Old English Poems*, 3rd ed. (New York: Norton, 2001) 9–14.

28. For a concise overview see Frantzen, *King Alfred* 31–39.

29. See Robin Flower, A. H. Smith and Corpus Christi College (University of Cam-bridge) Library, *The Parker Chronicle and Laws (Corpus Christi College, Cambridge, MS. 173): A Facsimile* (London: Oxford University Press, 1941).

30. See Sweet 25.

31. Matthew 5:17 reads: "nolite putare quoniam veni solvere legum aut prophetas non veni solvere sed adimplere" (refuse to think [I] come for to destroy the laws of the prophets, [I] do not come to destroy, but to fulfill [them]).

32. On the possible disingenuousness of Alfred's claim of humility, see Wormald, *Making* 277–85.

33. See Sweet 7.

34. On the respective probable dates of the texts, see Frantzen, *King Alfred* 11, 22–23.

35. Sweet 7.

36. Sweet 5, 7.

37. Sweet 7.

38. When Jesus first disperses the apostles to spread God's word, he does not want them to appeal to all nations, "sed potius ite ad oves quae perierunt domus Israhel" (but rather go to the sheep that have been lost of the house of Israel) (Matthew 10:6). Only after his death and resurrection does Jesus command his disciples to spread holy law among "omnes gentes" (all nations) (Matthew 28:19).

39. God, Himself, does not inscribe the famous tablets of the Ten Commandments until Exodus 31:18.

40. See Matthew 5:21, 27, 33, 38, 43.

41. On the relationship between written and unwritten law as it applies to Judeo-Christian and Germanic cultural practice, see Wormald, "*Lex*" 105–38; Wormald, *Making* 416–29, 82–83.

42. Alfred would be familiar with this concept as it appears in his translation of the *Regula pastoralis*: "Þæm lareowe is to witanne ðæt he huru nanum men mare ne beode ðonne he acuman mæge" (The teacher is to understand that he not at all inform a man more that he can endure), Sweet 458.

43. See, for example, s. a. 878 (A). Following Guthrum's defeat at Edington, Alfred "onfeng æt fulwihte" (received him at baptism). See Janet Bately, ed., *The Anglo-Saxon Chronicle: A Collaborative Edition*, vol. 3 (Cambridge: Brewer, 1983) 51.

44. See, for example, s. a. 900 (A): Alfred's accession in which he "feng [...] to Wesseaxna rice." See Bately, *Anglo-Saxon Chronicle* 48.

45. See *Af El.* 49.9.

46. Bately, *Anglo-Saxon Chronicle* 1.
47. Ine is the brother of Alfred's great-great-great-great-grandfather. For a genealogical table derived from the *Chronicle*, see Michael Swanton, ed., *The Anglo-Saxon Chronicle* (New York: Routledge, 1996) 288–89. On the legitimizing function of royal genealogies, see David Dumville, "Kingship, Genealogies and Regnal Lists," *Early Medieval Kingship*, ed. I. N. Wood (Leeds: University of Leeds Press, 1977) 72–104.
48. Here I speak of that portion of Mercia that is not under Danish control at the time: Mercia west of the Alfred-Guthrum border. See map in Abels, *Alfred* 351.
49. On Offa's "lost" code, see Patrick Wormald, "In Search of King Offa's Law-Code,'" *People and Places in Northern Europe, 500–1600: Studies Presented to Peter Hayes Sawyer*, eds. I. N. Wood and N. Lund (Woodbridge: Blackwell, 1991) 25–45; Wormald, *Making* 106–08.
50. Æthelberht's law code is extant only in the twelfth-century *Textus Roffensis*. See P. H. Sawyer, ed., *Textus Roffensis: Rochester Cathedral Library Manuscript A. 3. 5* (Copenhagen: Rosenkilde and Bagger, 1957) 1–3.
51. See *Anglo-Saxon Chronicle* entry for 871: "Ða feng Elfred Eðelwulfing his broður to Wesseaxna rice" (Then his [Æthelred's] brother, Alfred, son of Æthelwulf, ascended to the throne of the West Saxons)(Bately *Anglo-Saxon Chronicle* 48).
52. On the Mercian submission, see Simon Keynes, "King Alfred and the Mercians," *Kings, Currency and Alliances: History and Coinage in Southern England in the Ninth Century*, eds. M. A. S. Blackburn and Simon Keynes (Woodbridge: Boydell, 1998) 19–34. On the Kentish submission to Ecgbert, and its disposition under him and his descendants, see Abels, *Alfred* 29–33; Kirby 155–57, 74, 76; Yorke 97–99.
53. As the *Anglo-Saxon Chronicle* shows, in 886 Alfred "gesette" (occupied) the Mercian walled town of London, and then "befæste þa burg Eþerede aldorman to haldonne" (entrusted the fort to [Mercian] ealdorman Æthelred to keep) (Bately, *Anglo-Saxon Chronicle* 53). On Mercia's relationship with Wessex, see Abels, *Alfred* 180–87; Keynes, "King Alfred and the Mercians" 1–45; Kirby 176–78.
54. See Abels, *Alfred* 92–94.
55. See P. H. Sawyer, *Anglo-Saxon Charters: An Annotated List and Bibliography*, Royal Historical Society Guides and Handbooks, vol. 8 (London: Royal Historical Society, 1968) 151–54.
56. See Af *El.* 49.9: "Ic ða Ælfred cyning…"
57. Æthelberht had some, but less, influence over the South and West Saxons adjoining his territory. On the geographical boundaries of Æthelberht's rule, see Kirby 24–30.
58. See Alfred P. Smyth, *King Alfred the Great* (Oxford: Oxford University Press, 1995) 529–31, 75–77.
59. The Venerable St. Bede, *Bede's Ecclesiastical History of the English People*, eds. and trans. Bertram Colgrave and R.A.B. Mynors (Oxford: Clarendon, 1969) 76.
60. Bede 150.

Chapter 2

1. My use of the term "secular" refers to those elements of Anglo-Saxon society apparently derived from feud-based Germanic, heroic, and pagan cultural traditions as opposed to those indebted to Latinate Christianity. For a concise overview of the relationship between Christian and pagan elements of Anglo-Saxon culture, see Roberta Frank, "Germanic Legend in Old English Literature," *The Cambridge Companion to Old English Literature*, ed. Michael Lapidge (Cambridge: Cambridge University Press, 1991) 88–106; Katherine O'Brien O'Keeffe, "Heroic Values and Christian Ethics," *The Cambridge Companion to Old English Lit-*

erature, ed. Michael Lapidge (Cambridge: Cambridge University Press, 1991) 107–25; John D. Niles, "Pagan Survivals and Popular Belief," *The Cambridge Companion to Old English Literature*, ed. Michael Lapidge (Cambridge: Cambridge University Press, 1991) 126–41.

2. On the function of the representation of the king in relation to power, see Louis Marin, *Portrait of the King*, trans. Martha M. Houle, Theory and History of Literature, ed. Jochen Schulte-Sasse, vol. 57 (Minneapolis: University of Minnesota Press, 1988) 5–15.

3. See entry for *bot*, Antonette Di Paolo Healey, Richard L. Venezky and Angus Cameron, eds., *Dictionary of Old English* (Toronto: Published for the Dictionary of Old English Project Centre for Medieval Studies University of Toronto by the Pontifical Institute of Mediaeval Studies, 1986) 1982–87.

4. For a fundamental explanation of the Anglo-Saxon *bot* system of compensation for injury or death, see Pollock and Maitland 46–49, 449–53. For the role of *bot* as an element in feud-based Anglo-Saxon culture, see Paul Hyams, *Rancor and Reconciliation in Medieval England* (Ithaca: Cornell University Press, 2003) 79–80. For a working explanation of feud in medieval England, see Hyams, *Rancor* 8–9.

5. On the roots of these elements in Icelandic culture, see Jesse L. Byock, *Feud in the Icelandic Saga* (Berkeley: University of California Press, 1982) 1–10; William Ian Miller, *Bloodtaking and Peacemaking: Feud, Law, and Society in Saga Iceland* (Chicago: University of Chicago Press, 1990) 221–57.

6. For further discussion of the role of feud in Anglo-Saxon culture, see especially the following works of Paul Hyams: *Rancor and Reconciliation in Medieval England* (Ithaca: Cornell University Press, 2003) 79–80, 98–110; "Feud in Medieval England," *Haskins Society Journal* 3 (1991) 1–21; "Feud and the State," *Journal of British Studies* 40 (2001) 1–43; "Was There Really Such a Thing as Feud in the High Middle Ages?" *Vengence in the Middle Ages: Emotion, Religion and Feud*, eds. Susanna Throop and Paul Hyams (Farnham: Ashgate, 2010) 151–75. See also, John G. H. Hudson, "Feud, Vengence and Violence in England from the Tenth to the Twelfth Centuries," *Feud, Violence and Practice: Essays in Medieval Studies in Honor of Stephen D. White*, eds. Belle Tuten and Tracey Billado (Farnham: Ashgate, 2010) 34–40; John M. Hill, *The Anglo-Saxon Warrior Ethic: Reconstructing Lordship in Early English Literature* (Gainesville: University Press of Florida, 2000) 10–16, 47–60.

7. See Liebermann, *Gesetze*, *Af El*. 11–13, 16–29,34–36, 42; *Af*. 1–33, 35–42, 44; and *Ine* 2–13, 18, 20–25, 28–32, 34–44, 46–51,53–54, 56–57, 60, 62–63, 67–68, 71–76.

8. See Michel Foucault, *Discipline and Punish: The Birth of the Prison*, trans. Alan Sheridan (New York: Pantheon, 1977).

9. A "two-hynd man" is one whose life is valued at 200 shillings. For a summary explication of *bot*, *wer*, and *wite*, see Pollock and Maitland 46–49.

10. See Wormald, "*Lex*" 105–15.

11. Danish aggression against the West Saxons continued throughout Alfred's career, even as Alfred accepted the submission of Mercia and Wales during the 880s. See Keynes and Lapidge 262–63.

12. On this reading of Alfred's *Domboc*, see Wormald, *Making* 277–85, 416–29.

13. See Wormald, "*Lex*" 134–38; Wormald, *Making* 429.

14. See Rosamond McKitterick, ed., *The New Cambridge Medieval History: Volume II c. 700–c. 900* (Cambridge: Cambridge University Press, 1995) 15–16. McKitterick claims such a nation-identifying function of law for the early legislation of the Franks, Visigoths, Lombards, and Saxons, among others. See also Wormald, *Making* 48–49, 131–34, 416. This process, in itself, does not differentiate Alfred from the Carolingians. Rather, as shall be seen, the difference between the Carolingians and Alfred lies in the ultimate image cultivated as a result of this operation.

15. Keynes and Lapidge argue that the variations on Alfred's title as *Angul-Saxonum rex* (king of the Anglo-Saxons) "impl[ies] an aspiration to wider political authority" (227). See also, Keynes, "King Alfred and the Mercians" 14–18, 28. Smyth questions this conclusion,

arguing that the title *Westseaxna cyning* (king of the West-Saxons) more accurately reflects contemporary usage as defined by genuine charters of the period. See Smyth 384–91.

16. *Af El.* 49.7, "7 eac swa geond Angelcyn" (and also throughout the English race).

17. On kingship and national identity, see Foot 25–49; Patrick Wormald, "Bede, the *Bretwaldas*, and the Origin of the *Gens Anglorum*," *Ideal and Reality in Frankish and Anglo-Saxon Society: Studies Presented to J.M. Wallace-Hadrill*, ed. Roger Collins (Oxford: Blackwell, 1983) 99–129; Patrick Wormald, "*Engla Lond*: The Making of an Allegiance," *Journal of Historical Sociology* 7 (1994) 1–24.

18. See Benedict Anderson, *Imagined Communities: Reflections on the Origin and Spread of Nationalism*, 2nd ed. (London: Verso, 1991).

19. See, for example, the laws of Æthelberht (*Abt* 21), Hlothere and Eadric (*Hl* 1), Wihtræd (*Wi* 25), Ine (*Ine* 23), and Alfred (*Af* 30).

20. For example, "monegra meniscra misdæda bote gesetton" (they [the bishops and wise men] set the compensation of many human misdeeds) (*Af El.* 49.8). Although the bishops may have acquiesced to the payment of *wergild*, it certainly did not come from any scriptural source.

21. On the power of narrative in creating national identity, see Homi Bhabha, "Dissemination: Time, Narrative, and the Margins of the Modern Nation," *Nation and Narration*, ed. Homi Bhabha (New York: Routledge, 1990) 291–322.

22. See R. R. Davies, *The First English Empire: Power and Identities in the British Isles, 1093–1343*, The Ford Lectures Delivered in the University of Oxford in Hilary Term 1998 (Oxford: Oxford University Press, 2000) 199–200; Marin 9–15.

23. Alfred translates the following verses from the book of Exodus: 20:1–3, 7–9, 11–17, 23; 21:1–36; 22:1–11, 16–28, 28–29, 31; 23:1–2, 4, 6–9, 13. These verses contain the Decalogue and portions of the Book of the Covenant, which expands upon the strictures of the Ten Commandments. He also translates Acts 15:22–29, describing the apostolic mission to Syria, Antioch, and Cilicia. Finally, punishments by the Church are represented in the laws by such terms as *amænsumian* (to excommunicate) (*Af El.* 1.7), *scrifan* (to shrive) (*Af El.* 1.8), *geandettan* (to confess) (*Af El.* 5.4), and *unhadian* (to unfrock) (*Af El.* 21).

24. In the translations, the concept of Christian mercy is expressed by variations of the words *mildheort* (literally "mild-heart") or *milts* (mercy).

25. Samuel Fox, ed., *King Alfred's Anglo-Saxon Version of Boethius: De consolatione philosophiae*, 2nd ed. (New York: AMS, 1970) 228.

26. Claudio Moreschini, ed., *Boethius: De consolatione philosophiae, Opuscula theologica* (Munich: Saur, 2000) 126.

27. Sweet 403. Throughout Chapters 52 and 53, Alfred is again translating various forms of the Latin *misericordia* (mercy, pity), as well as the Latin *pietas* (piety, kindness). See J. P. Migne, ed., *Patrologiæ Cursus Completus, Series Latina*, vol. 77 (Paris: Garnieri Fratres, 1849) 104–09.

28. Thomas Carnicelli, ed., *King Alfred's Version of Saint Augustine's Soliloquies* (Cambridge: Harvard University Press, 1969) 50. The Latin reads: "postremo ut liberes" (finally, that you set [me] free). See Gerard Watson, ed., *Saint Augustine: Soliloquies and Immortality of the Soul* (Warminster: Aris & Phillips, 1990) 22. Although Alfred is demonstrably the author of the translation of the *Soliloquies*, the addition of mercy to the passage may or may not be his as there is no firm idea as to what his exemplar looked like. On Alfred's authorship of the translation, see Carnicelli 38–40; Frantzen, *King Alfred* 68–69; Whitelock, "Prose" 71–73, 80–89; Pratt, *Political Thought* 328–32. On the state of Alfred's exemplar, see Frantzen, *King Alfred* 69–72; Smyth, 537–38.

29. Carnicelli 61–62. No parallel text exists in the Latin. See Carnicelli 100–01; Watson 36.

30. Fox 212.

31. Moreschini 119.

32. See Carnicelli 48.

33. On Alfred's authorship of the preface, see Carnicelli 38–39.

34. Again, Alfred uses forms of *mildheortnesse* and *miltsian* to translate the Latin forms of *misericordia* and *pietas* through Chapters 16 and 17. For comparison, see Migne 32–38; Sweet 97–127.

35. Sweet 101.

36. The Latin phrase reads: "aliis misereri debuisset" (he ought to feel pity for others) (Migne 33).

37. Sweet 101.

38. Sweet 127. Alfred here uses *mildheortnes* to translate the Latin *clementia* (clemency, mercy). See Migne 38.

39. On the role of mercy in the *Domboc*, see Wormald, *Making* 422–23; Treschow *passim*; Pratt, *Political Thought* 232–38.

40. On Alfred's connection and debt to the Carolingians, see Chapter 1, n. 3.

41. Treschow, for example, acknowledges the limit of Fulk's influence to only "a small part of the framework of Alfred's prologue" (103). He also notes the fundamental difference between Hincmar's and Alfred's respective admissions of mercy into jurisprudence, citing Hincmar's *De regis persona et regio ministerio* and *Capitula in synodo apud S. Macram ad Hincmaro* (Treschow 103–05). For more detailed discussions of the influence of Hincmar and Fulk on Alfred's law-giving, see Wormald, *Making* 423–27; Pratt, *Political Thought* 223–30.

42. See Godden 206–26.

43. See Foucault 47–48.

44. See Abels, *Alfred* 274–84; Pollock and Maitland 37–52; Wormald, *Making* 118–25.

45. See, for example, the repetition of specific punishment language in *Af El.* 13: "swelte se deaðe" (let him suffer the death).

46. *Af El.* 42.

47. On Anglo-Saxon law and property rights, see Pollock and Maitland 56–60.

48. See especially the discussions of Cynewulf and Cyneheard, and of Byrhtnoth in Hill 74–88, 115–28.

49. Bately, *Anglo-Saxon Chronicle* 50.

50. William Stevenson, ed., *Asser's Life of King Alfred*, 2nd ed. (Oxford: Clarendon, 1959) 37. On the use of *obsides*, see Keynes and Lapidge 246, n. 91.

51. "non occides" (Do not murder) (Exodus 20:13).

52. Exodus 21:13 normally reads: "qui autem non est insidiatus sed Deus illum tradidit in manu eius constituam tibi locum quo fugere debeat" (However, he who has not laid in wait, but God hands over that man into his hand, I shall have for you [the killer] a place to which to escape).

53. On the possible necessity of killing in feud, see Byock 106–13; Pollock and Maitland 46–55.

54. On negotiating the Biblical views on vengeance in a feud-based culture, see Hyams, *Rancor* 44–48.

55. Fox 212; Sweet 101.

56. See Matthew 26:14–16, 27:3–5; Mark 14:10–11; Luke 22:3–6; Acts 1:16–25.

57. Although Byock is speaking specifically of the medieval Icelanders of the eleventh century, the concept of adapting Christianity to local customs has been widespread throughout history.

58. The Anglo-Saxon practice of the *bot* system is feud-based insofar as *bot* defines a set of socially appropriate compensations for various transgressions. As Byock argues, the aim of feud resolution was "to return the community to a workable arrangement [through finding] a compromise that could be lived with" (102). This compromise hinges on socially

dictated appropriate compensation, which could range from the killing of the offender to the acceptance of remuneration.

59. Sweet 7.

60. Sweet 7.

61. See Acts 15:1–21.

62. See Acts 15:22–35.

63. Sweet 459.

64. *Af El.* 49.7.

65. Although the practice of allowing monetary compensation for wrongs is easily found in the Old Testament (see, for example, Exodus 21:18–22:15), I have yet to find any direct teaching of Jesus approving of this custom.

66. See Sarah Hamilton, *The Practice of Penance* (Woodbridge: Boydell, 2001) 41–43, 60–64.

67. See Allen J. Frantzen, *The Literature of Penance in Anglo-Saxon England* (New Brunswick: Rutgers University Press, 1983) 41–44.

68. Frantzen, *Literature* 127–29.

69. Grimbald was a priest sent from Fulk, the Archbishop of Rheims, to Alfred's court around 886. On Fulk and the penitentials, see Frantzen, *Literature* 127–28. On Grimbald's coming to Alfred's court, including the authenticity of Fulk's letter, see Keynes and Lapidge 26–27, 93, 182–86, 260 n., 331 168.

70. See Stanley 219; Wormald, *Making* 277–88.

71. This, of course, is keeping in mind the collaborative nature both of legislating and the production of the manuscript. On the cooperative nature of legislating, see Abels, *Alfred* 261–63; Smyth 421–51. On the cooperative nature of manuscript production, see Carol Braun Pasternack, *The Textuality of Old English Poetry*, ed. Michael Lapidge, Cambridge Studies in Anglo-Saxon England 13 (Cambridge: Cambridge University Press, 1995) 12–21.

72. Alfred cites the laws of his "foregengan" (fore-goers) as originating "oððe on Ines dæge, mines mæge, oððe on Offan Mercna cyninges oððe on Æþelbryhtes" (either in Ine's day, kinsman of mine, or in Offa's [time], king of Mercia, or in Æthelberht's [time]) (*Af. El.* 49.9).

73. On Anglo-Saxon oath-taking and breaking, see Abels, *Lordship* 83–90; Abels, *Alfred* 148–50, 277–82; Thomas Charles-Edwards, "Anglo-Saxon Kinship Revisited," *The Anglo-Saxons: From the Migration Period to the Eighth Century*, ed. John Hines (Woodbridge: Boydell, 1997) 175–76; Keynes and Lapidge 306, n. 6–7; H. R. Loyn, *The Governance of Anglo-Saxon England, 500–1087*, The Governance of England 1 (Stanford: Stanford University Press, 1984) 72; Stanley 221; Frank Merry Stenton, *Anglo-Saxon England*, 3rd ed. (Oxford: Clarendon, 1971) 311–13; Wormald, *Making* 283–84; Yorke 247.

74. Wihtræd proclaims a king's word incontrovertible, even "buton aþe" (without oath) (*Wi* 16).

75. See Stanley 216–21.

76. For *að* see Healey, Venezky and Cameron 687.

77. In Alfred's laws, "Dryhten" consistently applies to the heavenly Lord, while "hlaford" is specifically used to denote an earthly ruler. This distinction between the two is instructively encapsulated in *Af El.* 37: "Ne tæl ðu ðinne Dryhten, ne ðone hlaford þæs folces ne werge þu" (Do not slander your [heavenly] Lord, nor curse the [earthly] lord of the people).

78. The use of the male pronoun throughout the law code specifically address men as its audience. See, for example, *Af.* 1: "æghwelc mon *his* að 7 *his* wed wærlice healde" (each man carefully keep *his* oath and *his* pledge [my emphasis]). As Alfred would most likely know, swearing in God's name is forbidden in Matthew 5:34: "non iuare omnino" (do not swear at all).

79. On the general nature of the *comitatus* relationship in the Anglo-Saxon period, see Hill 16–18, 111–28; O'Keeffe 112–14; Pollock and Maitland 29–34; Stenton 289–300.

80. For a more detailed account, see Abels, *Alfred* 34–44; Stenton 298–303; Wallace-Hadrill 141–51; Yorke 26–61.

81. See, for example, *Wi* 19–24, *Ine* 19, *A Gu.* 3.

82. See, for example *Wi* 23: "Gif man Gedes þeuwne esns in heora gemange tihte, his dryhten hine his ane aþe geclænsie" (If one accuses a bond-servant among a crowd, his lord shall clear him by his own oath).

83. See, for example, *Wi* 21: "ceorlisc man hine feowra sum his heafodgemacene on weofode; 7 ðissa ealra að sie unlegnæ" (a churlish man [may clear himself], himself one of his four fellow-servants at the altar; and the oath of all of these shall be unquestionable).

84. See the examples provided by Julia Smith, "Religion and Lay Society," *The New Cambridge Medieval History: Volume II c. 700–c. 900*, ed. Rosamond McKitterick (Cambridge: Cambridge University Press, 1995) 669–72. See also Frantzen, *Literature* 97–107.

85. On Alfred's laws and penance in ninth-century England, see Frantzen, *Literature* 94–129.

86. For the reconstruction of this law's first clause, "Gif he þonne þæs weddige þe him riht sie to gelæstanne 7 þæt aleoge," see Whitelock, *English Historical Documents* 409, n. 2; Wormald, *Making* 171–72, n. 38–39.

Chapter 3

1. For an overview of Cnut's conquest, see M. K. Lawson, *Cnut: The Danes in England in the Early Eleventh Century*, The Medieval World (New York: Longman, 1993) 9–48, 81–116; Stenton 380–87. On *I–II Cnut*, see Lawson, *Cnut* 61–63; Pauline Stafford, *Unification and Conquest* (London: Arnold, 1989) 108, 38–41; Dorothy Whitelock, "Wulfstan and the Laws of Cnut," *English Historical Review* 63 (1948) 433–44. The code dates to 1020 or 1021, four or five years following Cnut's accession to the English throne. On the date, see Wormald, *Making* 364–65. Three Old English versions of *I–II Cnut* pre-date the Norman Conquest: London, British Library Cotton Nero A i. (mid-eleventh century); Cambridge, Corpus Christi College 383 (late eleventh, early twelfth century); and London, British Library Harley 55 (mid-twelfth century). On the dates, see Ker 210, 110, 323. Post-conquest Latin versions appear in the *Quadripartitus* manuscripts. See Wormald, *Making* 236–44.

2. Most likely, the actual author of the law code was Wulfstan, archbishop of York and bishop of Worcester (1002–23). See Dorothy Whitelock, "Wulfstan's Authorship of Cnut's Laws," *English Historical Review* 70 (1955) 72–85; Wormald, *Making* 330–66, 88–97, 449–65.

3. Wulfstan's date of birth is unclear. He became bishop of London in 996, and served as Archbishop of York from 1002 until his death in 1023. On Wulfstan's authorship, see Wormald, *Making* 330–45. Wormald's argument rests on comparisons of content, style, and even handwriting with known Wulfstanian documents.

4. All citations from *I–II Cnut* are taken from Liebermann's transcription of Cotton Nero A. i., the earliest manuscript witness of *I–II Cnut*: see Liebermann, *Gesetze* I. 278–371. The translations are my own.

5. On the history of *að* and *wedd*, see; Pratt, *Political Thought* 233–38 The code *I Cn.* 19.1 also appears prior to *I–II Cnut* in a code of King Æthelred's (*V Atr.*), but its source is ultimately Alfredian. Archbishop Wulfstan wrote legislation for both kings, Æthelred and Cnut, during their respective reigns. Liebermann notes Wulfstan's reliance on *Af.* 1 in the Æthelred law that enjoins a man to "word 7 weorc fadige mid rihte, 7 að 7 wedd wærlice healde" (guide his words and works properly, and carefully keep his oath and pledge) (*V*

Atr. 22.2). Citations from *V Atr.* are taken from Liebermann's transcription of Cotton Nero A. i., the earliest manuscript witness: see Liebermann, *Gesetze* I. 236–45. The translations are my own.

6. See Whitelock, *English Historical Documents* 462–63; Wormald, *Making* 359.

7. On the inclusion of the phrase "oððe þurh reaflac," see Whitelock, *English Historical Documents* 462 n. 5.

8. On the specific debts of Cnut to "Edward-Guthrum," see Whitelock, *English Historical Documents* 461–62; Wormald, *Making* 359. On the Danish term "*lahslit* 'breach of the law' [...] the term given in the Danelaw to a fine varying with the rank of the offender," see Whitelock, *English Historical Documents* 446 n. 6.

9. In his "Sermo in .XL." (Sermon for the first Sunday of Lent), Wulfstan states: "Ðonne is Lenctentid eallum cristenum mannum huru nedbehfe rihtlice to gehealdanne, forðam nis ænig man on life swa wær þæt he over ealne geares fæc him swa wel wið deofol gescyldan mæg swa swa he beðorfte. Ðonne is Lencten us eallum to dædbote gescyft þæt we geornlice on þam fæce þa þing wið God ælmihtigne gebetan þe we to unrihte oðrum tidum gedoð þurh deofles lare" (Then is the Lenten-time indeed necessary for all Christian men to hold correctly, because not any living man is so careful that he, over all his space of years, can protect himself so very well against the devil just as he needed. Then Lent allots atonement to us all, so that in that space of time we then earnestly atone for the thing which we unrightly do at other times against God almighty, through the devil's teaching). See Dorothy Bethurum, ed., *The Homilies of Wulfstan* (Oxford: Clarendon, 1998) 233.

10. Wulfstan, for example, significantly ignores the whole of Alfred's historical preface presenting Mosaic law and the new dispensation through Christ, emphasizing the connection between Anglo-Saxon legislation and early Christianity.

11. Alfred specifically devotes his fourth law to lord-treachery (*Af.* 4–4.2), but numerous other laws also deal with less grievous breaches of lord-subject responsibilities. For example, *Af.* 1–1.8 deals with the breaking of oaths, *Af.* 3 with the breaking of the "cyninges borg" (king's bail), *Af.* 7–7.1 with the breaking of the peace in the king's hall, and *Af.* 40 with "burgbryce" (breaking into the house) of the king. For a general overview of the importance of the relationships between king, lord, thegn, and subject, see Abels, *Lordship* 58–96; Pollock and Maitland 32–34; Stenton 298–314.

12. See Byock 99–113; Pollock and Maitland 46–48.

13. Karl Jost, ed., *Die "Institutes of Polity, Civil and Ecclesiastical": Ein Werk Erzbischof Wulfstans von York* (Bern: Franke, 1959) 50.

14. Bethurum 275.

15. See Lawson, *Cnut* 56–63; M. K. Lawson, "Archbishop Wulfstan and the Homiletic Element in the Laws of Æthelred II and Cnut," *The Reign of Cnut: King of England, Denmark and Norway*, ed. Alexander R. Rumble, Studies in the Early History of Britain (London: Leicester University Press, 1994) 152–64; Whitelock, "Wulfstan" 450.

16. On Cnut's concern for social stability, see Lawson, *Cnut* 207–10.

17. A comparison of the *Anglo-Saxon Chronicle* entries relevant to the respective conquests of Cnut and William the Conqueror finds Cnut treated with greater acceptance and respect that William was. See *Chronicle* entries for the years 1017- 36 in comparison to those of 1066-87.

18. On the date of the *Instituta Cnuti*, see Wormald, *Making* 116, 404–05. The text is found in twelve manuscripts (Liebermann's Cb, Ct, Di, H, Jo, Lb, Pa, Pl, Rl, S, T, Va) variously dating from the mid-twelfth to sixteenth centuries. See Liebermann, "On the *Instituta*" 101–07; Liebermann, *Gesetze* I. xviii-xlii, 279–367, 612–17.

19. The bracketed titles are the currently recognized scholarly names of these pieces of legislation. See Wormald, *Making* 391–95.

20. See Wormald, *Making* 391–95.

21. See Wormald, *Making* 402–06.

22. This includes his translations of the verbs "betan" and "gebetan" (both meaning "to compensate for a wrong").

23. See R. E. Latham and D. R. Howlett, *Dictionary of Medieval Latin from British Sources: Fasicule III, D-E* (London: Oxford University Press, 1975) 770–71.

24. Although Cnut is a Danish ruler in England, his legislation can be considered Anglo-Saxon in character, as its author is the Anglo-Saxon archbishop, Wulfstan of York.

25. See Wormald, *Making* 393–95.

26. The *Instituta* translator renders these pairs as "rex et archiepiscopus," "archiepiscopus et filius regis," "episcopus et comes," and "rex et episcopus" (*In Cn* III 56–57), respectively.

27. *Af.* 15–17, 19–19.2, 20, 23–23.2, 29–31.1, 38–39.2, 44–77; *Ine* 9, 13.1, 14–15, 58–59.

28. Although unstated here, Alfred elsewhere allows exculpation through monetary compensation Cf. *Af.* 4.2.

29. A "twelve-hide man" is a man whose wergild is 1200 shillings. See Pollock and Maitland 34.

30. See, for example, the catalogue of Nero A. I in Ker 210–11.

31. Ine's law code follows that of Alfred's in the *Domboc*. It is only found as part of Alfred's *Domboc*, and is taken to operate as an integral part of the text.

32. *Ine* 13.1 cites thieves as comprising an group of up to seven renegade men. From seven to thirty-five such men is a band, and above that is considered a marauding army.

33. The intervening laws, *In. Cn.* III 42–63.1, are drawn from the *Grið* and *Geþyncðu* groups. See Liebermann, *Gesetze* I. 615–16.

34. Although Wormald sees the possibility for a contemporaneous addition of Book III to Books I and II by Wulfstan or members of his circle, he ultimately argues for its later addition by a later eleventh-century compiler during the reign of William I. Compare Wormald, *Making* 352 to 404–05.

35. Lawson, *Cnut* 56–63; Lawson, "Archbishop" 152–64; Whitelock, "Wulfstan" 450.

36. See Wormald, *Making* 364–66, 463–65.

37. On the identity and station of the author of the *Instituta Cnuti*, see Liebermann, "On the *Instituta*" 82–88.

38. See Wormald, *Making* 404–05. Wormald, *Making* 404–05.

39. On the use of the term *Angelcynn*, see Foot 25–49; Kathy Lavezzo, "Another Country: Ælfric and the Production of English Identity," *New Medieval Literatures*, ed. Rita Copeland, vol. 3 (Oxford: Oxford University Press, 1999) 67–94; Wormald, "Bede" 99–129; Wormald, "*Engla Lond*" 1–24.

40. Cnut's kingdom of "eall Angelcynes" (all the Anglo-Saxons) includes "West Seaxan" (Wessex), "East Englan" (East Anglia), "Myrcean" (Mercia), and "Norðhymbran" (Northumbria). See the *Anglo-Saxon Chronicle* (E), entry for 1017. For representative examples of the translator's use of *Angli*, see *In Cn Inscr.*, *In Cn* III 2, 8, and 45.4.

41. See Bhabha 2–4, 302–08.

42. It is only here that Wormald's view of early law as primarily ideological seems to fit the case of the *Domboc*. See Wormald, "*Lex*" 105–15.

43. See Wormald, *Making* 244; Richard Sharpe, "The Dating of the *Quadripartitus* Again," *English Law Before the Magna Carta*, eds. Stefan Juranski, Lisi Oliver, and Andrew Rabin, Medieval Law and Its Practice 8 (Leiden: Brill, 2010) 81–93. On the identity and station of the compiler, see Patrick Wormald, "'Quadripartitus,'" *Law and Government in Medieval England and Normandy: Essays in Honour of Sir James Holt*, ed. John Hudson (Cambridge: Cambridge University Press, 1994) 139–45.

44. See Wormald, *Making* 240–41.

45. Liebermann presents the text of the *Domboc* and the *Quadripartitus* translation of it as parallel transcriptions in his *Gesetze*. His tracking of changes from the Old English to the Latin show only the most superficial of emendations, usually for the sake of contextual

clarity or grammatical sense. Q, like Wulfstan, uses the Latin *emendare* to stand for the concept of *bot* throughout his translation, emphasizing the monetary nature of the dictated reparations for wrongs against people or property.

46. See Wormald, *Making* 465–68.

47. On the content and organization of the *Quadripartitus*, see Wormald, *Making* 236–44.

48. On classifying the ruling class of England in the late-eleventh to early twelfth-century as specifically Anglo-Norman, see John Gillingham, *The English in the Twelfth Century: Imperialism, National Identity, and Political Values* (Woodbridge: Boydell, 2000) 124–27, 50–56.

49. See M. T. Clanchy, *From Memory to Written Record* (Oxford: Blackwell, 1993) 200–09, 18–19.

50. On Anglo-Saxon Latinity, see W. F. Bolton, *A History of Anglo-Latin Literature, 597–1066* (Princeton: Princeton University Press, 1967) 9–14, 62–63; Keynes and Lapidge 28–29; Patrizia Lendinara, "The World of Anglo-Saxon Learning," *The Cambridge Companion to Old English Literature*, eds. Malcolm Godden and Michael Lapidge (Cambridge: Cambridge University Press, 1991) 264–81.

51. On the Norman's self-conscious nature of managing the anxieties of conquest, see Bruce R. O'Brien, *God's Peace and King's Peace: The Laws of Edward the Confessor* (Philadelphia: University of Pennsylvania Press, 1999) 11–19.

52. See Stenton 673–78.

53. See Wormald, "*Lex*" 133–35.

54. Q states in his preface that his book is unfinished, containing "solo principio, non fine" (only a beginning, not an end) (*Quadr.* II *Praef.* 13).

55. The project of compiling legislation is eventually completed with the *Leges Henrici Primus*. On the plan and execution of the *Quadripartitus*, see Wormald, *Making* 236–44, 411–15.

56. These labels are Liebermann's, but will serve to clarify the discussion.

57. See Richard Sharpe, "The Prefaces of '*Quadripartitus*,'" *Law and Government in Medieval England and Normandy: Essays in Honour of Sir James Holt*, eds. George Garnett and John Hudson (Cambridge: Cambridge University Press, 1994) 149–50; Wormald, *Making* 243–44.

58. All citations from the *Dedicatio* and the *Argumentum* are taken from Sharpe, "Prefaces" 151–72.

59. See Wormald, *Making* 243–44. However, Sharpe does not find a pre-1100 date to be a necessary condition: see Sharpe, "Prefaces" 149–50.

60. On the poor contemporary estimation of William II, see M. T. Clanchy, *England and Its Rulers, 1066–1272*, 2nd ed. (Oxford: Blackwell, 1998) 41–45.

61. The *Argumentum* is extant in manuscripts of the first and second drafts of the entire *Quadripartitus*. See Sharpe, "Prefaces" 149–50; Wormald, "'*Quadripartitus*'" 125–33.

62. See Wormald, *Making* 244. For an argument citing the consistently dour tone between both the *Dedicatio* and the *Argumentum*, see Sharpe, "Prefaces" 150.

63. "The laws that go by King Edward's name, derived from the institutes of Cnut in the first place..." (*Arg.* § 1). Further, Q claims that Edward "would be received as king only if he guarantee to them [the thegns of all England] upon oath that the laws of Cnut and his sons should continue in his time with unshaken firmness" (*Arg.* § 9).

64. Q is specifically referencing the issuance of Cnut's Winchester code (*I–II Cnut*). See *Arg.* § 4.

65. See Sharpe, "Prefaces" 163 n. 99.

66. The text is taken from Liebermann, *Gesetze* I. 522. The translation is my own.

67. See, for example *Arg.* § 18 in which Q juxtaposes Henry I's England with the shortcomings of the French, the Normans, and the Danes, among others.

68. Liebermann, *Gesetze* I. 539.

69. The *Textus Roffensis* was probably created around the year 1123–24 at the Benedictine monastic cathedral at Rochester, making it a relatively close contemporary of the *Quadripartitus* and the *Instituta Cnuti*. See Ker 443; Wormald, *Making* 245.

70. For technical descriptions of the complete contents of the *Textus Roffensis*, see Ker 443–47; Sawyer, *Textus Roffensis* 15–18.

71. See Mary P. Richards, *Texts and Their Traditions in the Medieval Library of Rochester Cathedral Priory*, Transactions of the American Philosophical Society, vol. 78, Part 3 (Philadelphia: American Philosophical Society, 1988) 48.

72. On the relative importance of the pagan nature of this convention of lineage, see Dumville 77–79.

73. The text is taken from Sawyer, *Textus Roffensis*. The translation is my own.

74. Liebermann presents the texts of the *Domboc* from both the earliest manuscript (CCC 173) and the *Textus Roffensis* as parallel transcriptions in his *Gesetze*. His tracking of the changes between the two manuscripts (roughly 200 years apart) show only the most superficial of emendations, usually for the sake of contextual clarity or grammatical sense.

75. See Sawyer, *Textus Roffensis* 101ʳᵛ.

76. Wormald argues for *Hadbot*'s inclusion based on similarity of content. See Wormald, *Making* 247–48.

77. For the charter, see Alistair Campbell, ed., *Charters of Rochester* (London: Oxford University Press, 1973) 1. On its spurious nature, see Campbell, xv, xii; Richards, *Texts* 54.

78. In the thirteenth-century *Leis Willelme*, William I is cited as preserving "les leis e le custumes" (the laws and customs) that "reis Edward *sun cusin* tint devant lui" (king Edward, *his cousin* [my emphasis], held before him [William I]) (*Leis Wl Prol.*).

79. See Wormald, *Making* 244,52,481–83. See also O'Brien 17–19, 132–34.

Chapter 4

1. See Richard Helgerson, *Forms of Nationhood: The Elizabethan Writing of England* (Chicago: University of Chicago Press, 1992) 65–104.

2. For an example of the struggle in accommodating the Anglo-Saxon past to Early Modern sensibilities, see the treatment of the mid-fifth-century British queen Boadicea: Jodi Mikalachki, *The Legacy of Boadicea: Gender and Nation in Early Modern England* (New York: Routledge, 1998) 1–18, 115–49.

3. On the nature and reach of Parker's influence, see May McKisack, *Medieval History in the Tudor Age* (Oxford: Clarendon, 1971) 26–49; R. I. Page, *Matthew Parker and His Books* (Kalamazoo: Medieval Institute Publications, 1993) 1–92; Benedict Scott Robinson, "'Dark Speeche': Matthew Parker and the Reforming of History," *Sixteenth Century Journal* 29.4 (1998) 1066–72.

4. On the volume of Parker's collection, see Page 1–42; Robinson, "'Dark Speeche'" 1070–72.

5. As a result with his break from the Roman Catholic Church, Henry VIII dissolved monasteries throughout England in the late 1530s into the early 1540s. See David Knowles, *Bare Ruined Choirs: The Dissolution of English Monasteries* (Cambridge: Cambridge University Press, 1976) 153–250.

6. He was able to secure royal printing commissions for those printers in his favor, such as John Day. He financed Day's creation of the first Anglo-Saxon font, and provided the manuscripts leading to six of the nine sixteenth-century Anglo-Saxon publications. See W. W. Greg, "Books and Bookmen in the Correspondence of Archbishop Parker," *The Library* 16.3 (1935) 258–59.

7. Parker's relationship with the Tudors stretched back to Henry VIII's rule. He served as chaplain to both the king himself, and earlier to Elizabeth's mother, Anne Boleyn. Parker was one of Boleyn's chaplains from 1535 until her death the next year. He became one of Henry VIII's chaplains in 1537. See V. J. K. Brook, *A Life of Archbishop Parker* (Oxford: Oxford University Press, 1962) 15–16. His success was in no small part due to his connections with the royal house. His rise to the archbishopric of Canterbury was one of the new queen's first acts. On the relatively compulsory nature of this election, see Brook 68.

8. On the nationalistic nature of the Anglican Church's connection to early Britain, see Patrick Collinson, "The English Nation and National Sentiment in the Prophetic Mode," *Religion and Culture in Renaissance England*, eds. Claire McEachern and Deborah Shuger (Cambridge: Cambridge University Press, 1997) 15–45; Arthur Ferguson, *Clio Unbound: Perception of the Social and Cultural Past in Renaissance England* (Durham: Duke University Press, 1979) 104–15, 129–244.

9. See Helgerson 12–13.

10. See Anderson 12–19, 37–46. Anderson dates the beginning of this process to the advent of print in the sixteenth century. However, I would extend this function to manuscript production as well, especially in the case of royal manuscript production, such as was the case with the *Domboc*. Although perhaps operating on a smaller scale, and complicated by scribal error and emendation, effective manuscript production generally renders the same kind of effects as later print production.

11. The *Testimonie* is paginated by leaf. Leaf one is the title page. Leaves 2ʳ through 19ᵛ contain the preface to the text. Ælfric's "Sermo de sacrificio in die pascae" fills leaves 19ʳ through 62ᵛ (The Anglo-Saxon text appears on the verso leaves while an English translation appears on the recto). For the text, see Malcolm Godden, ed., *Ælfric's Catholic Homilies. The Second Series: Text*, vol. 5 (Oxford: Oxford University Press, 1979) 150–60. Leaves 62ʳ through 73 contain two epistles on Easter from Ælfric to Wulfsige and Wulfstan, respectively (The Anglo-Saxon text again appears on the verso leaves while an English translation appears on the recto). For the texts, see Bruno Assmann, ed., *Angelsächsische Homilien und Heilgenleben*, vol. 3 (1889; Introd. Peter Clemoes, Darmstadt: Wissenschaftliche Buchgesellschaft, 1964) 86–109, 33–42. The Latin version of Ælfric's letter to Wulfstan follows on leaves 74–75. Leaves 76ʳ through 78ᵛ contain an approbation of the previous material by Archbishops Parker and thirteen other bishops. The remainder of the text, leaves 78ʳ through 88, contains the Lord's Prayer, the Creed, and the Decalogue (the latter appears on leaves 85–88). For the texts, see Assmann 144; Peter Clemoes, ed., *Ælfric's Catholic Homilies. The First Series: Text*, vol. 17 (London: Oxford University Press, 1997) 324–25; Liebermann, *Gesetze* I. 26–29; Benjamin Thorpe, ed., *The Homilies of the Anglo-Saxon Church: The First Part, Containing the Sermones Catholici, or Homilies of Aelfric*, vol. 2 (New York: Johnson Reprint, 1971) 596. The final leaf is a guide to Anglo-Saxon characters and an end paper.

12. See the term "circle" characteristically used, for example, in Grant 9–23; Simon Keynes, "Anglo-Saxon History: A Select Bibliography," *Old English Newsletter: Subsidia* 13 (1998); McKisack 26–49.

13. Although he began his inquiries after old documents in earnest upon his accession to archbishop in 1559, the Privy Council's support did not become official until 1568. See McKisack 26–34.

14. When citing specifics from the texts, I will refer to the author as Joscelyn, as he was most likely the executor of the *Testimonie*. However, when speaking of the wider effects and influences of the *Testimonie*, I will refer to the text as Parker's insofar as Joscelyn was in Parker's employ and acting directly under the Archbishop's hand. On Joscelyn's authorship of the *Testimonie*, see Timothy Graham, "John Joscelyn, Pioneer of Old English Lexicography," *The Recovery of Old English: Anglo-Saxon Studies in the Sixteenth and Seventeenth Centuries*, ed. Timothy Graham (Kalamazoo: Medieval Institute Publications, 2000) 83; Robinson, "'Dark Speeche'" 1062.

15. See Graham 83–140, esp. 26, 37.
16. See Graham 132–33.
17. On priests' ability to marry, see Aelfric, *A Testimonie of Antiqvitie* (New York: De Capo, 1970) 8–9, 14–15. For emphasis on the "Saxon tongue," see Aelfric 78, 80–81, 87.
18. See Michael Murphy, "Religious Polemics in the Genesis of Old English Studies," *Huntington Library Quarterly* 32 (1969) 244–45.
19. See Aelfric 16–17.
20. Joscelyn has *Af. El. Pro.*-9 printed on pages 85–86 of the *Testimonie*.
21. See Robinson, "'Dark Speeche'" 1075–83.
22. On the Second Nicene Council and the debate over images, see David Ganz, "Theology and the Organization of Thought," *The New Cambridge Medieval History: Volume II c. 700–900*, ed. Rosamond McKitterick (Cambridge: Cambridge University Press, 1995) 773–77; Thomas Nobel, "The Papacy in the Eighth and Ninth Centuries," *The New Cambridge Medieval History: Volume II c. 700–900*, ed. Rosamond McKitterick (Cambridge: Cambridge University Press, 1995) 577–78.
23. According to Joscelyn, the story is the entry for the year 792, see Aelfric 88. Joscelyn's version of the tale was drawn from, among other sources, the *Flores historiarum*, an edition of which Parker first published in 1567: see Matthew Paris, *Flores historiarum*, ed. Matthew Parker (London: Thomas Marsh, 1570) 282–83.
24. King Alfred explicitly justifies the reproduction of books "þa þe niedbeðearfosta sien eallum monnum to wiotonne" (which are most necessary for all men to know). See Sweet 7.
25. See Grant 18–19; Retha Warnicke, *William Lambarde: Elizabethan Antiquary, 1536–1601* (London: Phillimore, 1973) 136–37.
26. The *Archaionomia* begins with an introductory section (32 pages) containing an epistle to the reader, a guide to Anglo-Saxon characters, a section defining unfamiliar terminology, a map and description of early Britain, and errata. The Anglo-Saxon laws follow (122 pages); the original text on the left, and a Latin translation on the facing page. Lambarde presents the laws of Ine, Alfred (including his treaty with Guthrum), Edward (including his treaty with Guthrum), Æthelstan, Edmund, Edgar, Æthelred, and Cnut. A final section (35 pages) contains the laws of William the Conqueror and Edward the Confessor solely in Latin. The text concludes with an alphabetical index of Latin legal terms.
27. My thanks to J. Holland for assistance in translating Lambarde's Latin. For a plausible alternative translation of this passage, emending the text to read "peruulgarem" (to publish), see Rebecca Brackmann, "Laurence Nowell's Edition and Translation of the Laws of Alfred in London, British Library Henry Davis 59," *The Heroic Age* 14 (2010): §14 n.10. Web. <http://www.heroicage.org/issues/14/brackmann.php#a10>.
28. See Greg 243–79; McKisack 27–54; Warnicke 32.
29. On Lambarde's use of Parker's manuscripts, see Grant 20; McKisack 78–80; Warnicke 23.
30. There is some debate as to Nowell's biography. Recent scholars have ascertained that the *Dictionary of National Biography*'s entry for Laurence Nowell actually conflates two people: Nowell the antiquary and Nowell the Dean of Lichfield. Although the life-histories of two individuals have been largely disentangled, some details remain foggy. The birth of Nowell the antiquary, for example, is only roughly pegged to the decade between 1510–20. This would make him approximately twenty years older than Lambarde. For the details and discussion of Nowell's identity and biography, see Carl Berkhout, "The Pedigree of Laurence Nowell the Antiquary," *English Language Notes* 23.2 (1985) 15–26; Grant 11–17; Thomas Hahn, "The Identity of the Antiquary Laurence Nowell," *English Language Notes* 20.3 (1983) 10–18; Warnicke 23–28. On Nowell's role in the translation of the *Quadripartitus*, see Brackmann, "Nowell's Glossary" 252–67.
31. The original manuscript dates to the turn of the eleventh century. Nowell's transcript is London, British Library Additional MS 43703.

32. See Ker 230–34.

33. On Nowell's transcript, generally, see Grant 25–39. On Lambarde's deviations from the Nowell transcript, see Grant 94–161.

34. See Warnicke 23.

35. On the date of Nowell's request and subsequent trip to the Continent, see Grant 14–15; Warnicke 23–24. On Nowell's leaving his possessions in Lambarde's care, see Grant 14–15.

36. Heraclitus' fragment 100 reads as follows: "Μαχεσθαι χρη τον δημον υπερ τον νομον οκως υπερ τειχεος" (People ought to fight to keep their law as to defend the city walls). See Heraclitus, *Fragments: The Collected Wisdom of Heraclitus*, trans. Brooks Haxton (New York: Viking, 2001) 66–67.

37. For an overview of the origins and progress of this debate, see Helgerson 65–104.

38. Within his *A Dialogue between Reginald Pole and Thomas Lupset*, Thomas Starkey identifies English common law as both "barbarous" and originating with the Normans. His solution is to accept Roman civil law in its place. See Thomas Starkey, *A Dialogue between Reginald Pole and Thomas Lupset*, ed. Kathleen Burton (London: Chatto and Windus, 1948) 175.

39. See Helgerson 65–70.

40. Parker received the Council's letter in July of 1568, while Lambarde dates his "Epistola" September 1568. As he thanks Parker for the use of his library in the creation of the *Archaionomia*, the two men certainly had close contact during this period. Lambarde, in publishing his work, is acting as a deputy of Parker, carrying out the Queen's wish as expressed to Parker through the letter from the Privy Council.

41. This text is inserted on G.iiii.ᵛ, between the Anglo-Saxon texts "Ne lufa þu oþre fremde godas ofer me" (You shall not love other strange gods over me) and "Ne minne noman ne cigþu on idelnesse" (You shall not call my name in vain). It is set off from the text through the use of italics and indentation, and signaled by the graphic: ☞. The corresponding section of G.iiii.ʳ is left blank.

42. Notation pagination follows that of the original text. See Aelfric. The text was originally published 1566/67 (London: John Day).

43. See Michael J. Curley, *Geoffrey of Monmouth*, Twayne's English Authors Series, ed. George Economou (Boston: Twayne, 1994) 10.

44. See *Af. El.* 49–49.9.

45. See William Haller, *Foxe's Book of Martyrs and the Elect Nation* (New York: J. Cape, 1963) 224–49.

46. See Haller 206–08.

47. See Helgerson 70–72.

Appendix

1. For a complete discussion of the manuscript history of the *Domboc*, and an overview of my interpretation of the text, see the introduction.

Works Cited

Abels, Richard Philip. *Alfred the Great: War, Kingship and Culture in Anglo-Saxon England.* The Medieval World. New York: Longman, 1998.

_____. *Lordship and Military Obligation in Anglo-Saxon England.* Berkeley: University of California Press, 1988.

Aelfric. *A Testimonie of Antiqvitie.* New York: De Capo, 1970.

Anderson, Benedict. *Imagined Communities: Reflections on the Origin and Spread of Nationalism.* 2nd ed. London: Verso, 1991.

Assmann, Bruno, ed. *Angelsächsische Homilien und Heilgenleben.* 1889. Introd. Peter Clemoes. Vol. 3. Darmstadt: Wissenschaftliche Buchgesellschaft, 1964.

Attenborough, F. L., ed. *The Laws of the Earliest English Kings.* Cambridge: Cambridge University Press, 1922.

Barker, Kenneth L., and Donald W. Burdick, eds. *The NIV Study Bible, New International Version.* Grand Rapids: Zondervan, 1985.

Bately, Janet, ed. *The Anglo-Saxon Chronicle: A Collaborative Edition.* Vol. 3. Cambridge: Brewer, 1983.

_____. *The Literary Prose of King Alfred's Reign: Translation or Transformation? Old English Newsletter: Subsidia.* Vol. 10. Binghamton: CEMERS SUNY-Binghamton, 1984.

Berkhout, Carl. "The Pedigree of Laurence Nowell the Antiquary." *English Language Notes* 23.2 (1985): 15–26.

Bethurum, Dorothy, ed. *The Homilies of Wulfstan.* Oxford: Clarendon, 1998.

Bhabha, Homi. "Dissemination: Time, Narrative, and the Margins of the Modern Nation." *Nation and Narration.* Ed. Homi Bhabha. New York: Routledge, 1990. 291–322.

Bolton, W. F. *A History of Anglo-Latin Literature, 597–1066.* Princeton: Princeton University Press, 1967.

Bourdieu, Pierre. *Practical Reason: On the Theory of Action.* Stanford: Stanford University Press, 1998.

Brackmann, Rebecca. "Laurence Nowell's Edition and Translation of the Laws of Alfred in London, British Library Henry Davis 59," *The Heroic Age* 14 (2010): §14 n.10.

_____. "Laurence Nowell's Old English Legal Glossary and His Study of the *Quadripartitus.*" *English Law Before the Magna Carta.* Eds. Stefan Juranski, Lisi Oliver and Andrew Rabin. *Medieval Law and Its Practice* 8. Leiden: Brill, 2010. 251–72.

Brook, V. J. K. *A Life of Archbishop Parker.* Oxford: Oxford University Press, 1962.

Butler, Judith. *Excitable Speech: A Politics of the Performative.* New York: Routledge, 1997.

Byock, Jesse L. *Feud in the Icelandic Saga.* Berkeley: University of California Press, 1982.

Campbell, Alistair, ed. *Charters of Rochester.* London: Oxford University Press, 1973.

Carnicelli, Thomas, ed. *King Alfred's Version of Saint Augustine's Soliloquies*. Cambridge: Harvard University Press, 1969.

Charles-Edwards, Thomas. "Anglo-Saxon Kinship Revisited." *The Anglo-Saxons: From the Migration Period to the Eighth Century*. Ed. John Hines. Woodbridge: Boydell, 1997.

Clanchy, M. T. *England and Its Rulers, 1066–1272*. 2nd ed. Oxford: Blackwell, 1998.

———. *From Memory to Written Record*. Oxford: Blackwell, 1993.

Clemoes, Peter, ed. *Ælfric's Catholic Homilies. The First Series: Text*. Vol. 17. London: Oxford University Press, 1997.

Colgrave, Bertram, and R.A.B. Mynors, eds. *Bede's Ecclesiastical History of the English People*. Oxford: Clarendon, 1969.

Collinson, Patrick. "The English Nation and National Sentiment in the Prophetic Mode." *Religion and Culture in Renaissance England*. Eds. Claire McEachern and Deborah Shuger. Cambridge: Cambridge University Press, 1997. 15–45.

Cox, Jeffrey, and Larry J. Reynolds, eds. *New Historical Literary Study: Essays on Reproducing Texts, Representing History*. Princeton: Princeton University Press, 1993.

Curley, Michael J. *Geoffrey of Monmouth*. Twayne's English Authors Series. Ed. George Economou. Boston: Twayne, 1994.

Davies, R. R. *The First English Empire: Power and Identities in the British Isles, 1093–1343*. The Ford Lectures Delivered in the University of Oxford in Hilary Term 1998. Oxford: Oxford University Press, 2000.

Douglas, David C., and George Greenaway, eds. *English Historical Documents c. 1042–1189*. 2nd ed. Vol. 1. Oxford: Oxford University Press, 1979.

Dubrow, Heather, and Richard Strier, eds. *The Historical Renaissance*. Chicago: University of Chicago Press, 1988.

Dumville, David. "Kingship, Genealogies and Regnal Lists." *Early Medieval Kingship*. Eds. P. H. Sawyer and I. N. Wood. Leeds: University of Leeds Press, 1977.

Ferguson, Arthur. *Clio Unbound: Perception of the Social and Cultural Past in Renaissance England*. Durham: Duke University Press, 1979.

Firchow, Evelyn Scherabon, and Edwin H. Zeydel, eds. *Einhard: Vita Karoli Magni*. Coral Gables: University of Miami Press, 1972.

Flower, Robin, A. H. Smith, and Corpus Christi College (University of Cambridge). Library. *The Parker Chronicle and Laws (Corpus Christi College, Cambridge, MS. 173) a Facsimile*. London: Oxford University Press, 1941.

Foot, Sarah. "The Making of *Angelcynn*: English Identity before the Norman Conquest." *Transactions of the Royal Historical Society* 6 (1996): 25–49.

Foucault, Michel. *Discipline and Punish: The Birth of the Prison*. Trans. Alan Sheridan. New York: Pantheon, 1977.

Fox, Samuel, ed. *King Alfred's Anglo-Saxon Version of Boethius: De consolatione philosophiae*. 2nd ed. New York: AMS, 1970.

Foxe, John. *The Unabridged Acts and Monuments Online*. 1583. Sheffield: HRI Online Press, 2011.

Frank, Roberta. "Germanic Legend in Old English Literature." *The Cambridge Companion to Old English Literature*. Eds. Malcolm Godden and Michael Lapidge. Cambridge: Cambridge University Press, 1991. 88–106.

Frantzen, Allen J. *King Alfred*. Twayne's English Authors Series. Ed. George Economou. Boston: Twayne, 1986.

———. *The Literature of Penance in Anglo-Saxon England*. New Brunswick: Rutgers University Press, 1983.

Fulk, Robert D. "Localizing and Dating Old English Anonymous Prose, and How Inherent Problems Relate to Anglo-Saxon Legislation." *English Law Before the Magna Carta*. Eds. Stefan Juranski, Lisi Oliver, and Andrew Rabin. Medieval Law and Its Practice 8. Leiden: Brill, 2010. 59–79.

Ganz, David. "Theology and the Organization of Thought." *The New Cambridge Medieval History: Volume II c. 700–900*. Ed. Rosamond McKitterick. Cambridge: Cambridge University Press, 1995. 758–85.

Gillingham, John. *The English in the Twelfth Century: Imperialism, National Identity, and Political Values*. Woodbridge: Boydell, 2000.

Godden, Malcolm, ed. *Ælfric's Catholic Homilies. The Second Series: Text*. Vol. 5. Oxford: Oxford University Press, 1979.

_____. "Biblical Literature: The Old Testament." *The Cambridge Companion to Old English Literature*. Ed. Michael Lapidge. Cambridge: Cambridge University Press, 1991. 206–26.

Graham, Timothy. "John Joscelyn, Pioneer of Old English Lexicography." *The Recovery of Old English: Anglo-Saxon Studies in the Sixteenth and Seventeenth Centuries*. Ed. Timothy Graham. Kalamazoo: Medieval Institute Publications, 2000. 83–140.

Grant, Raymond J. *Laurence Nowell, William Lambarde, and the Laws of the Anglo-Saxons*. Costerus New Series. Ed. Erik Kooper. Vol. 108. Amsterdam: Rodopi, 1996.

Greg, W. W. "Books and Bookmen in the Correspondence of Archbishop Parker." *The Library* 16.3 (1935): 243–79.

Hahn, Thomas. "The Identity of the Antiquary Laurence Nowell." *English Language Notes* 20.3 (1983): 10–18.

Haller, William. *Foxe's Book of Martyrs and the Elect Nation*. New York: J. Cape, 1963.

Hamilton, Sarah. *The Practice of Penance*. Woodbridge: Boydell, 2001.

Hastings, Adrian. *The Construction of Nationhood*. Cambridge: Cambridge University Press, 1997.

Healey, Antonette Di Paolo, Richard L. Venezky, and Angus Cameron, eds. *Dictionary of Old English*. Toronto: Published for the Dictionary of Old English Project Centre for Medieval Studies University of Toronto by the Pontifical Institute of Mediaeval Studies, 1986.

Helgerson, Richard. *Forms of Nationhood: The Elizabethan Writing of England*. Chicago: University of Chicago Press, 1992.

Heraclitus. *Fragments: The Collected Wisdom of Heraclitus*. Trans. Brooks Haxton. New York: Viking, 2001.

Hill, John M. *The Anglo-Saxon Warrior Ethic: Reconstructing Lordship in Early English Literature*. Gainesville: University Press of Florida, 2000.

Howe, Nicholas. "Historicist Approaches." *Reading Old English Texts*. Ed. Katherine O'Brien O'Keeffe. New York: Cambridge University Press, 1997. 79–100.

_____. *Migration and Mythmaking in Anglo-Saxon England*. New Haven: Yale University Press, 1989.

Hudson, John G. H. "Feud, Vengence and Violence in England from the Tenth to the Twelfth Centuries." *Feud, Violence and Practice: Essays in Medieval Studies in Honor of Stephen D. White*. Eds. Belle Tuten and Tracey Billado. Farnham: Ashgate, 2010.

Hyams, Paul. "Feud and the State in Late Anglo-Saxon England." *Journal of British Studies* 40 (2001): 1–43.

_____. "Feud in Medieval England." *Haskins Society Journal* 3 (1991): 1–21.

_____. "Neither Unnatural nor Wholly Negative: The Future of Medieval Vengence."

Vengence in the Middle Ages: Emotion, Religion and Feud. Eds. Susanna Throop and Paul Hyams. Farnham: Ashgate, 2010. 203–19.

_____. *Rancor and Reconciliation in Medieval England*, Ithaca: Cornell University Press, 2003.

_____. "Was There Really Such a Thing as Feud in the High Middle Ages?" *Vengence in the Middle Ages: Emotion, Religion and Feud.* Eds. Susanna Throop and Paul Hyams. Farnham: Ashgate, 2010. 151–75.

Jost, Karl, ed. *Die "Institutes of Polity, Civil and Ecclesiastical": Ein Werk Erzbischof Wulfstans von York.* Bern: Franke, 1959.

Juranski, Stefan, Lisi Oliver, and Andrew Rabin, eds. *English Law Before the Magna Carta.* Medieval Law and Its Practice 8. Leiden: Brill, 2010.

Ker, N. R. *Catalogue of Manuscripts Containing Anglo-Saxon.* rev. ed. Oxford: Oxford University Press, 1990.

Keynes, Simon. "Anglo-Saxon History: A Select Bibliography." *Old English Newsletter: Subsidia.* Vol. 13, 3rd rev. ed. Kalamazoo, MI: Medieval Institute, 1998.

_____. "The Cult of King Alfred." *Anglo-Saxon England* 28 (1999): 225–356.

_____. "The Fonthill Letter," *Words, Texts, and Manuscripts: Studies in Anglo-Saxon Culture Presented to Helmut Gneuss on the Occasion of his Sixty-Fifth Birthday.* Eds. Michael Korhammer, Karl Reichl, and Hans Sauer. Cambridge: Brewer, 1992. 53–97.

_____. "King Alfred and the Mercians." *Kings, Currency and Alliances: History and Coinage in Southern England in the Ninth Century.* Ed. Simon Keynes. Woodbridge: Boydell, 1998. 1–45.

_____, and Michael Lapidge, eds. *Alfred the Great, Asser's Life of King Alfred and Other Contemporary Sources.* Harmondsworth: Penguin, 1983.

Kirby, D. P. *The Earliest English Kings.* rev. ed. London: Routledge, 2000.

Knowles, David. *Bare Ruined Choirs: The Dissolution of English Monasteries.* Cambridge: Cambridge University Press, 1976.

Lambarde, William, ed. *Archaionomia, sive De priscis Anglorum legibus libri, sermone anglico, vetustate antiquissimo, aliquot abhinc seculis conscripti, atq: nunc demum, magno iurisperitorum, & amantium antiquitatis omnium commodo, e tenebris in lucem vocati.* London: John Day, 1568.

Latham, R. E., and D. R. Howlett. *Dictionary of Medieval Latin from British Sources: Fasicule III, D–E.* London: Oxford University Press, 1975.

Lavezzo, Kathy. "Another Country: Ælfric and the Production of English Identity." *New Medieval Literatures.* Ed. Rita Copeland. Vol. 3. Oxford: Oxford University Press, 1999. 67–94.

Lawson, M. K. "Archbishop Wulfstan and the Homiletic Element in the Laws of Æthelred II and Cnut." *The Reign of Cnut: King of England, Denmark and Norway.* Ed. Alexander R. Rumble. Studies in the Early History of Britain. London: Leicester University Press, 1994. 141–64.

_____. *Cnut: The Danes in England in the Early Eleventh Century.* The Medieval World. New York: Longman, 1993.

Lendinara, Patrizia. "The World of Anglo-Saxon Learning." *The Cambridge Companion to Old English Literature.* Ed. Michael Lapidge. Cambridge: Cambridge University Press, 1991. 264–81.

Liebermann, Felix, ed. *Die Gesetze der Angelsachsen.* 1903–16. Aalen: Scientia, 1960.

_____. "King Alfred and Mosaic Law." *Transactions of the Jewish Historical Society* 6 (1912): 21–31.

_____. "On the *Instituta Cnuti Aliorumque Regum Anglorum*." *Transactions of the Royal Historical Society* 7 (1893): 77–107.

Loyn, H. R. *The Governance of Anglo-Saxon England, 500–1087.* The Governance of England; 1. Stanford: Stanford University Press, 1984.

Lucas, Peter, ed. *Exodus.* Exeter: University of Exeter Press, 1994.

Maitland, Frederic William. *Domesday Book and Beyond: Three Essays in the Early History of England.* Norton Library; N338. New York: Norton, 1966.

Marin, Louis. *Portrait of the King.* Trans. Martha M. Houle. Theory and History of Literature. Ed. Jochen Schulte-Sasse. Vol. 57. Minneapolis: University of Minnesota Press, 1988.

McKisack, May. *Medieval History in the Tudor Age.* Oxford: Clarendon, 1971.

McKitterick, Rosamond, ed. *The New Cambridge Medieval History: Volume II c. 700–c. 900.* Cambridge: Cambridge University Press, 1995.

Migne, J. P., ed. *Patrologiæ Cursus Completus, Series Latina.* Vol. 77. Paris: Garnieri Fratres, 1849.

Mikalachki, Jodi. *The Legacy of Boadicea: Gender and Nation in Early Modern England.* New York: Routledge, 1998.

Miller, William Ian. *Bloodtaking and Peacemaking: Feud, Law, and Society in Saga Iceland.* Chicago: University of Chicago Press, 1990.

Moreschini, Claudio, ed. *Boethius: De consolatione philosophiae, Opuscula theologica.* Munich: Saur, 2000.

Murphy, Michael. "Religious Polemics in the Genesis of Old English Studies." *Huntington Library Quarterly* 32 (1969): 241–48.

Nelson, Janet. "'A King Across the Sea': Alfred in Continental Perspective." *Transactions of the Royal Historical Society* 5th ser. 36 (1986): 45–68.

——. "The Political Ideas of Alfred of Wessex." *Kings and Kingship in Medieval Europe.* Ed. Anne Duggan. London: King's College London Centre for Late Antique and Medieval Studies, 1993. 123–58.

Nichols, Stephen G., and Siegfried Wenzel, eds. *The Whole Book: Cultural Perspectives on the Medieval Miscellany.* Ann Arbor: University of Michigan Press, 1996.

Niles, John D. "Pagan Survivals and Popular Belief." *The Cambridge Companion to Old English Literature.* Eds. Malcolm Godden and Michael Lapidge. Cambridge: Cambridge University Press, 1991. 71–87.

Nobel, Thomas. "The Papacy in the Eighth and Ninth Centuries." *The New Cambridge Medieval History: Volume II c. 700–900.* Ed. Rosamond McKitterick. Cambridge: Cambridge University Press, 1995. 563–86.

O'Brien, Bruce R. *God's Peace and King's Peace: The Laws of Edward the Confessor.* Philadelphia: University of Pennsylvania Press, 1999.

O'Keeffe, Katherine O'Brien. "Heroic Values and Christian Ethics." *The Cambridge Companion to Old English Literature.* Ed. Michael Lapidge. Cambridge: Cambridge University Press, 1991. 107–25.

Page, R. I. *Matthew Parker and His Books.* Kalamazoo: Medieval Institute Publications, 1993.

Paris, Matthew. *Flores historiarum.* Ed. Matthew Parker. London: Thomas Marsh, 1570.

Pasternack, Carol Braun. *The Textuality of Old English Poetry.* Cambridge Studies in Anglo-Saxon England. Ed. Michael Lapidge. Vol. 13. Cambridge: Cambridge University Press, 1995.

Pollock, Frederick, and Frederic William Maitland. *The History of English Law before the Time of Edward I.* 2nd ed. London: Cambridge University Press, 1968.

Pope, John C., ed. *Eight Old English Poems.* 3rd ed. New York: Norton, 2001.

Pratt, David. "Written Law and the Communication of Authority." *England and the Continent in the Tenth Century: Studies in Honor of Wilhelm Levison (1876–1947).*

Eds. David Rollason, Conrad Leyser, and Hannah Williams. Studies in the Early Middle Ages 37. Turnhout: Brepols, 2011. 331–50.

Richards, Mary P. "Anglo-Saxonism in the Old English Laws." *Anglo-Saxonism and the Construction of Social Identity.* Ed. John D. Niles. Gainesville: University Press of Florida, 1997. 40–59.

_____. "The Manuscript Contexts of the Old English Laws." *Studies in Earlier Old English Prose.* Ed. Paul Szarmach. Albany: State University of Albany Press, 1986. 171–92.

_____. *Texts and Their Traditions in the Medieval Library of Rochester Cathedral Priory.* Transactions of the American Philosophical Society. Vol. 78, Part 3. Philadelphia: American Philosophical Society, 1988.

Robinson, Benedict Scott. "'Dark Speeche': Matthew Parker and the Reforming of History." *Sixteenth Century Journal* 29.4 (1998): 1061–83.

Robinson, Fred C. *The Editing of Old English.* Cambridge: Blackwell, 1994.

Ryan, Kiernan, ed. *New Historicism and Cultural Materialism: A Reader.* London: Arnold, 1996.

Sawyer, P. H. *Anglo-Saxon Charters: An Annotated List and Bibliography.* Royal Historical Society Guides and Handbooks. Vol. 8. London: Royal Historical Society, 1968.

_____, ed. *Textus Roffensis: Rochester Cathedral Library Manuscript A. 3. 5.* Copenhagen: Rosenkilde and Bagger, 1957.

Schütt, Marie. "The Literary Form of Asser's *Vita Alfredi.*" *English Historical Review* 62 (1957): 209–20.

Sharpe, Richard. "The Dating of the Quadripartitus Again." Eds. Stefan Juranski, Lisi Oliver, and Andrew Rabin, Medieval Law and Its Practice 8. Leiden: Brill, 2010. 81–93

_____. "The Prefaces of '*Quadripartitus.*'" *Law and Government in Medieval England and Normandy: Essays in Honour of Sir James Holt.* Ed. John Hudson. Cambridge: Cambridge University Press, 1994. 148–72.

Smith, Julia. "Religion and Lay Society." *The New Cambridge Medieval History: Volume II c. 700-c. 900.* Ed. Rosamond McKitterick. Cambridge: Cambridge University Press, 1995. 64–84.

Smyth, Alfred P. *King Alfred the Great.* Oxford: Oxford University Press, 1995.

Stafford, Pauline. *Unification and Conquest.* London: Arnold, 1989.

Stanley, Eric Gerald. "On the Laws of King Alfred: The End of the Preface and the Beginning of the Laws." *Alfred the Wise: Studies in Honour of Janet Bately on the Occasion of Her Sixty-Fifth Birthday.* Ed. Malcolm Godden. Rochester: Brewer, 1997. 211–21.

Starkey, Thomas. *A Dialogue between Reginald Pole and Thomas Lupset.* Ed. Kathleen Burton. London: Chatto and Windus, 1948.

Stenton, Frank Merry. *Anglo-Saxon England.* 3rd ed. Oxford: Clarendon, 1971.

Stevenson, William, ed. *Asser's Life of King Alfred.* 2nd ed. Oxford: Clarendon, 1959.

Swan, Mary, and Elaine M. Treharne, eds. *Rewriting Old English in the Twelfth Century.* Cambridge: Cambridge University Press, 2000.

Swanton, Michael, ed. *The Anglo-Saxon Chronicle.* New York: Routledge, 1996.

Sweet, Henry, ed. *King Alfred's West Saxon Version of Gregory's Pastoral Care.* 1871. 2 vols. London: Oxford University Press, 1958.

Thorpe, Benjamin, ed. *The Homilies of the Anglo-Saxon Church: The First Part, Containing the Semones Catholici, or Homilies of Aelfric.* 1846. Vol. 2. 2 vols. New York: Johnson Reprint, 1971.

Treschow, Michael. "The Prologue to Alfred's Law Code: Instruction in the Spirit of Mercy." *Florilegium* 13 (1994): 79–110.

Veeser, Aram, ed. *The New Historicism.* New York: Routledge, 1989.

_____, ed. *The New Historicism Reader.* New York: Routledge, 1994.

Wallace-Hadrill, J. M. *Early Germanic Kingship in England and on the Continent.* Oxford: Clarendon, 1971.

Walzer, Michael. *Exodus and Revolution.* New York: Basic Books, 1985.

Warnicke, Retha. *William Lambarde: Elizabethan Antiquary, 1536–1601.* London: Phillimore, 1973.

Watson, Gerard, ed. *Saint Augustine: Soliloquies and Immortality of the Soul.* Warminster: Aris & Phillips, 1990.

Whitelock, Dorothy, ed. *English Historical Documents c. 500–1042.* 2nd ed. Vol. 1. Oxford: Oxford University Press, 1979.

_____. "The Prose of Alfred's Reign." *Continuations and Beginnings: Studies in Old English Literature.* Ed. Eric Gerald Stanley. London: Nelson, 1966. 67–103.

_____. "Wulfstan and the Laws of Cnut." *English Historical Review* 63 (1948): 433–52.

_____. "Wulfstan's Authorship of Cnut's Laws." *English Historical Review* 70 (1955): 72–85.

Wormald, Patrick. "Bede, the *Bretwaldas,* and the Origin of the *Gens Anglorum.*" *Ideal and Reality in Frankish and Anglo-Saxon Society: Studies Presented to J.M. Wallace-Hadrill.* Ed. Roger Collins. Oxford: Blackwell, 1983. 99–129.

_____. "*Engla Lond*: The Making of an Allegiance." *Journal of Historical Sociology* 7 (1994): 1–24.

_____. "In Search of King Offa's "Law-Code."" *People and Places in Northern Europe, 500–1600: Studies Presented to Peter Hayes Sawyer.* Ed. N. Lund. Woodbridge: Blackwell, 1991. 25–45.

_____. "*Lex Scripta and Verbum Regis*: Legislation and Germanic Kingship, from Euric to Cnut." *Early Medieval Kingship.* Ed. I. N. Wood. Leeds: University Leeds, 1977. 105–38.

_____. *The Making of English Law: King Alfred to the Twelfth Century.* Oxford: Blackwell, 1999.

_____. "'*Quadripartitus.*'" *Law and Government in Medieval England and Normandy: Essays in Honour of Sir James Holt.* Ed. John Hudson. Cambridge: Cambridge University Press, 1994. 111–47.

Wright, Charles. "Moses, *Manna Mildost.*" *Notes and Queries* 31.229:4 (1984): 440–43.

Yorke, Barbara. *Wessex in the Early Middle Ages.* Studies in the Early History of Britain. London: Leicester University Press, 1995.

Index

Index

Edward "the Elder," king of the English: law code 77–78
Einhard 16–17; *Vita Karoli* 11, 16
Elizabeth I, queen of England 5, 83–85, 90–93, 96, 98–99, 102; Privy Council 86, 96
Eucharist 86–87
Exodus, Old English 11, 15, 20–23

feud 1, 36, 38, 48–52, 55–57, 61–64, 67, 69, 72, 103–4
folcriht ("common law") 24, 36, 48
"Fonthill Letter" 3
Foxe, John 98; *Acts and Monuments* 98
Fulk, archbishop of Rheims 44

genealogies 5, 78–80, 102
Geoffrey of Monmouth, *Historia regum Britanniae* 97
Gregory I "the Great," Pope 42–43; *Regula pastoralis* (*Pastoral Care*) 3, 23–25, 26, 40–43, 48, 50–51, 101
Grið and *Geþyncðu* 66–68
Grimbald of St. Bertin 53

Hadbot 66, 80
Henry I, king of England 12, 60–61, 72–76, 78, 81, 102; *see also Quadripartitus*
Henry VIII, king of England 84
Hibernensis 53; *see also* penance, penitentials
Hincmar, archbishop of Rheims 44
Hlothere and Eadric, kings of Kent 78, 80
homilies 63, 65, 87; *see also* Ælfric, Wulfstan

idolatry 88–89, 97
Ine, King of the West Saxons 2, 4, 8–10, 18–19, 22, 29–31, 36, 54, 68, 70, 72, 95, 106
injury, personal 7–8, 31, 36, 39, 48, 67, 70
Instituta Cnuti 2, 4, 8–10, 12, 60, 66–73, 77–78, 82, 102
Israelites 20–23, 28–29, 98–99

Joscelyn, John 86–90, 96–99

Kent 8, 18, 30–33, 80–81
kingship 1, 3–5, 10–12, 15–17, 19–33, 35–44, 47, 50–57, 59–60, 64, 71, 79, 104

Lambarde, William 2, 12, 84, 89–99,

102–3; *Archaionomia* 2, 5, 12, 84, 90–97, 103
law books and codes *see Grið* and *Geþyncðu*; *Hadbot*; *Instituta Cnuti*; *Mircne Laga*; *Norðleoda Laga*; *I-II Cnut*; *Quadripartitus*; *Textus Roffensis*
Liebermann, Felix 105–6

manuscripts 5–10, 59, 81, 83, 105–6; Cambridge, Corpus Christi College 173 (the "Parker Chronicle") 2, 8–9, 24, 105; London, British Library Cotton Otho B.xi 8–9, 86, 92; Rochester Cathedral Library A.3.5 *see Textus Roffensis*
Mary I, queen of England 5, 83
Mercia 30–33, 38, 66, 81, 95, 103
mercy 25, 40–52, 56
Mircne Laga 66
Moses 7, 15, 18–24, 26–29, 54, 57, 90, 95–98, 101, 103, 106; Mosaic law 18–29, 36, 40, 44–51, 57, 65, 69, 94, 95
murder 37, 48–49, 70–71

Norðleoda Laga 66, 68
Norman Conquest 2, 4–6, 12, 59–61, 65–67, 71–74, 76–77, 80, 82, 87, 89, 102, 104
Nowell, Laurence 9, 86, 91–92, 96, 99

oaths 21, 47, 54–56, 62, 64, 67; oathhelpers 55
Offa, king of Mercia 29–31, 54, 95
Old Irish Penitential 53; *see also* penance, penitentials
I-II Cnut 2, 4, 12, 60–71, 82, 102

Parker, Matthew, archbishop of Canterbury 2, 12, 84–92, 96–99, 102; *De Antiquitate Britannicae Ecclesiae* 85
penance, penitentials 52–56; *see also Hibernensis*; *Old Irish Penitential*; *scrif*
Protestant Reformation 83–99, 102–104

Quadripartitus 2, 5, 8–10, 12, 60, 72–78, 79, 82, 102

Rochester Cathedral Priory 5, 12, 60, 78, 80–82, 102

scrif ("penance") 55–56; *see also* penance, penitentials